The Board of Directors:

Perspectives and Practices in Nine Countries

By Jeremy Bacon and James K. Brown

*A Research Report from The Conference Board's
Division of Management Research
Harold Stieglitz, Vice President*

Acknowledgments

The Conference Board is especially grateful to those organizations and individuals outside the United States who contributed research assistance for this report. In the order in which their countries are presented in the report, they are:

Prof. Dr. Eberhard Witte, Institut für Organisation, Universität München, Federal Republic of Germany

Sveriges Industriforbund (Federation of Swedish Industries), Stockholm, Sweden, in particular Dr. Per-Martin Meyerson

The Confederation of British Industry, London, England

The Institut de l'Entreprise, Paris, France, and M. J.P. Leguay of MANORGA S.A., Paris

The Ekonomic ve Sosyal Etüdler Konferans Heyeti (The Economic and Social Studies Conference Board), Istanbul, Turkey, and Prof. Mustafa Aysan of Istanbul University

The Conference Board in Canada

Avison Wormald of Lansberg, Wormald y Asociados, Caracas, Venezuela

Keizai Doyukai (Japan Committee for Economic Development), Tokyo, Japan

* * *

A number of members of The Conference Board staff besides the principal authors made important contributions to this report. Phyllis McGrath conducted a number of interviews as background for the chapter on the United States. Burton W. Teague wrote much of the German chapter. Rochelle O'Connor provided vital editorial and coordination help. Lillian Kay dealt with an unusually difficult editing schedule. Leslie Joseph tabulated and analyzed material from several countries. G. Clark Thompson was instrumental in arranging research assistance in Europe and Japan. And the project was conceived and guided by Harold Stieglitz.

Contents

Foreword

WERE PRIVATE ENTERPRISE less successful, were its influence less pervasive, possibly it would command less attention. But business as an institution of twentieth-century industrialization has done its job of creating added value most handsomely. And in doing its job, it has assumed a major — if not dominant — role in shaping the socio-economic environment of industrialized societies all over the world. Only government surpasses business in the number of people whose expectations, frustrations, and realizations can be traced to its decisions.

It seems little wonder, then, that those who give direction to business effort should be a focal point of those who are affected by their decisions. In the world of corporate business, the board of directors is the body of people that has ultimate authority for determining how a particular company will interact with society. There is little question that, in highly industrialized societies, that body continues to be under pressure for reform. The impact of the much talked about Bullock Report, for example, is not restricted to the United Kingdom where it originated. It has found avid readers in other countries.

At issue is the governance of the corporation — to whom is the board of directors accountable? Only to the shareowners it legally represents, or to other noninvestor groups or constituencies? And if, in the complex environment of the present period, its legal accountability is an anachronism, how does the accountability to this broader constituency become manifest — and with what effect?

Answers to such questions have emerged — the codetermination of the Federal Republic of Germany being the outstanding example. But it is also apparent that the answers are good for only limited periods of time. In country after country, new or revised answers are sought — with varying degrees of intensity — that fit the peculiar socio-economic dynamics of that nation.

Corporate governance is clearly an issue vital to the movement toward "a new International World Order." Inasmuch as the Sixth International Industrial Conference, convening in 1977, has chosen that as its theme, this Conference Board investigation of the board of directors was designed to explore and clarify the pressures and responses that are emerging in various countries.

The study is, of necessity, incomplete. New pressures, different responses, occur even as we go to press. Obviously, the study was ambitious in scope and could only be completed — within a limited time — with generous and enthusiastic cooperation of both the IIC, which financed the study, and individuals and organizations in the nine countries that provided information and analysis of their respective countries (see box, page ii). But the primary responsibility for this report and its contents lies with Jeremy Bacon and James K. Brown of The Conference Board, its principal authors.

KENNETH A. RANDALL
President

Part I
Overview

Chapter 1
Changes in Board Practices

THE BOARD OF directors, long a bastion of the capitalistic system, is proving to be vulnerable, like other institutions, to upheavals in the economic, political and social environments of countries around the world. Developments are occurring that are changing the meaning of what it is to be a member of a board of directors, and of what is involved in managing a company. In many instances these developments are altering the relationship between the board and management to a profound degree.

These important changes are being experienced in different degrees of intensity and variety in the nine countries included in this report. But the board of directors is present, in some form, in all of them. The law or laws of a country may be general, or even ambiguous, where boards of directors are concerned, but wherever the law makes it possible to conduct business in a divided-ownership and limited-liability corporate form, it also requires the existence of a body or organ to oversee the company's activities and protect the interests of its shareholders.

Of the many aspects of board practices mentioned in this report, the key issues, the critical questions that have surfaced, are these:

(1) What is the board's proper role? Does it "direct," as the title "director" at least implies? If so, what does the term "direct" mean? Is "supervise" a better term for what a board should do? (The German Aufsichtsrat is usually translated as a supervisory board or council, and its function is spelled out in the law and distinguished from that of management.) Can, or should, a board "manage," which North American law generally grants it full authority to do — but which it rarely does, especially in a company of major size?

(2) To whom should directors of a company be responsive in carrying out their duties? In many countries the premise that companies are run solely to produce a profit for their owners is being challenged; in some countries in this survey the concept that a company must be responsible to employees, customers, the community, and the general public is already thoroughly institutionalized, while in others it is being pressed in varying degrees.

(3) What changes, if any, are called for in the makeup or role of boards of directors, and how should they be implemented? Significant changes have already taken place in some European countries, particularly in board membership but also in board structure. Yet further changes are being called for, just as "reforms" are being pushed across the Atlantic, where changes have also been in progress but largely without compulsory legislation (with certain exceptions in Canada). Just what changes are necessary or would be beneficial, and the extent to which they should be codified in law, are major concerns in several countries.

Significant Changes in Board Practices

Three changes that have already taken place or are in progress concerning boards of directors are especially significant, as viewed by executives and board members in the countries surveyed. One is the addition of workers, employees with nonmanagement positions, as voting members; a second is the adoption of the two-tier structure in place of the single board; and the third is the emergence of an independent and assertive role for a growing number of boards, especially in the United States but in other countries as well. These changes are examined in detail in this chapter.

Workers as Directors

Among several changes observed affecting boards of directors in the countries surveyed for this report, the addition to the board as full voting members of employees below the management level is probably the most significant, and certainly the most widely discussed. At present, worker directors are found in only a minority of these countries. Whether the election of nonmanagement employees to boards of directors truly constitutes a trend may have to await the results of the current proposals in Britain, and in the longer run may depend on what the European Economic Community (EEC) endorses in terms of suggested or required board makeup for member countries. It is not considered an issue in the two North American countries surveyed, although executives there are quite familiar with the practice through their experience with overseas customers or through foreign subsidiary operations of their own companies.

Among the nine surveyed countries, only three — West Germany, Sweden and France — provide for worker board members in private-sector companies, and in the case of France the procedure is a voluntary one and has not been adopted by a large number of companies to date. Turkey and Venezuela do provide for employee directors in the case of government-owned companies. Employee board members are not found in Britain with the much-publicized exception of British Steel and a few other companies where it has been tried on an experimental basis. (The Bullock Committee, appointed by the British government to explore ways of improving industrial democracy in that country, has proposed that nonmanagement employees be added to British boards in substantial numbers. See pages 64 to 65 for details on how this would be done.) The EEC has put forth a draft version of a formula for board membership in member countries that would include employees, but this proposal is at present in abeyance.

The practice of placing nonmanagement employees on a board of directors is a German innovation. Its history in that country goes back to the early 1920's, when it was put into effect under law — to a limited extent — as an extension of the concept of employee participation in decision making, especially through works councils. But worker board membership in its present form and scope really dates from the period just following World War II, first in the coal and steel industries at the insistence of occupation forces (under a law passed in 1951), and shortly thereafter in other industries at the insistence of the labor unions. The German practice of employee board membership is known by the term *Mitbestimmung,* a word that is difficult to translate into other languages. The three present forms of worker board membership found in Germany are described in Chapter 3 on that country, beginning on page 27. For most companies of substantial size, the formula provides for employee board members in equal numbers with directors representing shareholders.

Even though Germany has more than a quarter century of experience with Mitbestimmung, the practice can still be said to be in a state of change in that country. The Codetermination Act of 1976 is a recent and major challenge for most major companies, since it requires a 50 percent proportion of employee representatives on the board instead of the one-third proportion that prevailed under prior law for major companies outside the coal and steel industries. The election procedures spelled out in the law are so detailed and difficult to put into effect that many, if not most, of the companies required to change their board composition under the law will not as yet have achieved the new required makeup, even though this report is being published more than a year after the law went into effect. And many Germans believe that the effect of the new law will not be known for a number of years.

On the other hand, although it mandates major changes that place a large number of new worker directors on German boards, the law — to the bitter disappointment of the German labor movement — does not change the essential ultimate voting control of shareholders over company affairs. And by placing employee directors on a supervisory board that by law does not have authority to make management decisions, the German practice stops short of forcing full-time management to share decision making at the top management level with workers.

In Sweden, the only other country included in this survey that makes nonmanagement employee board membership mandatory (if requested by unions representing a specified proportion of employees), the worker directors do not serve on a supervisory body but sit beside shareholder representatives on a single board having full authority over company affairs. Thus the Swedish approach does put workers into the essential management decision-making process. But only two nonmanagement employee board members are provided for under the law, and thus they have no veto power, nor even what is considered to be a major influence, on the decision-making process in the boardroom. (It has been pointed out that because the Swedish law applies the selection of two employee directors down to companies as small as those having 25 employees, the relative importance of this law will be greater for smaller companies that tend to have smaller boards.) And Swedish boards do not meet frequently, as a rule, which also limits the involvement of worker directors.

Critics of the Bullock majority report proposals in Britain express concern that the formula for employee board membership put forth by the committee would exceed both the German and Swedish systems in terms of influence granted to employees as board members. Under the Bullock formula, nonmanagement employee directors would have equal representation with directors chosen by shareholders, and would not serve on a supervisory board but on a single board. And the process for selecting employee directors would be completely in the hands of the trade unions. (For a detailed discussion of the Bullock proposal and arguments for and against it, see pages 64 through 66 in Chapter 5.)

The EEC formula put forth in draft form has two of the important charactistics of the German system, in that workers and shareholder representatives would have equal numbers of seats, and they would sit on a supervisory board. But the EEC formula adds a third group, equal in size to the other two, consisting of outsiders who are acceptable to both the employee side and shareholder side. This co-approval (or co-veto, if you will) approach to board membership is found in the Netherlands (a country not included in the present survey), and is included in the Bullock formula but with the independent faction reduced in size compared with the shareholder and employee sides. The EEC is not presently doing much about following up its draft, and opinion differs on when, or even if, it will put into effect rules governing its member countries that will require some form of employee board membership.

The chief claims made for adding workers to boards of directors are:

(1) Workers are really partners with shareholders in the sense that labor is a partner with capital in the running of the company. That partnership should extend to membership on boards of directors.

(2) Worker board membership will lead to improved decision making because decisions will be based on better information that can only be supplied by employees from their immediate experience with the work situation.

(3) Improved availability of information to employees, made possible through their participation on the board, will lead to an improved performance at the shop level and elsewhere in the company.

Proponents of employee board membership can point to a certain amount of evidence that supports their view.

The German experience demonstrates, at the very least, that the system can work. Germany's much-envied record of economic growth and the absence of serious labor disruptions in the post-World War II period are sometimes cited as being partly due to Mitbestimmung. German executives who have lived through it seem to find the system a workable one, if not necessarily one they would choose if they had an option. Swedish executives, too, many of whom gained experience with workers in the boardroom during a three-year trial period that preceded the 1976 legislation in that country, tend to say that the system works and that it does improve the quality and quantity of information on which boards can made decisions.

And two of the most feared potential drawbacks of employee presence in the boardroom have not come to pass, at least as major problems. One is the use of employee board membership to disrupt management decision making or escalate labor-negotiations matters to the level of the boardroom. The other is the fear that employee access to sensitive or confidential information about the company and its prospects might lead to information leaks that could prove harmful to the company.

Worker board membership does receive a good deal of criticism, however. Even some people who favor the concept feel that it lacks effectiveness in many cases, but they place the blame not on the system but on the fact that, even under the 50-50 formula in Germany, employee directors still lack full parity of decision-making power with shareholder representatives on the board. And some advocates point out that membership on a supervisory body or council, instead of on a single board, denies workers board membership in the true sense.

Another criticism voiced by people who believe that worker board membership is a sound idea is that managements find ways to thwart it. In particular they refer to the fact that management controls the information available to employee directors, and that managements are sometimes guilty of withholding selected information from these directors, or of providing it only at the last minute and, therefore, making it all but useless.

More numerous are critics who find that the system itself is not a good one. One of the arguments raised against having nonmanagement employees on the board of directors — and this problem is cited even by those who feel that the system can be made to work — is that it adversely affects the management decision-making process. In most cases the objection is that the presence of employees on the board has the effect of slowing down decision making. In part this is because diverse viewpoints have to be reconciled before a decision can be reached. But the point is also made that workers from the shop-floor level are not trained or equipped to deal with matters that normally come before a board of directors, and that their inexperience and the need to clarify matters for them to a greater extent than usual lead to longer deliberations. The impediment to swift decision making is considered especially harmful where employees sit on a single board, but the problem exists with supervisory boards as well.

A different objection regarding decisions where employee board members are concerned is that their presence can lead to the making of bad or incorrect decisions. This problem, or potential problem, seems to occur in situations where the board of directors must consider matters that will affect large numbers of employees and have a major impact on the company's employees or a major segment of them. Employee directors in such situations are under great pressure to try to prevent the board from deciding on a course of action that will adversely affect their fellow employees. And because they also serve as an early warning system for employees where such matters are concerned, their presence on the board can help to bring about early challenges from organized labor to proposals not felt to be in the workers' best interest.

This last potential for adversely affecting the decision-making process in the boardroom would seem to be the reason for another drawback that is mentioned in having employees serve on the board. Many executives, as well as employees and union members, feel that there is a strong motivation on the part of management to avoid the potential roadblock represented by employee directors by making decisions outside the confines of the boardroom. There is a temptation for key executives to confer among themselves informally rather than to risk confrontation or challenge at the board level. The 1976 Swedish legislation that provides for nonmanagement employee board membership takes this potential problem into account by providing that where there are management committees with authority to consider major company matters, employees have the right to be present at meetings of those committees.

Another problem mentioned in placing nonmanagement employees on boards of directors is the time involved before such a director can acquire the experience and also the confidence to make a genuine contribution in boardroom deliberations and decision making. This problem can be aggravated in situations where employee directors serve specified terms and then are replaced by others. Both Germany and Sweden have programs for training employees for board service, but executives sometimes complain that these programs are costly — including the cost of time away from the employee's basic job — and that the training can have only limited success.

Another objection raised to the presence of non-management employees on the board is that it diminishes the control of shareholders over decisions made concerning company assets, and therefore interferes with the traditional legal right of owners' control. This threat to the right of ownership involved in the purchase of shares was raised vigorously in Germany during consideration of the 1976 legislation, and was evidently a factor in the formula that was finally arrived at, which, although it provides for equal representation for employees and shareholder representatives, also contains features that give a slight edge in voting potential to the shareholder side. Even this formula is being challenged in the courts as effectively depriving shareholders of some control over their assets. Some Germans express concern that this aspect of equal board representation for employees will put German companies at a disadvantage in attracting investment capital. British critics of the Bullock Committee's proposals in that country have voiced the same concern.

The argument that workers who are chosen to serve on boards of directors are placed in a difficult position is one of the most often mentioned criticisms. The worker director is faced with having to decide on matters with which be may be quite unfamiliar; he finds himself in an atmosphere in which he may feel that he is not really considered an equal; he may find himself confronted with a sense of conflict in having to decide on issues that may have quite different priorities for the company as a whole and for his fellow employees; and he may even find that his service as a director results in suspicion or loss of confidence among his fellow employees, who may no longer make him privy to their own thinking on the one hand — or may see him as consorting with the enemy on the other. It has been said that there are cases where Swedish unions, which control the selection of nonmanagement employee directors in that country, have refrained from placing key people on boards for fear of having them compromised or diminished in effectiveness through this process.

Placing blue-collar workers on the board has another disadvantage, some people feel strongly; it leaves out the middle-management ranks. This point of view emphasizes the important role played by managers below the top rank in running a company, and suggests that the position of these people has already been weakened by various worker participation arrangements. To add the further indignity of keeping them out of the boardroom while the lower ranks of employees are let in only makes their position in the company more difficult, it is argued. The 1976 German legislation guarantees at least one seat on the supervisory board to a senior executive or manager, although the definition of what level is meant is not yet clear.

The single objection to worker board membership that is voiced with the strongest feeling by executives in conversation and is made a great deal of in statements by employer organizations is that the system gives unions too much power. Even in Germany, where unions do not control the selection process for all worker directors as they do in Sweden and as it has been proposed they do in Britain, it has been shown that unions are nonetheless very influential in the process. And the 1976 legislation grants board seats to representatives of unions, even though those representatives may not work within the company itself. The fact that Swedish unions have been granted the power to select employees for board service is tempered somewhat by the fact that board membership for employees is essentially limited to two seats, and by the attitude of unions that makes it possible for management to negotiate important issues, including board representation. On the other hand, the traditional union situation in the United Kingdom is one of fragmentation and confrontation; this is a major cause of the struggle by the industrial community in the U.K. to prevent the imposition of the system proposed by the Bullock Committee, which would place the machinery for worker-director election entirely in the hands of the unions.

Finally, two general observations are often made by executives and by students of the subject about the practice of placing nonmanagement employees on boards of directors. One is that employee board membership should not be seen as a substitute for more basic forms of employee participation in the decision-making process of a company. According to this widely expressed point of view, providing for worker directors can accomplish little if there is not at the same time, and preferably already well-established, a system at lower levels of the company that gives employees a formal and effective means for making their viewpoints heard concerning matters that affect them. The German works-council system, a concept that dates back to the mid-nineteenth century in that country and which has extensive authority under present-day law, is often cited as a reason for the successful implementation of Mitbestimmung in that country. Sweden also has a well-integrated system for incorporating the employee point of view in the decision-making process, a system

that serves as an underpinning for the presence of union-appointed employees on the board. But Britain does not have such a system, a fact that is often mentioned as a reason why the Bullock proposal for employee board representation could not succeed.

The other general comment made about employee board representation is that the preoccupation with a formula, in terms of numbers of representatives, may be misguided and tend to obscure or ignore an important reality concerning how boards of directors operate. Stressing how many votes each side can muster suggests that boards of directors take votes frequently on issues before them. In practice, however, it is found that boards seldom decide issues by formal voting procedure. The decision-making process at the board level is generally one of arriving at a consensus, preferably complete agreement, in an atmosphere in which strong objection can defer or even defeat an issue without the benefit of any formal voting procedure. This perception of how directors arrive at decisions leads to the belief that the very presence of workers on a board is more important than how strong they are in number.

Prior to the 1976 legislation, most major German companies operated with supervisory boards having one-third worker representation. It is argued that even though the employees on such boards could not stalemate issues in terms of having equal number of votes with shareholder representatives, their presence frequently led to consensus decisions that might well have differed from decisions that would have been made in their absence. But it is also true that the management-and-employers side in the struggle that preceded the 1976 legislation in Germany fought to prevent the extension of the coal and steel formula to other industries, because they did not wish equal representation with shareholder representatives to become the general practice. The fear was that true parity of voting power would result not in consensus but in stalemates that would not only hamper board effectiveness but could even negate the control of shareholders over company affairs.

The Two-Tier Board Structure

The two-tier structure, in which a supervisory board or council appoints and oversees a management or executive board, is generally found where board membership (on the supervisory board) has been granted or provided to nonmanagement employees. But it can also exist without employee board representation, as it does in the Netherlands. And it is possible to give workers board membership without at the same time establishing a two-tier structure; Sweden is an example of this. Thus the concept of two bodies dividing the top-management function of a company can and does exist separately from that of nonmanagement employee board representation, and can be considered a concept in its own right.

The following characteristics, or consequences, of the two-tier approach to top management organization are observable:

(1) A two-tier structure separates in a tangible way the direct management of a company and the function of supervising and overseeing the management function. In countries with a single board, these functions are perceived as separate and to some extent are carried out separately. But since some individuals bear the responsibility for both they can become muddled and the supervisory function may become weakened in the process.

(2) The physical separation into two bodies not only results in delineating and defining the two functions of management and supervision, but assures that one person is not asked or expected to do both. Perhaps it would be more valid to say that one person is prohibited from doing both.

(3) The two-tier structure changes — and to an important degree diminishes — the role of the traditional director or board member. The supervisory body is not granted direct managerial authority over company affairs. The members of the supervisory board are, therefore, one step removed from the ability to control directly most events in the company. This leaves them with quite a different role to play from that performed by directors serving on a single board, who usually have full authority to act directly in company matters.

(4) Presumably it insulates supervisory board members from the degree of liability that, in some countries at least, attaches to serving as a director on a single board.

The net effect of establishing a two-tier system is not easy to assess. One result that seems to occur is that management is given a clear and also stronger authority over company affairs. This is said even in France, where traditionally the combination president-chairman position has been one of considerable authority. But this does not mean that the supervisory board is without potential or real authority, influence or impact. This is attested to by comments in Germany, where the system originated and has prevailed for years. For example, it is still possible for a major shareholder to make his wishes known effectively through the instrument of the supervisory board. Also, the law gives the supervisory board approval power over certain key decisions in the financial area that assure that management is answerable to its wishes. And, of course, it has the power not only to appoint but also to dismiss members of the management board.

The role of banks in Germany adds a dimension of importance to the supervisory board in that country. German banks can and do purchase shares of companies for their own account. In addition, German banks customarily contact their customers who own shares of these companies in which the bank itself has invested and who are holding or keeping their shares in the bank's custody, requesting that the bank be given power to vote the customers' shares along with its own. This tends to make banks emerge as key shareholders in many corporations, with the expected result that they hold board seats on the supervisory boards of those companies. This situation may coincide with that of large loans made to the company by the bank, the combined effect being one in which banks exert considerable influence, made tangible through membership or chairmanship of supervisory boards.

Although the two-tier board structure is often seen as a radical departure from the North American viewpoint, Europeans find a similarity to the two-tier structure in the management organization of some major U.S. corporations. They suggest that when a board of directors consists largely of outside directors, who are limited by time and the amount of information they can acquire to a kind of supervisory role, and when there is also a strong and active management or executive committee that meets frequently and has considerable authority over management affairs, the result is very similar to the results found under the two-tier system. The big difference is that the U.S. board retains full authority over the company's affairs, unlike the supervisory board, which does not have such authority.

Some critics of the two-tier system are skeptical of its motivation. They feel that it is put into effect primarily to ensure that worker directors cannot be elected to the essential management body of the company. Also, the comment is heard in Germany that some companies in that country have gotten into serious difficulties because of the inability of the supervisory board system to provide effective oversight. The combination of lack of authority, limited information about company affairs, and infrequent board meetings gives the supervisory board little opportunity or capability to monitor management performance or corporate affairs effectively, in this view.

Revival of Board Independence and Authority

The third development in directorship practices that has major significance, particularly in the view of study respondents in the United States where this trend seems to be most evident, involves more of a change of attitude than one of board makeup or structure. A growing number of boards have begun to reassert the primacy of authority that critics of the board system in that country (and elsewhere) believe has been largely usurped by corporate managements. The impetus for this trend has come from external factors but its implementation, unlike the two changes described above, has not been imposed from outside: It is the achievement of directors themselves. And to a large extent this shift in the balance of power has been accomplished with a minimum of resistance from management — sometimes with management's help — although in some cases it has led to the replacement of the chief executive.

The underlying factors in this trend, all dealt with in some detail in the chapter on the United States (and also reflected in material on other countries), include:

• *An increase in the climate of potential liability for directors.* Members of boards in that country are clearly concerned about the increased chances of involvement in lawsuits and other difficulties to which they are now exposed as directors. They have responded, in many cases, by involving themselves more seriously in their responsibilities, and in the process have restored to the board a degree of control over the company and its affairs that was lacking.

• *A loss of public confidence in big business and its leadership.* Scandals of national and international proportions involving major corporations, and a growing uneasiness over the size and power of corporate giants, have led to what some see as a crisis of confidence that worries U.S. business leaders and board members. One hoped-for result of strengthening the board's authority is that shareholders and the general public — and the government — will be reassured that corporate abuses of power can be self-corrected.

• *An increase in criticism of the board as a viable institution.* The board's passivity or ineffectiveness has been increasingly singled out as a weak spot in the free-enterprise system. One response to this criticism on the part of some boards has been a reassertion of board authority and a stronger stance by individual directors in the performance of their duties and in their position relative to management.

• *The possibility of government intervention.* The U.S. business community wants very much to prevent further encroachment of government on the freedom of companies to manage their own affairs and make their own decisions. Undoubtedly, some of the emphasis by U.S. business leaders on restoring authority and legitimacy to the board — and it should be emphasized that this trend is evident among some of the top U.S. companies — stems from a conviction that if business does not get its own house in order it will be forced to do so, on undesirable terms, by government.

Given these factors behind the increase in board authority and independence in a number of major U.S. firms, here are four of the specific responses by boards that achieve this result:

• *The audit committee has risen to prominence.* For many observers of the United States boardroom scene, the new emphasis given to the audit committee of the board is the single most important and significant development in board practices in that country. This committee, almost always consisting entirely of outside directors, has become a primary tool by which the board (1) monitors corporate performance, and (2) acquires corporate information outside the usual channel — essentially the chief executive. In the process it has come to represent the board's independence as well as the company's financial credibility.

And some companies have expanded the role of this committee, which has traditionally been that of arranging for and verifying the company's annual financial audit (external and internal). Some audit committees now also have the job of overseeing corporate policy and behavior in such increasingly sensitive areas as social responsibility, ethical business conduct, and avoidance of conflict of interest for directors as well as employees. Where there is no policy the committee may be called upon to develop one. Audit committees have also been the instrument, in many cases, through which companies have conducted self-examinations to learn whether illegal or so-called unusual payments have been made to acquire or maintain business contracts.

A requirement by the New York Stock Exchange that all listed companies have an audit committee, made up of independent directors, by mid-1978 will not result in a major change, because most companies that are affected already have such a committee. But the ruling is an indication of the key role attributed to the audit committee in restoring independence and authority to U.S. boards.

• *Executive compensation and nominating committees have also gained ground.* Committees of outside directors charged with deciding on forms and levels of compensation for top executives in the company have become almost universal in major firms. Their purpose is to make decisions in this area as objectively as possible, and to reassure shareholders that top management cannot unilaterally line its own pockets with unreasonable compensation. Similarly, committees of outside directors have begun to appear as the channel through which nominees for board vacancies are selected and evaluated. As yet found only in a minority of large firms, this committee helps to meet the objection that a chief executive chooses only friends or supporters for board seats when the choice is his, which it is in many companies. Nominating committees shift to the board at least some control over its own composition, which can be an important step toward a more independent board.

• *Directors are getting better company information.* Directors of United States corporations are asking for and getting more and/or more useful information about company affairs on which to base their decisions. The ability to get information, for a board as for any group or organization, or for individuals, is an essential ingredient in being able to make valid independent judgments on management proposals or other corporate affairs. (The audit committee is seen by many directors as the board's most important potential source of information.)

• *Boards are challenging management.* A climate has developed in the United States in which directors are showing a greater willingness to take serious issue with corporate managements and to face up to a change at the top when it is called for. The frequency of press reports that a corporate chief executive is leaving a company to "pursue other interests" (only infrequently is board displeasure with performance or disagreement on policy issues specified in such announcements, however) bears testimony to this change.

The effect of these changes in companies where they have occurred is a major one, in terms of the relationship of management to the board and in terms of the status of the board itself. And the extent to which these trends have begun to assert themselves in major U.S. corporations constitutes a significant change in directorship practices in that country. It remains to be seen whether this trend will be overshadowed by more sweeping legislative approaches that so far have not moved beyond the discussion stage and may never do so.

Reappraisal of the Board in a Changing Context

As significant as the changes described above are, or are felt to be, they do not necessarily involve a change in the concept of what a board does nor should do. For example, the legislation in Germany and Sweden that is bringing about important changes in board membership does not redefine or change the essential role of boards in those countries, although the changes in membership could well affect board practices in time.

Yet the fundamental concept of the board and its role, and its suitability and effectiveness as an instrument of corporate governance, are indeed being questioned in a number of countries. And the questions stem not only from incidents that amount to breakdowns in the system of which the board is at the center but also from a realization that the entire context in which boards — and companies — function has been undergoing major changes.

Questions Growing Out of Corporate Conduct

Basic doubts about the ability of boards of directors to govern the modern corporation have been raised by incidents that have aroused the concern and antagonism of people in and out of government. The United States can be used to illustrate this point perhaps better than any other country. The list of developments there that have led to a reappraisal of the board and its role include charges of widespread environmental damage; payment of bribes; providing poor and even dangerous products and services; misuse of company assets; improper use of privileged company information by insiders; connections between "big business" and government that lead to charges of favoritism; anticompetitive arrangements such as price fixing (and interlocking directorships); and the unexpected collapse of such major firms as Penn Central.

Inevitably, questions raised as a result of these developments lead to the boardroom. Where were the directors when all this was going on? Why didn't they know what was happening? If they did know, why didn't they put a stop to it, or replace top management? For some who have considered these questions, the answers suggest that the board as it now exists is no longer adequate to the challenge of overseeing the modern U.S. company. But for others the solution is to be found in breathing new life into the board and making it more effective.

The Reality of a Changing Environment

Directors do not exist or make decisions in a vacuum; they carry out their function in a real world that is increasingly one of change. Even if some of these changes do not bear directly on the board and its work, their cumulative effect is important to directors, because the concepts of management, of private enterprise, even of national boundaries, are in a state of flux. The question being raised is: Can boards as we have known them meet the challenge of such an altered environment?

A summary of major changes in the business and boardroom environment follows:

• *Greater social responsibility for companies.* Every reader will be familiar with at least some of the issues such as "consumerism," or demands for codes of conduct for companies, that have become part of running a present-day corporation. To the extent that companies must demonstrate a social responsibility in their operations, directors must take this newly important requirement into account in overseeing their companies.

• *Employee participation in decision making.* Despite the importance of the election of nonmanagement employees to boards of directors in some countries, many people see greater significance in the extent to which employees have gained the right to share in decisions concerning their jobs. The key to the importance placed on this trend is the fact that employees have gone beyond merely being *consulted* on matters and now have true co-decision authority in many areas, at least in some countries. This is more a concern for management than for the board, but it is bound to affect some board decisions too.

• *Employee participation in ownership and profits.* Steadily, and for the most part quietly, in several countries employees have become substantial shareholders in the companies for which they work. The bulk of this ownership is indirect, as in the case of profit-sharing or pension plans that own shares of the company's stock on the employees' behalf. Perhaps this is why there has been little indication to date that employees want to use their ownership position to pressure management on issues. But European employers are concerned about the possibility that proposals for "economic democracy," such as the one endorsed by the Swedish trade union confederation in 1976, will be implemented. The Swedish proposal is to convert some of each company's profits into a special form of equity and place it in a central national fund

that would be controlled by the trade unions. In due time the unions would gain effective control over Sweden's companies under this plan, and thus the employers in that country are trying to prevent it from being legislated.

• *Employee job security.* Whereas at one time managements had the almost unlimited authority to discharge employees, modern managements find that their hands are increasingly stayed when it comes to laying off workers. Recent legislation in Sweden significantly curtails managements' ability to discharge employees. And unions in general have fought for and achieved some measure of control over the firing of employees. In terms of industrial democracy, the restriction of the authority of managements to lay off employees means, among other things, that employees who believe they have cause to be critical of management feel secure in the knowledge that management will not be able to get rid of them by firing them, as was once a common practice.

• *Increased information to employees.* Among the countries reported on here, Germany and Sweden probably lead the way in providing a great deal more information about company affairs to employees than was once the case. Works councils and board membership are two channels for information, but there are also others. To manage in such an atmosphere, instead of one in which management has the luxury of secrecy, is a challenge — one in which directors can be directly involved.

• *Changes in corporate ownership patterns.* In some of the countries described in this report — Turkey and Venezuela, in particular — those who own a company are often directly involved with it and its affairs; ownership is a real and influential factor both for management and for the board. In other countries, however, ownership has moved away from this traditional pattern, in several respects:

• Companies have many, widely scattered owners, few or none of whom have substantial holdings (with the exception of institutional investors).

• Shareholders act as investors rather than owners and sell their shares if they are unsatisfied, rather than involve themselves in company affairs or challenge management.

• Institutional investors have become a dominant, although so far passive, factor in corporate ownership.

• Ownership has become increasingly multinational.

• In some countries, government investment in private-sector companies is substantial.

The fact that corporate ownership so little resembles its initial concept, where many large companies are concerned, has important meaning for directors. Most board members believe they have a responsibility to protect the interests of shareholders and yet are aware ownership has lost much of its significance. At the same time, other claims are being made on them as directors — to see that their companies are socially responsible, for example — that create a problem of multiple accountability for the modern director.

• *Government intervention and ownership.* National and lower level governments are having more and more of a say on how companies are run. New or revised legislation and aggressive regulation in a number of the surveyed countries have placed major demands on businesses, in terms of time and paperwork but also in terms of changed decision-making methods. Some laws — those specifying pollution-control standards, for example — have a major effect on investment decisions. And the process of nationalizing industries or companies and converting them to government ownership and management has been a major trend in some countries. For the director who is involved in either of these developments, the effect on how he views his responsibility and how he carries it out can be major.

• *Social contracts.* Sweden, Germany and Great Britain have experienced varying degrees of "social contracts," loosely defined here as agreements between business and labor, in coordination with government, to subordinate their own interests (wage increases, for example) to some extent so as to achieve goals in the common interest. Where a "social contract" is in effect, the options of management may be significantly limited in some areas of running the business (pricing, for example), and this becomes a concern of the board.

• *Internationalization.* One of the major realities of today's business environment is its international nature. The modern corporation crosses national boundaries with ease and as a matter of course. Whatever other implications this development may have — including the question of how the transnational company can be controlled and held accountable — it affects boardroom thinking and even board composition.

Out of the disappointments and uncertainties just described have evolved two main avenues of inquiry where boards of directors are concerned. One focuses on reassessing what the proper role of a board is supposed to be, including the possibility that this concept should be clarified and strengthened. The other inquiry concentrates on finding and implementing ways to make the board more effective in performing whatever is expected of it.

Direct, Supervise or Manage?

Among the surveyed countries, Canada and the United States illustrate most clearly the search for clarification of the board's function. One reason is that the two countries share what some call a legal fiction. State and provincial laws of each typically state that a board "shall manage the affairs of the corporation," and give the board more or less complete authority to do just that. But the legal concept is almost universally ignored and boards don't "manage"; that is left to managers, to whom the necessary authority is delegated.

The difference between practice and law rarely creates a problem because the system works, at least from one point of view. But the difference has received new attention because, to some proponents of reform, it represents an essential ambivalence in the concept of the board.

Dictionary definitions of terms such as "direct" or "manage" are not very helpful in this real-life situation. What is clear is that the chief executive of a widely traded Canadian or U.S. firm usually has a firm grip on corporate affairs and gets little interference from the board. Management runs the company from day to day, and management also initiates longer range plans and proposals; the board is largely passive and reactive (although it can influence management both by its advice and opinion and by the potential veto it holds over major proposals). Ownership, in the person of shareholders, is also generally passive. The typical chief executive officer in such a situation has very little "direction" from outside and a great deal of managerial authority.

A question that is being raised is whether a redefinition and clarification of roles is not needed as an essential step toward redressing the balance of power in corporations and restoring some authority to the board. But those who are raising this question are not suggesting that the board move into day-to-day company affairs; they seek closer supervision of duties that would still be delegated to management.

In Europe, the distinction between managing and directing or supervising is not an issue in some countries because it is not a problem. West German law makes the distinction pretty clearly, and in the process gives the supervisory board no managerial authority. In Sweden, where boards consist almost entirely of outsiders and meet infrequently — and where law prohibits combining the chief executive and chairman positions in one person — the distinction is also clear, although the Swedish board has the authority, if it chooses, to step in and make management decisions. The addition of nonmanagerial employees to Swedish boards does not change this distinction although it may result in matters being discussed at the board level that would not otherwise be dealt with there.

There does not appear to be a major thrust in France to change the practice of investing a great deal of authority in full-time management over company affairs, although there are proposals — in particular *La Réforme de l'Entreprise,* the report by the government-appointed committee headed by a former cabinet minister, Pierre Sudreau — for changing several aspects of how companies are run. France has had several years' experience with a voluntary two-tier board system; like the German system, where it is adopted it has the effect of sharpening the distinction between supervision and management, and of giving management a clear-cut mandate to run the company. In the still-prevailing single-board arrangement in France, the board consists of both managers and outsiders and, therefore, the distinction between supervision and management tends to be blurred, in the view of some French executives. But a different view says that many boards in that country are passive and do not interfere with management's prerogatives.

A reading of the chapter on the United Kingdom will show that keeping the management and supervision or direction functions discrete may be especially difficult in the traditional British board, where a majority are company executives. In this situation the ability of the board to provide a supervisory discipline depends more than it usually does on whether the executives who are also directors can successfully take a companywide perspective, rather than a departmental or divisional one, on matters that come before the board. Some British observers believe that this is difficult even for the best-intentioned executive and that British boards are not successful in directing or supervising themselves.

The eventual outcome of the Bullock Report's proposals (more accurately, the proposals of the majority of the Committee) may create quite a different environment for board-management relations in the United Kingdom, of course, but that outcome cannot be predicted at the moment.

In Turkey, as the chapter on that country explains, company ownership is often personally represented in the membership of the board. The same is true in Venezuela. In this structure, where the board has

ultimate authority and where the board can be said to be identical with the owners, distinctions between supervising and managing, where the board is concerned, may have little meaning or importance because of the direct influence of ownership on management decisions. Yet executives in both those countries express an awareness of the need to have a distinction. Since public ownership of companies (by individuals, in this case, not government) is on the increase in both countries, the pattern may change.

Board Ineffectiveness

Most criticism of the board and its performance does not concern its role as such but is centered on its ineffectiveness. In other words, directors know what they are supposed to do but they do not do it — or do too little of it to make a difference. Boards are ineffective in the following ways and for the following reasons, according to those who have raised this issue:

• *They lack objectivity and independence.* Directors are frequently selected by and tend to be sympathetic to top management. Or they have a business relationship with the company — as customer, or supplier, or provider of financial or legal services. In either case, they are not objective, independent overseers.

• *They lack true authority over management.* The board is supposed to be at the apex of the pyramid of authority; it should select (also dismiss) and monitor management. But in large modern companies the board's authority has been eclipsed by the power and effectiveness of professional managers, it is claimed, aided by the decentralization of ownership. Boards now defer to chief executives, instead of the other way around.

• *They lack a grasp of what is going on in the company.* Directors have been caught sleeping while illegal or ill-considered activities have plunged companies into financial or legal difficulties, or shareholders' interests have been abused. Recent scandals have reached international proportions and have raised embarrassing questions about how little knowledge directors have of companies in their charge. Critics say that directors rely too much on what management tells them and do not ask enough questions, and that this is a major cause of their ineffectiveness.

• *They do not work hard enough.* Most directors work hard, of course, but their time and effort is devoted primarily to their own business or profession. As busy people, they have little time to devote to serving on the board of someone else's company, with the result that directors do not work hard enough at it to do an effective job.

Proposals for Board Reform

Increasing concern over the effectiveness of boards of directors has produced a number of recommendations for changes designed to improve board performance and corporate governance in general. Some of these suggested reforms have greater applicability to some countries than they do to others, but most would probably be adaptable to each of the surveyed countries to some degree. And, in fact, a number of these changes are already taking place — voluntarily, in most cases, rather than under legislative mandate.

Proposals for reform of directorship practices include those in the following areas:

• *Selection procedures for directors.* One drawback to the director-selection process, it is often argued, is that the mail proxy system that has become necessary because of scattered ownership places the nomination and voting procedures under the control of incumbent managements. It is felt that this has led to a selection process that perpetuates boards comprised of directors who are sympathetic to top management; who, in fact, feel a sense of loyalty and obligation that prevents them from viewing management proposals objectively or from opposing management on important issues.

What is needed is better "corporate democracy," some say, and three major approaches have been suggested. One is to change the proxy system so that nominations for director positions can be accommodated from shareholders and others outside the company itself. And it is suggested that cumulative voting for directors be adopted by more companies. This is a system that allows shareholders to concentrate their votes on selected candidates rather than have their votes spread evenly over all candidates, which is what happens if they do not have the cumulative privilege. Cumulative voting is considered a more democratic system because it makes it at least theoretically possible to elect directors that management may not want.

A third approach to reducing management's control over the nomination of candidates for the board has become popular in recent years in the United States. It involves the establishment of a committee at the board level, usually consisting of outside directors, whose job it is to assess the need for new directors, to locate and evaluate possible candidates, and to recommend to the full board what person or persons should be approached and invited to stand for election. Such a committee is often called a nominating committee.

• *Criteria for selection of directors.* Who should serve on the board is a different matter from how they should be nominated and elected; to many the area of establishing criteria for choosing directors represents the opportunity for achieving the greatest improvement in board effectiveness. A common goal of many critics of board performance is to increase the number of true outsiders, meaning people who do not work for the company, have not done so in the past, and have no business connections with it. Another need that has been expressed is to approach the selection process with a thought-out goal of what mix of talents and experience on the board would best suit the company and its situation, instead of treating board service invitations as isolated decisions. Some countries in this survey have seen demands that boards be opened up to members who would represent consumer, environmental, community or other outside but concerned viewpoints. (Community representatives are found on some Swedish boards, but the general concept of special-interest board representation is generally stoutly resisted everywhere.) And, of course, nonmanagement employees, who already sit on boards in some countries, are seen by some not only as having a right to directorships as partners with representatives of capital but also as being able to add an important understanding of company affairs to board deliberations.

• *Training and information for directors.* One proposal for improving board effectiveness is to provide some form of training to newly elected directors. It might be an indoctrination program to give them important information about the company (its products or services, its plant locations); or it might be a program aimed at the director's job and familiarizing the new director with board procedures, the kinds of matters the board considers, the board decision-making process, and the kind of information that is made available to directors to help them. And directors in several countries feel that an improvement could be made in both the quantity and quality of the information they receive, and that better information could make them more effective as directors. Training is already available for workers selected for board service in Germany and Sweden.

• *Board leadership.* A board, like any group, needs leadership to be effective. Some criticism of board performance emphasizes the importance of having a leader — usually in the person of a chairman — who can and does motivate directors to contribute, and who can handle the process of integrating possibly conflicting points of view into an eventual consensus. There is a debate in progress in the United States on the basic question of whether the chairman of the board who is also the chief executive officer does not have excessive authority, and whether there is not an essential conflict when one person holds both positions. (In some countries the combined positions are not possible.)

• *Board committees.* The extensive use of committees of directors is very much a North American practice, where they are receiving new emphasis as a way to increase board awareness and effectiveness. Particularly in the United States, the use of an audit committee has received widespread approval, both as a means of gaining more information about company affairs for the board itself and as a means of ensuring that shareholders and others are receiving complete and timely information. Other committees that have become more popular in that country are the executive compensation committee, the social or public responsibility committee, and the nominating committee, as noted.

Chief Concerns of Directors

Those who serve on boards of directors are often in agreement with those who argue for change or improvement in directorship practices. The chapters on individual countries give every evidence of the awareness of directors and company managers of shortcomings in the performance of boards, and show that many of these directors and executives favor changes in the system. But it is also clear that they view some changes, both present and proposed, with alarm. Their chief concerns are outlined below.

Workers on the Board

Most respondents in countries where blue-collar employees do not serve on boards of directors are against the idea, citing the reasons that were spelled out at the beginning of this chapter. Respondents in Germany and Sweden, where workers do sit on boards, are not so negative about the concept, but Germans do express concern over the extension of the coal-steel parity representation idea to other industries under the 1976 law.

There seem to be two big worries about having workers in equal numbers with shareholder representatives, apart from slower decision making and other working problems. One is that it may deprive shareholders of their right, under the concept of private property, to control the use of the assets they own.

The other is that it will place too much effective power in the hands of organized labor.

The Growth of Union Power

The growth of the power of the unions is an almost universal concern of these who direct and run modern companies. As noted, much of the opposition to worker board representation is not aimed at the concept itself but at the added influence it gives to unions. This is especially true if unions are to be given the say over which employees will be selected for board service; such a feature in the Bullock proposal in Britain accounted for some of the loudest outcry against the committee's recommendations in that country.

Managements and supervisory board members in Germany are apprehensive that the presence of union delegates on the supervisory board, as provided for under the 1976 law, will not only give organized labor a stronger foot in the door at the top, but will also give the unions a built-in intelligence network that could put companies at a disadvantage in labor negotiations.

Constituency Representation

A board composed of directors who represent specific interests or groups outside the company, instead of sharing a common primary responsibility to represent the interests of shareholders, just will not work. That is the opinion of many directors and executives in various countries.

They strongly oppose the idea being put forward that board membership should be opened up to advocates or representatives of particular interests. It would destroy the necessary ability of boards to reach consensus decisions, they say, and the efficiency and effectiveness of boards would suffer.

Government Intervention

Concern about increasing government intervention in corporate affairs may be strongest in North America. Certainly United States managements and boards are alarmed over the extent of what they see as government encroachment on private-sector freedoms through legislation and regulatory enforcement. And they deplore the costs incurred in meeting government requirements in such areas as pollution control, the Occupational Safety and Health Act, and the Employee Retirement Income Security Act. A present concern is the possibility that Congress might entertain the idea of a federal incorporation requirement for large corporations. If such legislation were to be passed, it would very probably contain rules governing the makeup and possibly the duties of boards.

European respondents are accustomed to a considerably greater degree of government say in corporate affairs than their North American counterparts are used to. Still, German employers fought hard against the legislation that was eventually passed placing more workers on boards there, and in Britain the government move toward adding workers to boards in that country has met stiff resistance.

Changes in Liability and Accountability

Legal or financial liability is not a major concern of directors anywhere but in the United States, where it is the single greatest concern of many board members and has led to changes in practices (broadened provisions for indemnification for directors by companies, widespread use of directors' and officers' liability insurance, more active and inquisitive directors). Some directors outside the United States attribute the legal liability problem in that country to the fact that contingency fees for attorneys are permitted there. Both lawyers and clients are more prone to undertake lawsuits under such a system. The extensive use of class-action suits has also drawn many shareholders into the litigation process and made them conscious of the courts as a means of getting satisfaction when they believe that directors have not performed their duty or have acted contrary to the best interests of the shareholders.

On the other hand, directors in several countries share with those in North America a growing complexity in the concept of whom they are accountable to for their stewardship of a company. A director today in Sweden or Germany or the United Kingdom, just as in Canada and the United States, feels the pressure of having to serve more than one master. He or she must weigh factors other than what is best for the shareholder, and sometimes faces difficult choices between legitimate claims by more than one constituency — consumers, the community, employees, society as a whole. (The situation would be made considerably worse, many directors feel, if different constituencies were actually present as members of the board.)

The combination of major changes, pressures for reform, and chief concerns outlined in this chapter add up to an atmosphere for directors that is making board membership a serious and demanding responsibility. It is not too much to say that an all-but-honorary position is in the process of becoming a new profession — one that demands all the best qualities that lead to success in other professions. And it is possible that if the directorship function does not evolve in this direction quickly enough and effectively enough to match the corporation's changing environment, its legitimacy as the apex of the corporate structure may not survive the challenge it is facing in countries around the world.

Chapter 2
Board Comparisons

IN THIS CHAPTER, some comparisons are made among boards of directors and how they operate in the different countries under consideration. Comparisons are in some cases tentative because the information available from countries varies in detail. Nevertheless, there is clearly a core of agreement, a common perception of what a board of directors — or a supervisory board or council — is and does, from one country to the next. There are also distinctive differences in directorship practices, often based on national patterns.

Similarities in Boards and Board Practices

In terms of how boards resemble each other, four characteristics seem to be present regardless of the country being considered.

The Basic Legal Concept

The shared traditional legal concept of the board is that of a body chosen by the corporate owners to represent them and to have legal authority to act on their behalf in company matters. The obligation of directors to protect the interests of the shareholders is not as exact or demanding as that of legal fiduciaries; their two most clearly defined duties, as established by courts in several countries, are: (1) to be loyal to the interests of the shareholders and the company itself, and (2) to be prudent (but not necessarily expert) in their judgment in board matters, and diligent in performing their duties. These standards have not normally been difficult to meet — some say they are not rigid enough — but in recent years lawsuits and regulatory actions in the United States have established

somewhat higher norms there than before, along with higher exposure to liability.

Areas of Primary Involvement

Beyond the similarity of the basic concept and responsibility under law in different countries, there is also a degree of consistency in what boards do in carrying out that responsibility. Directors in most of the countries surveyed were asked to define the essential role of the board according to their own experience, and to cite the kinds of decisions a board must either make or approve to fulfill its function. Responses show that the director's job tends to center around the same areas of responsibility, whatever the country:

(1) Long-range corporate objectives;
(2) Corporate strategies or long-range plans for meeting objectives;
(3) Allocation of major resources;
(4) Major financial decisions, including changes in capitalization and capital investment programs;
(5) Mergers, acquisitions, divestments;
(6) Top management performance appraisal, succession, compensation.

Boards differ in dealing with these matters, from one country to the next, in how directly they get involved in them. This, in turn, seems to depend on the pattern of board membership. Direct shareholder representation on the board, such as is common in Turkey and Venezuela, tends to result in direct board involvement. Scattered and disinterested ownership, like that found in the major industrialized countries, leads to boards that have little direct involvement with company affairs. An exception to this latter statement is found in the United Kingdom, where a predominance of company executives on the typical board leads to relatively direct involvement by the board in management decisions. In Germany, the indirect role of the supervisory board is a built-in feature of the two-tier structure there.

The Importance and Influence of the Individual

Comments from directors in several countries stress that a board is not a faceless group but, rather, a group of individuals, who differ in their points of view and in their ability to make a contribution. What counts in the long run is the commitment, integrity and personal effectiveness of directors as individuals. This can be enhanced by strong leadership by the chairman, itself an individual factor.

Perhaps the single most important individual, however, in terms of the board's role and its relationship with management, is the chief executive officer. In any case, many board decisions depend in the end on a position taken by a single director — a position that can be quite lonely.

The Conflict of the Employee Director

In an earlier section on worker directors it was pointed out that the nonmanagement employee who is chosen to serve on the board faces difficulties in his role as a director. Company executives, too, who are not new to the boardroom and who make up a substantial proportion of many boards, even outside the U.K., have problems in serving as directors.

The first is that of adopting a companywide perspective and of representing the shareholders and others, rather than themselves and their employees. Some executives are not really able to achieve the shift in perspective and in attitude that is called for in the director's job.

The second problem for the executive who serves on the board, of course, is that he is in an awkward situation relative to the chief executive officer. In his daily corporate life he works for the chief executive and is subordinate to him. But as a member of the board of directors, the executive in theory is asked to appraise the performance of the chief executive, and in extreme cases is expected to share the board's responsibility for replacing the chief executive. The consensus is that this is an almost impossible position for the

employee director, and that as a practical matter he does not and cannot be expected to take issue with the chief executive at board meetings or act as his monitor or appraiser in any realistic sense.

There are those who believe that the presence of employees on boards of directors, with the exception of the chief executive himself, is poor practice. It places the director who is an executive in a difficult position and, to some extent, it gives the chief executive the ability to produce the votes that he needs for his own proposals.

Differences in Boards and Board Practices

While boards of directors in various countries appear to have the shared characteristics outlined above, there are also distinctive differences — in makeup and in practices — that are often national in flavor. The description of board differences that follows demonstrates, if nothing else, that the concept of a board of directors is flexible enough to work in a variety of forms and styles.

Two of the major differences between boards in different countries — the presence or absence of nonmanagement employees, and the two-tier versus single board structure — will not be repeated here (they are discussed on pages 4 through 8).

National Distinctions

Boards tend to bear the stamp of the business, social and political environment of their country. Worker representation on the board is quite different in Sweden from Germany, for example. The factors that govern the national characteristics of boards are set forth below.

• *Corporate ownership patterns.* It has already been mentioned that the number, geographic distribution, and absence or presence of major shareholdings included in the ownership of a company can vary significantly, and that this pattern of ownership can have a definite effect not only on the composition of a board but on its function. The pattern of ownership tends to differ strongly among the countries surveyed, ranging from the concentrated ownership-direct board representation pattern found in Turkey and Venezuela, for example, to the U.S. pattern of widely dispersed ownership and thus a lack of ownership control or influence over a board's membership or its role.

Where ownership is concerned, study cooperators in several countries consider the presence of an active and well-organized securities market to be important. A stock market serves as a discipline on corporate leadership because it provides a measuring stick of results. And it is important for directors, as well: Stock performance is an indication of the quality of the board's stewardship (in other words, a measure of board performance) and also a means by which the board can appraise management. A market also means that a dissatisfied owner can sell his or her shares conveniently.

• *Politics and legislation.* Political parties have had a profound effect on boards of directors in some of the countries included in this survey, particularly on their composition. Thus in Sweden, for example, the long reign of the Social Democratic Party included the passage of legislation that is bringing workers onto the boards of most Swedish companies. Germany's 1976 legislation expanding the equal representation of workers on German boards was the achievement of a consensus of the Christian Democratic Union and Social Democratic parties. Britain's Labour Party is responsible for the inquiry by the Bullock Committee that is apparently leading to the addition of workers to British boards. Unions have been active in promoting such legislation in these countries, of course.

Some countries have laws that limit the presence of foreign directors on domestic-company boards. Foreigners employed by Venezuelan companies may not serve as directors in that country. A number of Canadian jurisdictions require that Canadians be in the majority on the boards of Canadian-owned or -controlled corporations.

Another type of law governing directorships that is found in several countries limits the number of boards on which an individual can serve. No such law exists in the United States, but there have been some suggestions that one should be passed.

Countries place different emphasis on the use of legislation to govern conduct of boards and business. German laws for company conduct and board composition and responsibility are relatively detailed; by contrast, British cooperators refer to a tendency in their country to dislike legislative mandates (it is still a country without a formal constitution), and to rely instead on custom and codes of honor.

• *Social concerns and the company.* The degree to which the social welfare of employees is considered a responsibility of the company can have an effect on the board of directors. For example, the German society's long-standing and thorough-going concern for the social aspects of life — as distinguished, for example, from the economic aspect, which in the

corporate framework means primarily wages — is reflected in several ways in German company life. One pertinent example is the position of labor director (Arbeitsdirektor), a required member of the management board (Vorstand). In the coal and steel industries, this appointment cannot be made by the supervisory board unless the worker members of that board approve of the nominee. Thus, employees have control over the choice of the executive who has authority over personnel matters. (This position is a somewhat ambiguous one under the 1976 legislation for other industries, however.)

Other European countries, too, have a socially oriented approach to the management of companies. This has not been true, by and large, of Canada and the United States. However, demands for socially responsible corporate conduct have begun to make themselves felt on the free-enterprise view of business in those countries. In terms of board practices, this development has been at least one factor behind the appointment of women to the boards of many major U.S. companies, and the establishment of social responsibility committees of the board. The new emphasis on the audit committee is also attributable, in part, to this trend.

• *Labor relations and organized unions.* The organized labor movement in North America has so far shown almost no interest in membership on boards of directors, and in fact has taken a strong stand against it. Also, North American boards of directors are characteristically not involved in labor relations or negotiations in a company. The situation is obviously different in such a country as Germany, where under new legislation there will be union representatives (as distinguished from company employees) sitting side by side with shareholder representatives on major company supervisory boards. Although labor relations matters are not considered a direct responsibility of the supervisory board on which nonmanagement employees sit in Germany, German executives say that the presence of workers, and in particular of union people, on the supervisory board can affect the supervisory board's procedure and its effectiveness in deciding on issues that affect the welfare of employees.

• *Management philosophy and style.* It can be said that there are national differences in management styles, and that these differences are reflected in the boardroom. For example, the French businessman operates in an atmosphere that has traditionally been highly authoritarian; one French chief executive interviewed for this survey likened the French business hierarchy to the Prussian military tradition of strong authority. The powerful position of the Président-Directeur-Général in France is consistent with this authoritarian tradition.

In the United States, the increasing separation of ownership from corporate management, combined with other factors such as the enormous growth in size and complexity of major U.S. corporations, has led to the preeminence of the professional manager. The man who achieves the chief executive post in a major U.S. corporation is able to use the lack of cohesiveness among corporate owners, and the fact that the machinery for the selection and election of directors is in the hands of management, to shape a board of directors that will enhance and support his programs. There has evolved in the United States the tendency in major corporations for the chief executive to serve also as chairman of the board.

• *Management representation on the board.* Another considerable difference among countries is the extent to which management is represented on the board of directors. At one end of the scale in this regard are Sweden — where almost all board members come from outside the company, and where in some cases the chief executive is the only member of management who also serves as a director — and Germany, where no members of management are found on the supervisory board as a matter of law.

One step removed from this practice is that found in North America, where outside directors generally outnumber directors from management, at least in major corporations, but where executives hold a larger proportion of board seats than their counterparts in Sweden.

On the other hand, the executive or inside director has traditionally held the majority of seats on boards in the U.K., although some major U.K. companies have boards on which outsiders predominate. And in Japan it is unusual to have anyone on a company board who is not from within the company (or at least a former employee).

The proportion of executive or management directors to directors from outside the company is a subject of current debate in several countries. In North America, there has been a long-time trend toward including a larger proportion of outside directors on boards. Even so, there is pressure in Canada and the United States not only to increase the proportion of outside directors but also to select outsiders who are more clearly independent in terms of freedom of affiliation with the company. And there are many British directors and executives who feel that the effectiveness of that country's board system might be improved by increasing the proportion of outside or nonexecutive directors on British boards. Also, Turkey has been experiencing an increased use of outside directors on boards in connection with a trend toward publicly held companies; the purpose is to create a board structure that has a sufficient independence to reassure private investors.

• *The use of board committees.* The assignment of directors to board committees that are designed to examine in closer detail particular areas of company affairs of concern to the board remains primarily a North American phenomenon. In the United States and Canada, the use of board committees is a widespread and relatively formalized practice. In recent years, the audit and executive compensation committees have received new attention and certain relatively new committees have begun to appear, such as a nominating committee for the choice of director candidates and a social responsibility committee.

Board committees are not unusual in the U.K., but are not nearly as frequently found as they are in North America. Formal board committees are more or less rare in Sweden, but the convening of small groups of directors is apparently fairly common; the 1976 Swedish legislation on employee board membership requires that employees be permitted to attend meetings of committees in that country. In Turkey, where company ownership is often directly represented on the board, committees are rarely found.

Universal Differences

Not all differences between boards of directors reflect country characteristics; some stem from universally found factors, regardless of country.

• *Company factors.* The role played by a particular board of directors at a given time can reflect rather accurately the situation in which the company finds itself. For example, a company that is clearly in good health in financial and marketing terms and is being effectively led may well have a board of directors that is not very involved; on the other hand, a company in financial or other difficulties may find its board of directors taking a far more active role and interest than usual. Boards everywhere seem to be at their most involved and effective best when a company faces a crisis.

As a company develops in size and complexity, its board may find its agenda changing to place less emphasis on specific areas and to concentrate more on overall planning, perhaps also with a change in membership to reflect a need for new expertise such as that of international management. One particular corporate development that can get a board involved, both in the sense of a specific contribution and in the sense of a heightened concern, is the prospect of a merger or acquisition.

• *Human factors.* It is obvious that the role of any given board of directors can be strongly affected by human factors. One of these is the strength of the incumbent management, or, particularly, the force of personality of the chief executive.

The importance of a board that can work together and assume common goals and responsibilities is stressed by respondents in various countries. It is often mentioned as a reason why there should not be a selection of advocates to serve on a board of directors. There is a widespread feeling that a director who is on a board solely to represent a constituency or a point of view may create a problem in board effectiveness.

Board leadership is a factor that is often mentioned by directors in commenting on differences in roles and also in effectiveness among boards. In some cases leadership comes about through the process of group dynamics, in the sense that a natural form of leadership tends to assert itself in the boardroom as with any other group. But board leadership more often has an organizational basis in the person of a chairman. The person who serves as board chairman has both the opportunity and responsibility for maximizing effectiveness. If the chief executive has the confidence of the board, the board itself will normally play a relatively passive role. This might be called the "don't tamper with success" approach to the board's function. But it is also true that a hands-off board may be the chief executive's idea. The situation in which a strong chief executive has run a company for a long time and during his tenure has managed to place on the board directors who tend to be supportive of his administration, and who holds in addition the title of chairman of the board, is one that can lead to a relatively impotent board. This situation has received criticism recently in the United States, where it is felt to result in an unhealthy concentration of authority, with a resulting loss of effectiveness at the board level.

Table 2-1: Summary of Reported Data on Composition and Organization of Boards of Directors of Major Companies in Nine Countries

	Federal Republic of Germany[a]	Sweden	United Kingdom	France[b]	Turkey[c]	United States	Canada	Venezuela[c]	Japan
Board structure	Two-tier	Single board	Single board	Single board	Single board	Single board	Single board	Single board	Single board
Board size:									
Range	20	4-15M / 7-14N[d]	6-25M / 7-24N	3-12	3-11	7-33M / 8-27N	5-18M / 5-53N	3-18	8-50[e]
Median	20	9[d]	15M / 20N	10[f]	7	13M / 15N	12M / 13N	7	21.6[f]
Percentage of boards having a majority of outside directors	None	100%	30%M / 25%N	100%	100%[g]	83%M / 86%N	88%M / 86%N	Majority[g]	None
Workers serve as voting directors	Yes	Yes	No	No	No	No	No	No[h]	No
Union representatives serve as voting directors	Yes	No[i]	No	No	No	No	No	No	No
Number or proportion of worker or union directors on a board	50%	2	None	None	None	None	None	None	None
Groups other than shareholders entitled to *elect* or *appoint* directors:									
Works council or employees	Yes	No	No	No	No	No	No	NA	No
Unions	Yes	Yes[j]	No	No	No	No	No	No	No
Government (when nonowner)	No	Yes[j]	No	No	No	No[k]	No	No[l]	No[m]
Most common term to which directors are elected (years)	NA	1[n]	3-4	5	3	1	1	2	2
Median number of board meetings per year	NA[o]	5M / 5.5N	NA	5[f]	16.5	10	5M / 6N	12	12
Percentage of boards having former employees as members	NA	41%M / 44%N	39%M / 63%N	NA	26%	63%	10%M / 8%N	12%	13%
Percentage of boards having women as members	NA	10%	4%	1.5%	10%	28%M / 41%N	4%M / 20%N	24%	None
Retirement policies for outside directors:									
Percentage of companies that have a policy	NA	23%M / 38%N	NA[p]	q	9%	82%M / 89%N	NA	12%	9%[r]
Most common age specified	NA	70	70	72	NA	70	NA	63	NA
Median board age	NA	55M / 55.5N	54M / 56N	58[e]	50	58M / 59N	57M / 57.5N	48	58[e]
Board committees:									
Percentage of companies that have committees	NA	18%	90%	10%	13%	95%[e]	98%M / 89%N	29%	2%
Median number of committees per board	NA	1	NA	NA	1	3	2	1	3

Note: Where "M" and "N" are used, they stand for manufacturing and nonmanufacturing, respectively.

NA — not available

[a]Figures are for supervisory boards of largest category of company under 1976 Codetermination Act (more than 20,000 employees); for composition of other boards see Chapter 3. NA answers indicate that no survey was conducted relative to those questions.

[b]Figures are for single-board structure (conseil d'administration); for data on optional two-tier structure see Chapter 6.

[c]Figures are for private-sector companies; see appropriate chapter for data on boards of government-owned companies.

[d]Excluding financial institutions.

[e]Approximate.

[f]Average (mean), not median.

[g]"Outsiders" commonly are major shareholders, however.

[h]Two companies do have one nonmanagement employee director each.

[i]Unions choose nonmanagement directors from among employees.

[j]Limited to major firms specified by law.

[k]A few special companies have government-appointed directors.

[l]One reporting financial institution has a government-appointed director.

[m]One reporting company has two government-appointed directors.

[n]Workers commonly serve 3-4 year terms.

[o]Four or five meetings per year is common.

[p]Policies are common but statistics not available.

[q]Legal requirement governs in most companies.

[r]Percentage based only on companies that have outside directors.

Part II
Individual Country Perspectives
and Practices

Chapter 3
Federal Republic of Germany

The German Context

Government Control of and Involvement in Business

In the Federal Republic of Germany a division of powers exists between the federal government and the state government which is quite similar to federal-state relations in the United States. The federal government holds the predominant jurisdiction in most legal matters pertaining to business and commerce; the most important areas are corporation law, antitrust law, and social legislation.

German social legislation started in the last century and today constitutes a tight social security net. The corporation laws also date back to the 19th century and have an especially highly developed body of law concerning "corporations with limited liability." German business law focuses particularly on incorporation and accounting aspects. The antitrust laws are of post-World War II origin.

A special "public law" governs the behavior of companies owned by federal, state and local governments, as for instance the federal railway system, the federal mail and telephone system, public broadcasting, some insurance companies and banks. In addition, the federal and state governments hold shares in various "private" companies (for instance, electric utilities,

The context section of this chapter on Germany was prepared by Prof. Dr. Eberhard Witte of the Institut für Organisation, Universität München. Burton W. Teague of The Conference Board staff wrote much of the remainder of the chapter.

local mass transportation, and the steel industry). Two million people, that is roughly ten percent of the total work force, are employed by public companies. The number of government-owned companies is roughly equivalent to France, but less than it is in the United Kingdom.

In general, the private- and public-owned corporations are quite independent from government and run their own affairs. However, the government does participate in innovations by granting research funds for various projects, and indirectly influences such industries as agriculture and home building by specifying various macroeconomic parameters.

The Role of the Aufsichtsrat (Supervisory Board)

The most important legal forms of private companies are the Aktiengesellschaft (AG) and the Gesellschaft mit beschrankter Haftung (GmbH). The AG is roughly comparable to the corporation in the Anglo-Saxon world, or the Société Anonyme (S.A.) in France. There is no equivalent in the United States for the GmbH. By law the AG has to have an Aufsichtsrat, or supervisory board, whereas the GmbH has to have an Aufsichtsrat only if there are more than 500 employees. Thirty-five percent of the total German work force is employed in AG's or GmbH's. Partnerships do not have an Aufsichtsrat; however, they may have a body known as a Beirat that has similar functions.

The same law that applies to the Aufsichtsrat of the AG also applies to that of the GmbH. Therefore, the following discussion focuses only on the law with respect to the AG.

The management structure of a German AG is very different from its Anglo-American counterpart. Its main difference lies in the dual system of an executive or management board (Vorstand) and a supervisory board. A member of the Aufsichtsrat must not, at the same time, be a member of the Vorstand, and vice versa.

The Vorstand runs the company. It is responsible for the performance of the company and represents the company to the public, whereas the Aufsichtsrat supervises the activities of the Vorstand. The Aufsichtsrat is not allowed to interfere in the policymaking of the Vorstand. This organizational structure was chosen in order to have a clear division of responsibilities between the Vorstand and the Aufsichtsrat.

In addition to the supervisory function, two other prime tasks of the Aufsichtsrat are to hire the members of the Vorstand and to approve the yearly balance sheet and profit statement.

The laws governing the AG make it mandatory, furthermore, that certain types of business activities be approved by the Aufsichtsrat. These are mainly strategic decisions on investment and financing. Depending on how many of these decisions tend to be vetoed by the supervisory board, one can speak of a stronger or weaker Aufsichtsrat, which interferes more or less with the policymaking of the Vorstand. An ownership-oriented company will have a tendency toward a stronger Aufsichtsrat.

Employee demands for codetermination have resulted in a series of laws providing for employee representation on supervisory boards. Since mid-1976, three different laws determine the composition of supervisory boards of major companies. The provisions of these three laws are presented in some detail beginning on page 30. In summary, they are:

• The Codetermination Act (Mitbestimmungsgesetz) of 1976, which becomes fully effective in mid-1978, governs companies with over 2,000 employees that are not involved in coal mining or iron or steel production (most of Germany's major firms);

• The Codetermination Act (Montanmitbestimmungsgesetz) of 1951 applies to companies in the coal-iron-steel industry, if they have over 1,000 employees;

• The Works Constitution Act (Betriebsverfassungsgesetz) of 1952, which was last revised in 1972, covers companies whose employees do not exceed 2,000 in number and that are not engaged in coal, iron or steel.

Employees are given as many supervisory board seats as are shareholder representatives under the first two laws, although different formulas govern under each. The Works Constitution Act provides for one-third employee representation.

Shareholder representatives on supervisory boards are elected by the annual shareholders' meeting. In large corporations they are often bankers, businessmen or representatives of the public rather than direct delegates of the actual shareholders. The representatives of the employees are proposed by the employees or by the unions, which are entitled to some seats included on the employee side of the membership. The manner of election depends on the governing law.

Management-Labor Relations and Unionization

The relationship between management and the employees and unions is determined by the ongoing discussion on employee codetermination, which itself dates back to World War I.

Within the hierarchy of the company, employee codetermination is administered in two ways. The works council (Betriebsrat) looks after the social, personal and economic interests of the employees. A works council is elected in every factory and is the major vehicle for negotiating a balance among various interests. In pursuing the interests of the employees the works council works from the bottom to the top. On the other hand, the participation of the representatives of the employees in the supervisory board takes effect at the pinnacle of the hierarchy. In the coal-iron-steel industry, there is even a representative of the employees in the Vorstand, who is in charge of personnel and social matters (Arbeitsdirektor). He is, in effect, chosen by the representatives of the employees who are in the Aufsichtsrat. The election of union representatives into the Aufsichtsrat has been a major goal of the unions and is now a feature of the two laws governing the largest companies.

Roughly 40 percent of the employees belong to a union; this percentage is slightly higher among hourly workers and slightly lower among salaried personnel. The unions are stratified not by profession, but by type of industry. Therefore each company deals with only one union.

In accordance with the federal system of Germany, wage bargaining is carried on between representatives of the unions and of management on a regional basis without interference by the government. The unions usually strive for higher wages and social benefits and attempt to minimize the risk of layoffs. By international standards there is a low propensity for conflict or strike.

Ownership of Corporations

In Germany there has occurred a change from the owner-controlled to the management-controlled company, although with a time lag relative to the United States and the United Kingdom. More than 20 percent of the big corporations are completely dominated by professional managers; family-dominated companies are usually found only within the medium- and small-sized companies.

The owners vote on the distribution of the profit in the annual shareholders' meeting, on approving the activities of the Vorstand and Aufsichtsrat, on the selection of a certified public accountant, on changes of the bylaws, and on the necessary steps for capital procurement.

It is quite common, especially for small shareholders, to assign voting rights to a bank. Therefore, the banks have a large share of the votes at their command.

It is rare that a proposal by the Vorstand is voted down. This demonstrates the inability of the small shareholder to control the destiny of the corporation.

Recent Changes

Important changes with respect to the cooperation among the Aufsichtsrat, Vorstand, shareholders and employees can be expected from the Codetermination Act of 1976, which will become effective July, 1978, after a two-year transitional period and will affect more than 600 large firms. The supervisory board of these companies will have an equal number of representatives of shareholders and of employees, instead of the former one-third employee representation that most had. Also, a quarter to a third of the employee representatives will be "outside" union delegates who do not work for the company.

The unions argue that no true "parity" exists on the supervisory board between the representatives of the shareholders and the representatives of the employees under the 1976 act. One reason is that at least one of the employee representatives must be a senior manager. Also, if there is a tie vote, the chairman will have two votes in the event of a second tie. Since the chairman will normally be chosen by the representatives of the shareholders, no decision can be taken against the unified opinion of the shareholders' representatives.

The law calls for a clear majority of the Aufsichtsrat when appointing members of the Vorstand, in order to ensure a broad support for them. After a cumbersome procedure, however, members of the Vorstand can also be chosen by the shareholders' representatives against the votes of the employee representatives.

The effects of the new law on the cooperation between Vorstand and Aufsichtsrat are of primary concern when the organizational structure of the company is discussed. The broadened codetermination assumes that all groups involved have the same interest in the development of the company because the company is the source of their income. If this assumption does not hold true, important decisions may very well be critically delayed because a conflict of interest may arise in the supervisory board. This would curtail the maneuverability of the company. If the supervisory board becomes a place of conflict, it is possible that decisions will be made by circumventing it.

Composition and Organization of the Supervisory Board (Aufsichtsrat)

No survey was conducted in Germany to ascertain the size and composition of supervisory boards in that country, since these matters are specified by law there and not by company preference. Also, many of Germany's supervisory boards are in a process of change resulting from 1976 legislation that requires the addition of many new employee directors to boards by mid-1978. Essentially, this section describes the composition of German supervisory boards *as they will be* once the new law is fully effective.

German law prescribes the size, the makeup, and the manner of election of the supervisory board in great detail, varying the requirements according to the form of company organization, industry and company size. The laws are so complex and include so many variables that generalizations or simple statements are in danger of being incomplete or technically inaccurate. The following presentation is as complete and accurate as possible without restating the laws themselves verbatim.

Before the 1976 Legislation

Since shortly after World War II, most major German companies have had a two-tier board system with employees of the company sitting on the supervisory board as voting members. During that period, until the new legislation, two legal formulas for the composition of supervisory boards governed most major firms:

Chart 1: Companies with 2,000 or Fewer Employees (Works Constitution Act, 1952)

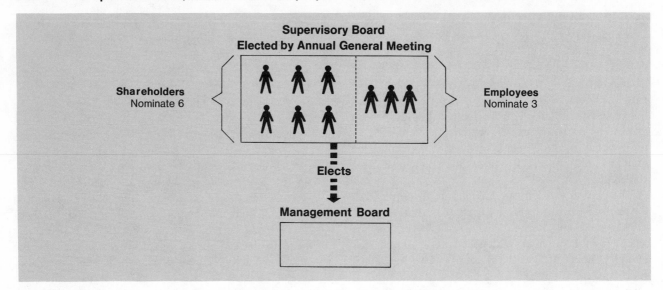

Supervisory Board
Elected by Annual General Meeting

Shareholders
Nominate 6

Employees
Nominate 3

Elects

Management Board

• For companies in the mining and steel industries, the formula was, and still is, equal representation for shareholders and for employees, with one additional neutral outside member acceptable to both sides; the actual size of the board depends on company size.

• For most other companies the formula has been one-third employee representation, two-thirds shareholder representation, with total board size again depending on company size. This formula was set forth under the Works Constitution Act — also called the Labor Relations Act — of 1952 (Betriebsverfassungsgesetz).

Since the 1976 Codetermination Act, the one-third/two-thirds pattern now applies only to companies regularly employing 2,000 or fewer. Since this report is basically concerned with the practices of major companies, this Works Constitution Act formula will not be explored here further, other than in Chart 1. But the two patterns for larger companies will be spelled out.

The Mining and Steel, or Montan, Formula (1951)

The Codetermination Act of 1951 for the coal mining and iron and steel producing industry (Montanmitbestimmungsgesetz) is based on a concept of equal representation of shareholders and labor (employees and also unions) on the supervisory board. Although the number of members on the board may be 11, 15, or 21, depending on the size of the operation, one of the members is a neutral outsider chosen by the rest of the members; the remainder of the board of 10, 14, or 20 members is equally divided between 5, 7, or 10

representatives each of the employees and the shareholders (see Chart 2).

Certain aspects of this law will be highlighted here, partly as a basis of comparison with the law that applies to major companies in industries other than coal and steel:

• The "odd" member must be neutral; he cannot be employed by the company, or be connected with organized labor, or have a financial stake in the enterprise. There is no such position provided for in the 1976 legislation.

• This position is not, at least not specifically under the law, that of chairman of the supervisory board. Rather, its importance lies in the ability to prevent 50-50 stalemates in board votes. This tie-breaking function is handled differently under the 1976 law.

• The supervisory board, as already noted, elects or appoints the members of the management board to their positions. One of these management board members must be a labor director (Arbeitsdirektor), or director for personnel and social affairs. Under this law, the labor director appointment must have the approval of a majority of the employee representatives on the supervisory board. The 1976 law does not give this kind of veto power to employee directors (and the labor director's position under that law is somewhat ambiguous).

The 1976 Codetermination Act

The Codetermination Act of 1976 (Mitbestimmungsgesetz 1976) extends the coal, iron and steel concept

Chart 2: Coal Mining and Iron and Steel Producing Companies (Codetermination Act, 1951)
Model for 11-Member Supervisory Board

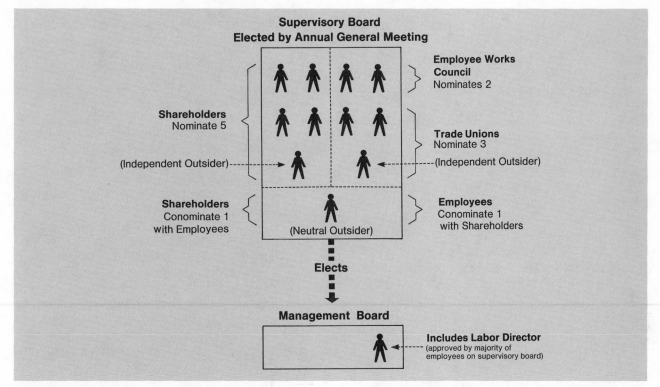

Supervisory Board
Elected by Annual General Meeting

Employee Works Council Nominates 2

Shareholders Nominate 5

Trade Unions Nominate 3

(Independent Outsider)----→ ←----(Independent Outsider)

Shareholders Conominate 1 with Employees

(Neutral Outsider)

Employees Conominate 1 with Shareholders

Elects

Management Board

Includes Labor Director
(approved by majority of employees on supervisory board)

---

of equal representation of employees and labor with the shareholders on the supervisory board to virtually all major industries, substantially ignoring the form of organization. The new law applies to the AG, GmbH, and KGaA — Kommanditgesellschaft: a limited commercial partnership — as well as profit-oriented trading cooperatives if they employ more than 2,000 persons in their undertakings. The scope covers combines of groups of companies (Konzern) and partial combines and syndicates (Teilkonzern) if the total employees in the group of companies exceed 2,000.

Companies covered by the 1976 Act that employ up to 10,000 employees are to have a supervisory board of 12 members, 6 of whom will be shareholder representatives, and 6 of whom will represent company employees and unions; those employing from 10,000 to 20,000 will have 16 members on the board with an eight-member split; and companies employing over 20,000 will have a 20-member board, with a 10-member split. (See Chart 3.)

Trade union representatives will hold two seats on a 12- or 16-member board, and three seats on a 20-member board. These directors need not be employees of the company — they represent the union (one that is actively involved at the company).

The remaining seats on the board open to employees (four, six or seven, depending on the board) must be filled by persons working for the company. These employee seats will be divided between three levels of employees, as specified in the law: wage earners (blue-collar), salaried employees (white-collar), and executive staff. Each of these groups is guaranteed at least one seat, with the rest of the vacancies to be filled according to the proportion of these employees in the company. (The definition of "executive" for this purpose is so far ambiguous and will need clarification in the courts.)

Each of these three employee groups will propose and elect their candidates or representatives in separate elections, as a rule. But the trade union representatives are to be proposed by the union. Generally, in companies employing less than 8,000 employees, the elections will be direct. When more than that number are employed, the vote of the employees as a whole will be for electors who, in turn, will vote for the members to serve on the board.

The chairman and deputy (vice) chairman are to be elected by the members of the board with a two-thirds majority. If a two-thirds vote cannot be mustered, the shareholders' representatives on the board must then

Chart 3: Companies with Over 2,000 Employees (Codetermination Act, 1976)
Model for Company with Over 20,000 Employees

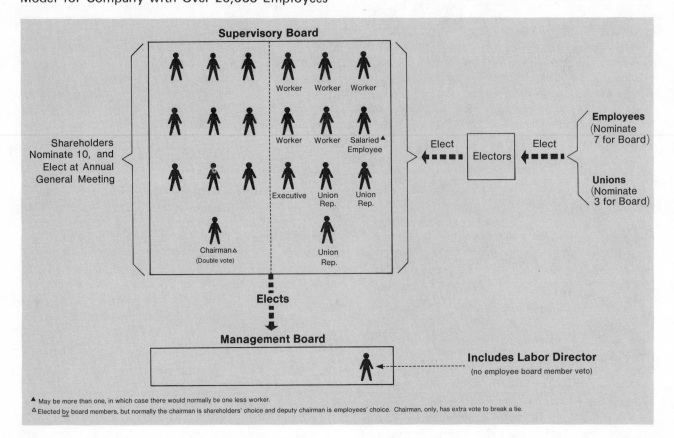

Supervisory Board

Worker   Worker   Worker

Worker   Worker   Salaried ▲ Employee

Shareholders Nominate 10, and Elect at Annual General Meeting

Executive   Union Rep.   Union Rep.

Chairman △ (Double vote)   Union Rep.

Elect ◄---- Electors ◄---- Elect

Employees (Nominate 7 for Board)

Unions (Nominate 3 for Board)

Elects

Management Board

Includes Labor Director (no employee board member veto)

▲ May be more than one, in which case there would normally be one less worker.
△ Elected by board members, but normally the chairman is shareholders' choice and deputy chairman is employees' choice. Chairman, only, has extra vote to break a tie.

take a separate second vote to elect the chairman. The result of this procedure, in all but unusual cases, will be that the chairman will come from the shareholder side of the board membership.

The importance of this is that when a vote of the supervisory board ends in a tie, and a second vote also results in a tie, the chairman can cast a second vote to break the deadlock. This right of the chairman is personal to him and may not be delegated, even to the deputy chairman, when the chairman is absent.

After the election of the chairman and the deputy chairman, the board will choose (and elect) the management board by a two-thirds majority. If that majority is not achieved, a mediation committee is formed, consisting of the chairman, the deputy chairman, and one shareholder's representative on the supervisory board and one labor representative on the board. They will propose a slate of candidates for the management board to be voted on by the supervisory board in plenary session. On this second vote, the election of the members of the management board will be by simple majority. If once again a majority cannot be

achieved, there will be another vote at which the chairman may cast his double vote to break a tie.

One of the members of the management board so elected will be designated the labor director (Arbeitsdirektor). The law does not spell out his duties, but it has been assumed he will be responsible for personnel and social matters, full time, or substantially full time, as is the practice in coal mining and the iron and steel industries. He may have other duties as well, since the law does say he will have equal powers of representation with the other members of the management board.

Shared Characteristics

The two laws just described governing the composition of the supervisory board in German companies obviously have distinctive differences, but there are also similarities under the German system as it applies to major firms:

• Employee representation is on the supervisory board of a two-tier system, not on a single or a management board;

- Employee representation, in membership if not in actual voting power, is equal to that of shareholders;

- A mechanism is provided for preventing deadlocks on important issues at the supervisory board level, which could potentially be very disruptive;

- Top management (the management board) is excluded from membership on the supervisory board, and thus is not in the position of supervising itself, as is the case in most countries.

Board Committees

The absence of a survey of German practices regarding supervisory boards makes comparison with board practices in other countries, such as the use of board committees, impractical. The use of committees of supervisory board members to specialize on selected board matters does not appear to a major practice, however, based on indirect evidence. But such committees are used to some extent; one example is the credit or loan committee found on the supervisory boards of some banks, whose responsibility is to examine and monitor loans and loan policies.

The Board Today and Tomorrow: Perspectives from Germany

Experience under Mitbestimmung

Germany has had workers serving on company supervisory boards for over 25 years. Other countries have paid a great deal of attention to the German system, not only to understand its mechanics but also to judge how well it works. The answer to the question of how well codetermination (Mitbestimmung) has served the German business system since World War II can depend very much on who is being asked. Even after a trial period of a quarter-century, German codetermination is a controversial subject.

Signs in Its Favor

Two characteristics of Germany's economic progress since the war's end would seem incontestable and are usually mentioned as signs that the presence of workers on supervisory boards has had positive results. One of these is the rebuilding of the industrial and financial might of Germany to a point of leadership — in economic strength and in stability, including currency stability — in Europe. At the very least, codetermination has not prevented this "industrial miracle" from taking place.

The other characteristic of the German postwar business environment that stands out, and that has contributed to growth and stability, is a remarkably low incidence of labor strife, evident in the accompanying table. The figures for Germany show that workers (and unionists) who have been elevated to director status have not used their positions on supervisory boards as a vantage point from which to throw a wrench into the peaceful negotiations between management and labor.

Table 3.1: Days Lost per Thousand Wage Earners, Nonagricultural Industries — Due to Labor Disputes

Year	Germany	Sweden	United States	Canada	Italy	United Kingdom	France	Japan
1965	2	1	388	416	567	127	71	201
1966	1	112	407	863	1,307	103	180	93
1967	19	0	649	641	683	122	295	60
1968	1	0	737	795	765	205	29	91
1969	12	35	626	1,170	3,186	302	150	115
1970	4	48	956	970	1,560	488	114	120
1971	207	250	681	414	924	625	282	178
1972	3³	3	374	1,075	1,347	1,102	237	150
1973	26	4	373	754	1,723	324	241	129
1974	49	16	629	1,156	1,476	659	204	270
1975	3	12[b]	415	1,335	1,886	270	237	225
1976	54[a]	NA	487	NA	NA	148	NA	NA

NA — not available.

[a]Estimated.
[b]Excludes agricultural strike involving 321,000 days lost by 7,000 workers.

Source: U.S. Department of Labor.

In conversation, at least, German executives show little genuine enthusiasm for the presence of workers on their supervisory boards, but on the other hand they can and do cite advantages of the system. One is that it gives the shareholder representatives on the board a source of direct information about what is going on in the company — important because the board does not meet often in most firms (four or five times a year, typically) and, therefore, has minimal contact with company affairs. Also, top management does not (cannot, by law) serve on the supervisory board and, therefore, is not necessarily routinely present to add information beyond what it presents in proposals.

Another positive feature of worker board representation, according to German executives, is that it gives the workers a better appreciation of other sides of issues confronting the company, aspects they might not otherwise consider or treat as legitimate.

Although surveys have shown that German workers do not count supervisory board membership to be as important, in terms of furthering their own interests, as, for instance, the works council, the union movement considers it to be very important, and believes that it has enabled union views to influence important company decisions. But the union goal has been to use the supervisory board to attain full parity with shareholders in decision making (to have an influence, or to be consulted but without voting parity, is not considered enough). That goal, despite a long struggle, has so far eluded the unions.

Reasons for Its Success

Before considering arguments for the opposite view — that the system of worker board representation has not worked well — it is appropriate to cite some factors that have contributed to whatever success can be claimed for Mitbestimmung. Some of these factors are part of the system itself, but others are part of the larger pattern of German life.

The system's two-tier concept, with workers on the supervisory board but not on the management board, gives workers representation without giving them direct involvement in management decision making. Some see this as a device for keeping employees out of the center of action, but others maintain that the separation of boards is a major reason why the presence of employees as directors has not disrupted the corporate system. Many Germans, and others, believe that a single board with a large proportion of nonmanagement employees could simply not function.

The management board in Germany has a clear and strong authority to run the company. Therefore, the system gives top management a powerful role to play. Only the management board has the legal authority to manage the company. The supervisory board cannot directly manage company affairs and, although the supervisory board has approval power over major decisions, it does not meet often and is not usually looking over management's shoulder.

Workers have been a one-third minority on most German boards on which they sit, so they have not been able to interfere with the wishes of the shareholder majority on those boards. This is a major reason why the unions pushed to extend parity representation to industries other than coal and steel. (The 1976 Codetermination Act does this but still keeps voting control on the shareholders' side.)

Labor unions in Germany have an unusually high sense of responsibility, and they have recognized that they have a common goal with industry and the rest of society to keep the economy strong. Some of this attitude is attributed to the common effort that was necessary to rebuild in the wake of World War II. But another reason mentioned for the responsible approach by the unions is the fact that they have emerged as a major factor in the economy as capitalists. The Trade Unions Federation (DGB) owns the fourth largest bank in the country, the largest construction company, and owns or is an investor in other enterprises. In any event, the unions have not used the foot in the boardroom door provided by codetermination to kick the props from under the effective management of companies.

Another reason given for the fact that worker supervisory board representation has not caused serious disruption is that German workers have other, and possibly more effective, means by which they can influence management thinking and decision making. The works council system exists under a detailed legal mandate; it gives workers a voice (outside the union structure) in many kinds of decisions in the company, and a formal and guaranteed access to company information through economic committees. Supervisory board membership does not have to serve as a relief valve for job-site frustrations or demands.

And the point is also made that, in many companies at least, the employees selected to serve on the supervisory board are not troublemakers but loyal veterans with long service in the company and a sense of identity with the company's goals and its success. Their presence on the board does not necessarily introduce an adversary situation or lead to conflict with the views of directors from the shareholder side.

Finally, it should be remembered that German management and labor have been conditioned to co-determination by a history that goes back over a century. During the nineteenth century a wave of liberal thought swept over Europe. One of its products was a concept that took root in Germany called the "constitutional factory," or the "factory republic." The theory was that employees should have a legally defined and authoritative role in consultation with management (Mitwirkung) through elected representatives, separate and distinct from trade unions.

This concept was accepted and made a part of German law as early as 1849, when the General Assembly at Frankfurt established an industrial code which provided for works councils (Betriebsrats). Although this was not implemented at the time, some large firms adopted the idea. The Imperial German Government instituted a weakened version of the concept during World War I, but the Nazis suspended it in 1933. At the end of World War II, the Allied Control Council restored works councils, and the Federal Republic of Germany continued and expanded on the program. It is from the foundation of the works councils that the codetermination laws have sprung.

Unfavorable Experience

Mitbestimmung cannot be described as a total success, and some say that on balance it is not a success at all, or that its drawbacks outweigh its advantages. From the point of view of German executives, the presence of workers on boards in that country has led to the following problems. (In citing them here it is necessary to repeat briefly points made in Chapter 1.)

Decisions — especially certain kinds of decisions — cannot be made as quickly and efficiently when there are workers on the board. The inexperience of workers in matters such as corporate finance is one reason; the need to convince them of the merit of decisions that they see as a threat to their own interests is another. One German cooperator told of taking five years to accomplish the closing of a money-losing plant because the presence of workers on the supervisory board forced debate and compromise on every step along the way. One view of the coal and steel industries, where worker representation on supervisory boards has been strongest, is that the performance of German companies in these industries has suffered from inability to respond to change and act quickly, because of the presence of workers on the board.

A related problem is that of companies being pressured into decisions that are not based on economic criteria, or that do not serve the best interest of the company or its shareholders. Examples are attempts by employees to influence decisions such as investments in production facilities outside the country, which could result in lost jobs in Germany.

Germans also say that workers have little background or experience that qualifies them to make the kinds of decisions they face as supervisory board members. This comment is made despite the training programs that have been used in that country to help workers function as directors. This aspect of worker board representation is usually not voiced as a serious objection, but rather as an indication that little advantage is gained by adding workers to supervisory boards.

There is a feeling that nonmanagement employees who serve on supervisory boards are placed in a difficult position in their role as director. They may simply have trouble handling themselves as equals of the prestigious business and financial representatives on the shareholder side. But they can also feel themselves on the spot between the management-shareholder side and the employee-union side on issues that come before the board, where they are legally charged with the responsibility to act in the best interests of the company as a whole. And they can experience a degree of distrust on the part of coworkers, some of whom may feel that serving on the board weakens one's loyalty to the cause of the employees.

One aspect of codetermination that troubles some Germans is the effect it may be having on investor confidence and, therefore, on investment decisions. Statistics show a decline in capital investment in Germany in recent years. Cause-and-effect is not proven or even measurable, but some believe the decline stems partly from investor concern over (1) the problems for management caused by codetermination, and (2) the weakening of ownership control over their invested assets that also results. The extension of parity worker board representation being brought about under the 1976 legislation has heightened concern on both scores. Finally, German executives are unhappy with the extent to which the trade unions (as distinguished from company employees) have gained power under codetermination.

The 1976 Codetermination Act

All political parties in Germany eventually supported the Mitbestimmungsgesetz of 1976, but only after years of debate, negotiation and compromise.

Organized labor and the liberal politicians had pressed for parity on the corporate Aufsichtsrat. Businessmen and conservatives had raised the constitutional question, pointing out that with parity investors would be deprived of property rights by the law. The right to vote on questions of policy with respect to the assets their shares represent is a property right. The Act, by injecting votes of persons other than shareholders, diminished that right, contrary to provisions in the Constitution, they maintained.

Some German lawyers believe that the compromise Act, by permitting the shareholders to elect the Chairman of the Aufsichtsrat and granting him two votes in order to break tie votes, satisfactorily answers the constitutional question. The courts have still to answer that question finally. It might be noted, however, that after 26 years the courts have not set aside the Montanmitbestimmungsgesetz of 1951. This could be due, though, to the special circumstances that exist in those coal mining, iron and steel industries.

The Act of 1976 does not absolutely guarantee shareholders control of their companies. The idea that it does is based on the fact that the chairman of the board is selected by the shareholders and has two votes. But this concept is based on the assumption that all the shareholder representatives and the chairman will always be present at every meeting, that they will never become ill or have an accident. It certainly is conceivable that a majority present at a given meeting could be labor representatives, who thus could vote for measures contrary to the interests of the owners.

The belief in shareholder control is based further on the fact that there will be at least one executive and one salaried employee on the labor side. Can these, even the executive, be counted on always to vote with the shareholders? The law provides they may not be discharged for any action they may take while acting on the board. And the interests of employees, even executive employees, may not always be congruent with those of the owners. The concepts of the two groups as to what is best for the company may at times diverge.

Still, from a shareholder's point of view, the compromise Act is significantly better than the 1951 Act. It differs from it in several important ways.

First, under the older law, there is a neutral board member (often chosen chairman); he is neither labor's nor the shareholders' representative. He is elected by the majority of the board, not by the shareholders' representatives as the chairman is under the new law. Generally he has been a cleric, an educator, or member of another profession who may be presumed to have no bias for either side. As such, he generally exercises little influence on policy.

Second, under the 1951 law there is no executive employee among the "labor" part of the panel. While executives may not always concur with the shareholders on every issue, the likelihood is far greater than if all were wage earners.

Third, although a labor director must be appointed (elected) to the management board (Vorstand) under the new law, his election and continuance in office do not depend on the approval of the majority of the labor members of the supervisory board, as is true under the older Act. Indeed, it appears that under the 1976 Act any of the members of the Vorstand may act in that capacity, including the chairman.

What Does the Future Hold?

Organized labor and the liberal politicians were both pleased and disappointed over the 1976 Act. They were disappointed by the fact that, in their terms, they did not achieve full parity with the owners of the businesses on the supervisory board; and they did not obtain the right to elect (or control the election of) the labor director. But they were pleased that they had taken a very long step in that direction by including all major German business in the codetermination net. Smaller, less publicly owned businesses were not included, possibly because too large a portion of the electorate might have become disenchanted with the concept. In any event, it is far easier to impose controls on big business than on smaller, more privately owned concerns. But full parity and an extension to all business may be included in future legislation. That the liberals consider the 1976 Act as just a step, however long, on the road to full parity was expressed by Chancellor Helmut Schmidt when he addressed the Trade Union I.G. Bau-Steine-Erden at Hannover on March 14, 1976: "Full parity is not achievable under the present political circumstances. But I think that the experience of the trade unions for over a hundred years has taught us the necessity of always concentrating every effort on what can be obtained at the given moment, in the awareness that tomorrow or the day after it will be possible, by building on what has been achieved today, to push forward another step."

Are There Alternatives?

But while they were congratulating themselves on their achievement, they were at the same time concerned over the possibility of widespread attempts on the part of owners to avoid the impact of the new Act. Labor Minister Walter Arendt offered a plea to businessmen when he addressed the Bundestag on the occasion of the third reading of the bill before the historic vote: "I should like here to ask the shareholders, the company managements, and the business and industrial federations to accept this law, to see the opportunity it contains for strengthening and further developing our economic and social order, and to cooperate on a basis of trust with the jobholders' representatives on the Supervisory Councils. Among other things this means not evading codetermination by organizational structuring. Let me say that would produce nothing but distrust . . ."

The law itself closed many, if not all, possible loopholes. Groups of companies are to be treated as one for the purpose of determining the number of employees, thus closing the avenue of divisionalizing corporations to keep the number of employees in any one division from reaching the qualifying limit. Limited partnerships are to be treated as corporations under this law. And, a point for foreign companies with German operations to ponder, if in a group of companies the controlling company is not subject to the law by reason of its legal form or because it is domiciled abroad, a company of the group which may be subject to the law can be deemed to be the controlling company even though it is only part of a chain of companies controlled from overseas. In that event, all of the employees of the entire group of companies may be counted to determine whether the German company is subject to the law.

But there are courses of action that can be taken to minimize the effect of the new law. While it was passed effective July 1, 1976, a transition period of two years was allowed before it becomes fully effective. During that time companies and their legal staffs have been considering many alternatives. They are reviewing their bylaws to minimize the catalog of items requiring the approval of the supervisory board. And since the voting margin of the shareholders is razor thin, great care is being taken to ensure the attendance of every shareholder member on the board. Some provision must be made, it is said, for the election of substitute members to vote in the absence of a member. It is particularly important to provide for replacement of the chairman by the shareholder members should the incumbent become incapacitated; otherwise. the advantage of the double vote could be lost.

While codetermination is only one factor in the determination of the form of doing business in Germany, some companies may be tempted to consider adopting the Kommanditgesellschaft auf Aktien (partnerships limited by shares). The impact of the new law on this form of organization is greatly mitigated. The company general partner (and it may be a GmbH company) may not be deprived of the management of the partnership, and a labor director does not have to be appointed (elected).

But there are risks associated with changes of this kind. First, there may be some adverse tax consequences. Second, there almost certainly would be some adverse labor relations consequences. And third, perhaps not the least, there could be some adverse public or customer reactions. The new law, albeit a compromise, passed the Bundestag by an overwhelming majority. Codetermination has a special ring to the German ear. It has had a long evolution, taking over a century to come to its present status. It now has great appeal to the general electorate, an assurance of a measure of control over one's own destiny, self-determination, so to speak.

Codetermination, then, can be seen as a part, and a relatively new part at that, of a social, legal and economic mosaic, based on long experience with joint consultation through the works council system, but probably not readily transportable to other countries. To transport one part of the mosaic without the rest — and without the decades of preconditioning German society underwent — could result in a shattering crash. This would be especially true in countries where labor relations is based on a concept of confrontation between management and labor. The chances of success in such instances do not appear to be great.

Indeed, it is not yet known whether codetermination will work in Germany on the broad scale visualized by the new law, which is not yet fully effective. Litigation over some of its terms has not reached a decisive level. Nor is its economic impact certain. If its critics are right, and codetermination is responsible for depriving the coal, iron and steel industries of the flexibility to close down unprofitable product lines, plants, unproductive facilities, and venture into new lines in other communities, then codetermination, when applied to virtually all of Germany's major industrial plants, may well mark the end of the German "Economic Miracle." Indeed, some informed observers believe that codetermination has already been a factor in channeling German investment capital into other countries.

Chapter 4
Sweden

The Swedish Context

Laws Affecting the Board of Directors

Virtually all business enterprises of any size are companies limited by shares (aktiebolag). Except for cooperative societies, such a company is the only form of business organization that must have a board of directors.

In Sweden there is no other form of business organization with limited liability share capital. Thus there is no Swedish equivalent of the French S.A.R.L., (Société à Responsabilité Limitée) or German GmbH (Gesellschaft mit beschrankter Haftung).

The rights and duties of directors of a company are set out in the Companies Act of 1975. Swedish companies have a single board system, and there is no legal provision for a two-tier board.

A board of directors is considered to have authority only as a group. The board may, however, authorize a director or the managing director (or any other person) to represent and sign for the company, unless this is prohibited by the articles of association.

The board of directors is responsible for the organization of the company and the management of its affairs. The directors must also see to it that the organization of the accounting and the management of assets includes satisfactory control.

The context section of this chapter and the survey material on which the description of the composition and organization of Swedish boards is based were provided by Dr. Per-Martin Meyerson of Sveriges Industriförbund (Federation of Swedish Industries), through the cooperation of that organization.

The day-to-day decisions and operations are normally the responsibility of the managing director of the company, who often bears the title of president and is the chief executive. He is appointed by the board, and is normally a member of it, although this is not a legal requirement.

The position of chairman of the board cannot be held (concurrently) by the person who is the managing director or president. Customarily, the chairman has been an outside director and the position has been a part-time one. The growth in size of companies — and groups of companies — has led to the fairly common practice of a chairman who spends full time on this position and has executive duties, but — it bears repeating — is not chief executive.

A director is not permitted to take advantage of the company for his personal gain, and he must not enter into legal transactions or undertake other measures that are likely to give an undue advantage to a shareholder or a third party to the detriment of the company or other shareholders.

Directors are not required by law to be shareholders themselves. If they are — in companies whose shares are listed on the stock exchange — they have to notify the Swedish Bank and Stock Exchange Inspection Board (Bankinspektioner) of their holdings. This is to give the Inspection Board an opportunity to see to it that the directors in these companies do not use privileged company information to take unfair advantage of buyers or sellers of the company's stock who lack the same information.

The board of directors is elected by the general meeting of shareholders, unless the articles of association provide that one or more directors shall be appointed in another way. Worker directors, however, are selected by trade unions. The directors' term of office shall be specified in the articles of association and may not be longer than four years.

The directors and the managing director must be resident Swedish citizens, but exceptions may be granted by the Board of Commerce (Kommerskollegium) for one-third of the board members and also for the managing director. The latter, however, must be a resident of Sweden. There are no laws that limit the number of boards on which a person may serve simultaneously.

Board Representation for Employees

According to the Act on board representation for employees in companies and cooperative societies, the employees have a right to appoint two members of the board (employee directors), and one deputy for each such director, in companies or groups of companies having a total of 25 or more employees in their service in Sweden. The trade unions elect the employee directors from among the employees within the enterprise, or in respect of parent companies, within the group.

An employee director has, in the main, the same rights and the same responsibilities as directors elected by the general meeting of shareholders.

Public Board Representation

According to the Act on public board representation in companies, cooperative societies, and foundations, the government has a right to appoint one member of the board (public director), and one deputy, in companies of great importance for the country. However, the Act will expire in 1979. It was introduced on a trial basis by the former socialist government. Except for some public directors who are already appointed in some holding companies, the present government has declared that it will not use its power under the Act to appoint public directors in companies.

Composition and Organization of the Board

A total of 77 Swedish companies provided information about the composition and organization of their boards, 61 of them in manufacturing industries and 16 in nonmanufacturing. They constitute a majority of the companies listed on the Swedish stock exchange, and range in size from four companies with annual turnover of under Skr 100 million to four companies

(three are banks) with turnover of Skr 10 billion or more.

All but one company provided this financial information, so that the distribution of the firms by size is as follows:

Size Categories	Number of Companies in Each Category	
	Manufacturing	Nonmanufacturing
(Turnover in millions of Skr)		
Under 200	12	1
200-999	22	5
1,000-2,999	14	5
3,000 and over	13	4
Totals	61	15

Board Size

The basic statistics regarding the sizes of the boards of these companies are:

Industry	Board Size (Number of Directors)		
	Range	Median	Mode
Manufacturing	4-15	9	9
Nonmanufacturing	7-25	11.5	7,9

Boards of the four banking and insurance companies that are included (a fourth of the nonmanufacturing companies) are unusually large and affect the median in the nonmanufacturing category. The boards of the four banking and insurance firms have 17, 18, 21, and 25 members. Leaving these companies out, the median board size becomes 9, the same as in manufacturing, and the maximum size in the range becomes 14. Only two out of 61 manufacturing companies reporting have boards with more than 12 members.

Board Composition

Outside directors (persons not presently working for the company) are in a majority on boards included in the survey. For manufacturing boards as a whole, about 38 percent of directors are full-time employees; for nonmanufacturing boards as a whole, the figure is about 40 percent.

In terms of nonmanagement employees, or workers, all but nine of the manufacturing companies have such directors and all but two nonmanufacturing firms do; they constitute about 19 percent of the total directors in each industry category.

Some other facts concerning board composition in participating Swedish companies:

• Women are found on eight boards, or about 10 percent of those reporting; one retailing firm has four female directors.

• A minority of companies (23 percent in manufacturing, 38 percent in nonmanufacturing) have policies that require an outside director to retire from the board at a prescribed age. The most popular age specified under such policies (both the median and mode in both industry categories) is 70.

• Median ages of boards in the two types of industries are also very similar: 55 in manufacturing, 55.5 in nonmanufacturing.

• Only three companies require that outside directors own stock in the company. Only two of these say there is a prescribed minimum of ownership — one share in one case, Skr 5,000 in the other.

• About 41 percent of the manufacturing companies and 44 percent of the nonmanufacturing companies have former or retired company employees on their boards. In about two-thirds of these companies, only one former employee is found on the board; the highest number reported is four.

• Reflecting the policy referred to in the previous section on the Swedish context, six companies, or 8 percent of the total, have one or more government-appointed directors on their boards. However, four of the six are the four companies in the banking and insurance industries, all of which have such directors: one has four; one has three; and the other two firms have two government-appointed directors each.

• One-year terms for directors are the common practice in these companies, except that worker directors often serve three- or even four-year terms.

• In terms of business or profession, outside directors serving on these Swedish boards have the following backgrounds, ranking the first six categories by number of directors:

Business or Profession	Number of Directors Mentioned for Each
Manufacturing company boards:	
Principal company owner or agent of owner	105
Manufacturing executive	81
Bank executive	43
Independent businessman, financier, consultant	38
Other financial executive	28
Educator	14
Nonmanufacturing company boards:	
Manufacturing executive	28

Business or Profession	Number of Directors Mentioned for Each
Principal company owner or agent of owner	15
Bank executive	11
Other financial executive	10
Merchandising executive	9
Government representative	8

Meeting Frequency

Information on how often boards of directors meet follows:

	Number of Regular Board Meetings per Year		
Industry	Range	Median	Mode
Manufacturing	4- 9	5	4
Nonmanufacturing	4-13	5.5	5

Boards of banks and insurance companies in the sample meet more often than do boards in other industries; the four firms involved meet typically 12 times a year (median and mode).

Committees

The use of committees of the board is a minority practice among cooperating Swedish companies and is rarely formalized. Fourteen companies (18 percent) report that they have such a committee; only one of these firms has more than one committee.

About half the committees reported have three members, of whom two, typically, are outside directors (one company has an all-outside-director committee of three). Outside directors are in a majority on all committees reported, which range in size from three up to eleven members (in a financial institution).

The names of committees reported are:

Name of Committee	Number of Companies Reporting
Presidium	3
Working or advisory committee	3
Executive committee	2
Finance committee	2
Committee for Preparation of Credits	1

The Board Today and Tomorrow: Perspectives from Sweden

Seven executives from leading Swedish firms — four chairmen, two presidents, and a managing director —

responded at some length to a questionnaire on Swedish directorship practices. Their comments were augmented by those of five other countrymen (including two presidents and a managing director) who were interviewed on the subject. The contribution of these cooperators accounts for much of the content of the discussion of board practices in this section. This group, while not large enough to constitute a broad cross section of Swedish industrial leadership, is significant in terms of its selected nature.

The Board's Basic Role

The Swedish participants, like those in other countries, were asked to describe the primary role that a board plays, as they have observed it in their own experience. Three areas of primary emphasis predominate in the answers given: financial matters, dealing with management, and policy matters. However, there is not a high degree of uniformity in the frequency of order in which these areas of responsibility are mentioned, and there are also differences in emphasis and in the degree of involvement of the board expected.

Finance is mentioned most often as an area in which the board has a responsibility. The board's role in financial affairs as indicated in these comments ranges from setting or monitoring policy, to providing financial contacts, to specific decisions such as payment of dividends. Here are some examples of the wording of the financial role of the board as mentioned by these respondents:

"Setting financial policy";
"Evaluating and authorizing major capital expenditures";
"Investment decisions, particularly concerning subsidiary companies outside the home country";
"Deciding financial reporting matters";
"Equity and long-term financing";
"Advising on banking activities."

In terms of frequency of mentions as a board role, relations with corporate management ranks second. The range of roles to be played by the board in dealing with management includes *appointing, supervising, evaluating* and *advising*. Clearly, the selection of the managing director or president — and replacing him if necessary — is seen as the most important of this set of board responsibilities. To quote one respondent: "The single most important function is to ensure that the best man is chosen to run the company."

In terms of giving advice to management, one respondent points out that this is especially valuable in matters in which management lacks experience of its own. The advisory role of the board is mentioned by several cooperators.

One managing director comments on the role of the board from a different viewpoint — that of management — when he says that the board should "actively support the managing director, wholeheartedly, in a business environment that is becoming more and more complicated."

The third kind of responsibility mentioned for boards is corporate policy. Of four respondents who single out policy, three feel that the board has an active or initiating role to play when it comes to policy; one bank chairman calls the board "the policymaking body of a corporation." But the three advocates of policy initiation at the board level do not necessarily see this as an all-inclusive role. For example, one says that the board should establish only certain (unspecified) policies; on the whole it controls rather than initiates. Another limits policy establishment for the board to financial matters.

Other areas indicated in which the Swedish board plays a role include:

Reviewing operations and their results;
Mergers, acquisitions and divestments;
Deciding on or reviewing corporate strategies;
Shareholder relations;
International contacts.

These executives were asked to comment on whether the essential role of the board differs from one company to the next. Two say it does not really differ, but most say that it does, although one of these believes that the essential role *should* be the same.

The reasons given for differences in the essential role of boards indicate two kinds of causes: people and situations.

From the people point of view, as a bank chairman puts it: "A board may be more or less active, demand more or less information from the management, meet more or less frequently." Another chairman says that the temperament and knowledge of the people involved affects what role a particular board will play. The performance and attitude of management, of course, are factors in this equation.

But boards also function differently because of circumstances. Mentioned most often is company size. Smaller companies not only have different kinds of problems but also tend to require a more direct kind of involvement by board members in company affairs. But circumstances and problems can vary from one company to the next without regard to size. One executive points out that there can be differences in financing, in production, in marketing, and in organization or structure among companies and that these can affect the board's function.

One chairman makes a comment that is echoed in virtually every country: "In difficult times and in a tight financial situation a board tends to become more active, more demanding."

Like respondents in other countries, these Swedish cooperators tend to agree that the board of a company owned or controlled by the government (not a common situation in Sweden, since over 90 percent of industry is privately owned) should have the same essential function as boards in private industry. But the following quote sums up the belief of some respondents that, as a practical matter, directors of government-owned companies do operate in a different atmosphere:

"In a nationalized or government-owned company, profitability is often somewhat differently interpreted, especially if the company has to work in a depressed branch, region or area. Political and social considerations often have a higher degree of influence in a government-controlled company than in a private company."

Board Effectiveness

Swedish cooperators have a fairly positive view of the effectiveness of the board system in that country, taken as a whole. Some simply say the system works well (three comments: very well, fairly well, satisfactory). But the majority say that boards vary considerably in effectiveness (as well as role) from one company to the next. One president feels that the system works well when there is strong ownership representation on the board, less well when there is not. Another respondent believes that board effectiveness depends on who the directors are and how much cooperation there is between the board and the chief executive. The chairman of a bank makes this general observation: "Perhaps the role of the board in many corporations has been declining in recent times, that of management increasing."

Asked to list those parts of their responsibility with respect to which boards tend to do best, Swedish executives cite the following:

Suggestions for Changes

"I would welcome a broader recruitment of directors than is traditional in Sweden, to make boards more representative of different kinds of expertise and different interests. More women, consumer representatives, younger people. As it is now, there are too many bankers and lawyers."

— A bank chairman

* * * *

"Directors should be given the opportunity and be able to take the time to be more deeply informed about the operations of the company they serve."

— A manufacturing president

* * * *

"Maybe the work of Swedish boards should be developed more in the divisionalized directions in which American boards are operating, so that members of the board could concentrate on some specific aspects of the life of the company."

— Managing director,
a manufacturing firm

Setting objectives and policies
Controlling corporate policies
Estimating future prospects for the company
Giving advice and information to management
Supervising management
Investment decisions (to which directors can bring unbiased views)
Initiating changes when necessary (based on the exposure of directors in their other capacities to trends and developments)
Providing important contacts (Says one chairman: "The Board knows everybody of importance to our business in the Nordic area.")
Dividend policy

They also acknowledge that there are tasks or areas in which boards tend to be less effective. A chairman cites the following shortcomings:

They tend to postpone uncomfortable decisions.
They are often too passive when it comes to changing a chief executive.

They are not effective at causing the company to give up unprofitable lines of business.

They tend to pay too much attention to short-term problems.

A managing director, perhaps speaking from his own experience, says that in the rare instances when a board intervenes in company operations, a lot of problems are created.

Appraising Board Performance

"The performance of the board is difficult to measure," comments one managing director of a major firm in responding to the question of how a board of directors is appraised, and by whom. Nevertheless, most respondents name some method or measure of board performance appraisal. Essentially, they seem to agree that judgment of the board's performance as a whole comes from outside the company, whereas the appraisal of the contribution made by an individual board member is an internal matter for the board itself. One chairman does believe that board appraisal can come from inside, by the directors themselves, and suggests that in some companies this is done annually.

For boards as a whole, appraisal comes from two main sources: shareholders (owners), and the financial and business community. They are guided by both general company performance, especially growth, and financial performance. Thus the measuring stick for judging the board is an indirect one, a reflection of how successful the company is. And the sign of success, or failure, is often seen in the price of the company's stock.

Shareholders can express their opinion by their decision on nominations for the board each year. They can also sell their stock, or buy more. A chairman among the respondents singles out one kind of shareholder, the large institutional holder, as being especially effective at appraisal because of the knowledge and expertise of its staff.

When it comes to appraising the performance of individual directors, the Swedish cooperators agree that the board itself is the best judge, and that appraisal from outside – even by shareholders – is rare. In fact, some say that an evaluation of individual directors and their performance is the exception rather than the rule, or simply is not done. When it is done, it is likely to be an informal process, perhaps based on a general feeling of directors and the chairman as to how their peers are contributing. But one cooperator suggests that even an informal appraisal by fellow board

---

How the Swedish System Works

The legislation passed in mid-1976 that governs worker board representation in Sweden includes the following characteristics:

• It applies to companies as small as those having 25 employees, but does not apply to banks or insurance companies;

• The union(s) can unilaterally decide that workers will be placed on the board of a company, but the union(s) must (1) represent more than half the company's employees, and (2) have labor agreements with the company;

• Where these conditions are met, the union(s) can elect employees of the company to serve on the board — they are not elected by shareholders;

• Deputies (one per employee director) are also entitled to attend board meetings and can participate in discussions but cannot vote, unless they are attending in place of the regular worker directors for whom they are deputies.

---

members *can* be effective: "During my ten years with the company we have 'fired' one director who did not perform."

To Whom Is the Board Accountable?

Almost every Swedish respondent says that his accountability as an outside director (and together they hold about 45 board seats in companies other than their own) is to the shareholders alone. The only comment suggesting a broader accountability, in terms of whose interests an outside director is obligated to represent, is this one from the managing director of one of Sweden's largest companies:

"The board and managing director must primarily take the responsibility for the survival and development of the company from an economic point of view. Recently the responsibility toward the employees, suppliers, distributors, dealers and other parties with 'interests' in the progress of the company has increased."

The fact that shareholders' interests are paramount to these Swedish directors might suggest that Swedish companies are run with only small regard for their employees — which is far from the truth. Swedish employers, like the government and society in general, consider the well-being of their employees to be very important. Wage and benefit levels in Sweden are very high — as is productivity. The annual reports of Swedish corporations often devote space to a discussion of personnel practices and emphasize improvements in this area. Even before legislation was passed giving employees the right to be consulted on major company issues and decisions, Swedish employees had some say in many matters affecting them.

One reason for the perception of the Swedish director — suggested in the responses above — that he is answerable as a director to the shareholders alone may be the concentration of corporate ownership in that country. A relatively small group of owners (people and organizations) control much of the industrial might of Sweden. Ownership is a clearly perceived and very real factor to the Swedish board member, especially by comparison with the diffused and disinterested pattern of ownership in larger countries.

Workers on the Board

At least some of the Swedish respondents have had experience with boards on which nonmanagement employees sit as voting members. In that country, as pointed out, workers do not become members of a nonmanaging supervisory board but take their place (as a definite minority) with management and shareholder representatives on a single board.

The respondents offer their opinions and the benefit of their experience with this system. For example, they were asked whether having workers on the board alters the board's working procedures. Most say no, but two testify that changes do occur. Says one: "The procedures tend to become more formal and cumbersome, smaller matters are taken up for discussion at the board level, board meetings are more time-consuming." States another: "Certain questions have to be treated outside the board but the number of such questions is less than one would expect."

This last statement gives some support to what some observers of the Swedish experience with workers on the board, and some union spokesmen, insist is true — that managements (and shareholder representatives) circumvent potential challenges on issues by worker directors by working informally outside the boardroom structure. As of 1976, the law presumably makes such a practice more difficult, because employees are now entitled to attend board committee meetings, although not normally as voting members.

On Worker Board Representation in Sweden

"The difficulty of speaking freely in board meetings decreases the role of the board as such in the management process. At the same time, worker representation increases the board's understanding of matters as they are really experienced by the employees of the company. It consequently gives the directors — and I am now speaking about outside directors — a more objective impression about the situation inside the company. This, of course, puts limitations on what the chief executive officer can tell the board about things going on inside the company (blaming it on others or taking the merit for himself, as the case may be). . . . But there is also the risk that if the employees on the board 'destroy' meetings, more power will pass to the chief executive and the chairman, as these two will then be the only body that can have open discussions and take decisions."

— The chairman of a manufacturing company

* * * *

"For decades, management and labor have been used to working together in works councils and other bi-partisan bodies, which has, no doubt, facilitated the introduction of the system of employee directors."

— A bank chairman

* * * *

"The wage earners' interest in board representation has presently been pushed in the background by the prospects of direct codetermination opened by new legislation and expected to be a part of future collective agreements." (A reference to 1977 legislation giving employees near-veto power over any important changes in the company of which they disapprove.)

— A manufacturing company presidnet

---

composition. "In large Swedish corporations, practically all directors are outside directors, in most companies including even the chairman," says one executive, and he, like the others, approves.

The comments of these Swedish executives coincide with other evidence that the addition of workers to Swedish boards is being accomplished with a minimum of disruption. The factors that have contributed to this include:

• A constructive attitude on the part of the unions, who actually select worker directors under that country's laws;

• The already-in-place mechanism, especially in works councils, for interaction and communication between management and employees — often described as essential to the success of employee board participation;

• The fact that the blue-collar directors, although they are voting members, are in a definite minority and therefore have only limited capability for opposing management proposals;

• The opportunity to become accustomed to the system during a voluntary three-year period beginning in 1973; and

• Training programs to help workers act as board members.

The unions have shown that they are willing to cooperate with management in implementing the system in situations that warrant it. For example, the president of a large manufacturing group points out that the unions have not always immediately enforced their right to place employees on a company's board, even though they meet the requirements of representation. In his own company, the unions agreed through negotiation that although workers would be added to boards of subsidiary companies of the group, the union would not exercise this right in connection with the parent-company board, at least initially.

Chapter 5
United Kingdom

The United Kingdom Context

Government Control of Business

In the United Kingdom the registration and control of business is regulated by central government statute, and the most important of the general regulations are embodied in three Acts of Parliament — the Companies Acts of 1948, 1967, and 1976. These Acts are primarily concerned with the requirements that have to be fulfilled:

(1) To form a company initially;
(2) To report annually both to shareholders and the Registrar of Companies;
(3) For the proper regulation of share capital and certain shareholders' rights;
(4) For the conduct of board meetings; and
(5) For winding up, liquidation or bankruptcies.

In addition, every company has a "Memorandum and Articles of Association," which is drawn up and agreed to by members (or shareholders) at the formation of the company, and which forms part of the legal framework within which the company must operate. There is very wide discretion within the Companies Acts' requirements as to what the "Memorandum and Articles of Association" shall contain, but as a minimum it will necessarily state:

The British context was prepared for this report by the Confederation of British Industry, which also provided the survey information on composition and organization of British boards.

(1) The purposes for which the company was formed;
(2) The share capital;
(3) The identity of officers to be authorized signatories on behalf of the company.

The "Memorandum and Articles of Association" may state a host of other things, most of which would be likely to be constraints imposed upon the directors in order to safeguard the shareholders' interests. For example, virtually all companies have an upper limit imposed beyond which the directors are not empowered to borrow money on behalf of the company without shareholder approval.

Quite apart from the general legal framework, which is intended to regulate the conduct of a business primarily with respect to the interests of shareholders — but also with respect to third parties such as creditors and debtors — there has been a very sharp increase in recent years in other forms of legislation to which companies must conform. These have been principally concerned with safeguarding the interests of employees and consumers. Although some of this legislation is clearly a tool for implementing the government's economic and social policies, the majority represents a reflection of a genuine need determined by public opinion. This legislation has covered matters such as health and safety, redundancy, pensions, prices and wages.

Government Involvement in Business

Government is involved in business in the United Kingdom at four levels:

(1) *Nationalized Industries.* There are 17 nationalized enterprises, wholly owned by the U.K. Government. These include most (but not all) of the transport, energy-producing, and telecommunications networks of the country. Among them, nationalized industries employ 2 million people and represent 11 percent of the GNP. Although they are intended to operate on principles similar to ordinary commercial organizations, this intent can frequently be prejudiced by political pressures insofar as, in practice, their boards are responsible only to the appropriate Secretary of State.

(2) *National Enterprise Board (NEB).* This is effectively a government-owned holding company, which was set up in 1975 with the intention of assisting in the implementation of the government's industrial policies. Its terms of reference are wide ranging; so far its activities have been largely (but not exclusively) confined to providing financial assistance to industrial "lame ducks" that happen to be of some strategic importance. (Examples: British Leyland, Chrysler Motors, Ferranti Ltd., and Alfred Herbert.) NEB owns a substantial proportion (usually more than 50 percent) of the shares of such companies, but in any event effectively controls each company's policies.

(3) *Share ownership.* The government is a substantial shareholder in a number of companies in the private sector. This has usually come about as a result of some accident of history, as opposed to a deliberate government policy. In these cases, the companies are run on strictly commercial lines, and government does not interfere in any way with the company's operation. There is usually at least one government-appointed director on the board. The best known example of this type of company is British Petroleum Company Ltd.; the government now holds about 31 percent of the ordinary share capital, having recently sold about 17 percent to the public, and The Bank of England owns about 20 percent.

(4) *Government financial assistance.* Under the Industry Act of 1972, government is empowered to provide financial assistance to companies for a wide variety of reasons. This assistance may be in the form of either share capital or loans. Although the finance so provided is typically rather a small proportion of the company's total capital, conditions attached to the provision of the money usually give government special monitoring powers over the company's activities. In this situation it is not unusual for government to nominate directors to the board.

Laws Affecting the Board of Directors

Virtually all business enterprises of any size are "limited companies"; of the three major forms of business organization, a "limited company" alone must have a board of directors (a minimum of two). (The other two types of business organization are sole proprietorships and partnerships. The partnership is particularly favored by professionals like lawyers, accountants and doctors.) As the name implies, a "limited company" is the only type of organization that has limited liability, which may be by share capital (most usually) or by guarantee (rarely).

Very few duties and responsibilities of a director are stated explicitly in Acts of Parliament. Essentially:

(1) The directors are responsible solely to the shareholders;

(2) Their function is to direct and control the business;

(3) Directors act in a fiduciary capacity to shareholders as a whole and do not represent special interests; and

(4) Directors are obliged to report annually on certain specific matters concerning the conduct of the business both to shareholders and to the Registrar of Companies.

In addition, directors are subject to any conditions or constraints set out in the Memorandum and Articles of Association.

In practice, many of the duties and responsibilities of directors have evolved over a period of many years as a result of case law (interpretations of the law tested in the courts) or official or semiofficial bodies whose pronouncements carry such general acceptance that they effectively guide directors in their decision making. Examples of the latter are the Monopolies Commission, the Takeover Panel, and the Stock Exchange. As a general guide, these duties and responsibilities may be summarized as follows:

(1) Directors have a duty of care to act with that degree of dilligence and skill which an ordinarily prudent man would exercise under similar circumstances.

(2) A board of directors is considered to have authority only as a group; directors have no legal power as individuals except for that delegated to them by the board. On the other hand, directors can be held liable as individuals for their actions, or failure to act, as board members.

(3) Directors are elected by members (shareholders), but are not always required by the Articles of Association to be shareholders themselves. However, it is not unusual for companies to require that directors own shares.

(4) It is usual for one-third of the members of a board of directors to retire each year by rotation; if eligible, they may be reelected. Those over 70 years of age are often reelected annually.

(5) There are virtually no legal restrictions on the nomination of persons for election to boards.

(6) There are no laws that limit the number of boards on which a person may serve simultaneously.

(7) Directors are forbidden from personally using the knowledge of privileged company information for their own gain.

(8) If a director has a personal interest in any matter under discussion on the board, he must declare his interest and not participate in the discussion and not vote on the matter. This type of "conflict of interest" will include matters concerning other companies with which he may be associated.

Management-Labor Relations and Unionization

The British Labour Party was founded very largely as a result of support from the trades union movement and this support is still a vital force in the present Labour Party. To this extent, the great majority (but not all) of the unions have direct political affiliations, and this inevitably flavors both attitudes and negotiations between labor and management.

About 40 percent of the working people in industry generally are members of trades unions, but this varies very widely from industry to industry, and company to company. Some companies and industries are "a closed shop" in which a worker must be a union member in order to be employed (most nationalized industries, motor industry, printing industry). However, in hotel and catering, agriculture, retailing and most smaller companies, union membership is low. A recent development is the increase of unionization among clerical and administrative workers and management.

In the U.K., managements must deal, as a rule, with a number of different unions within any one plant or company — often as many as 12 to 15. Although two unions — the Transport and General Workers Union and the Engineers Union — probably have 20 percent of all union members working in industry, they do not hold a dominant position; each union usually conducts its own negotiations quite independently of the others. In fact, there is often rivalry between them, and each pursues its own goals.

The great majority of unions are affiliated with the Trades Union Congress (TUC), which is primarily a consultative body. Although the TUC may pass resolutions and make recommendations to its affiliated member unions, these do not carry any force other than by agreement. For this reason, agreements arrived at between TUC leaders and government are of uncertain effect, because the TUC has only limited disciplines in order to ensure their implementation. In spite of this, however, the influence of the TUC on the formulation of government policy (especially that of a Labour Government) is considerable.

Ownership of Companies and Control of the Board

Most U.K. companies are owned by a large number of shareholders. On average, the number of shareholders in a particular company approximates the number of employees. Shareholders are comprised both of private individuals and of institutions like insurance companies, investment companies, pension funds, and merchant banks. Institutions are now believed to hold more than 50 percent of the equity of companies quoted on the London Stock Exchange. Clearing banks do not make equity investments on their own account, but their merchant banking subsidiaries may. It is rare for single individuals (or families) to hold more than a very small percentage of quoted equity: It is very common for them to do so if the company is unquoted.

As owners, the shareholders have the obligation to elect directors, which they do largely by proxy postal vote at the annual general meeting. Almost invariably, it is the existing board that nominates the people who are to be put up for election, and only rarely is one of these candidates defeated. Shareholders also have the power to remove directors, but such action is extremely unusual.

Two of the most common routine matters for which the approval of shareholders is required are the Annual Report and Accounts and the proposed dividend distribution. Shareholders' approval is also generally required for anything which may involve an alteration to the Memorandum and Articles of Association. The most common item for which companies have to obtain shareholders' consent is an increase in the authorized capital of the company, which in turn may be needed in order to satisfy an acquisition or possibly a "rights" issue.

Despite these requirements for shareholders' approval, the board of a company effectively controls it, not only because it controls the machinery of reporting, but also because virtually all shareholders — both individual and institutional — are passive and are strictly concerned with their dividends and the value of the shareholding. When shareholders are dissatisfied, they tend to sell their shares rather than call the board to account. The exception to this may be when a crisis overtakes a company, but even in that situation the matter is more likely to be resolved by conditions attaching to loan, debenture or preference-stock holders than by the holders of the equity shares.

In recent years, certain political factors (see below) are causing the whole question of the control of companies at board level to be reconsidered.

Current Concerns

Although some of the principal concerns of U.K. directors today arise from the political scene, there have also been certain underlying changes in the attitude of the general public toward industry and its role. The business enterprise is being asked to be more responsive to the needs of the public and to the well-being of its own employees. And board members (as well as company employees) are being challenged to meet somewhat higher standards of accountability than have prevailed in the past.

Two developments of particular concern to directors are:

(1) *Employee participation.* The idea that employees should be given a greater say in a company's affairs has gained popularity, and the Labour Party is committed to the concept of "industrial democracy." In order to pursue one aspect of this concept, the Bullock Committee was set up by the Secretary of State for Trade and has recommended that the larger U.K. companies should have boards of directors comprising equal numbers of shareholders and employee representatives, with an additional number of directors to be appointed by agreement between the shareholders' and employees' parties (the 2X + Y formula as it is called).

Were this proposal to be adopted, it would clearly require a complete revision of the whole of the existing concept of the duties and responsibilities of a director and the functions of a board. At this writing, the possibility of legislation that would require such a change can only be guessed at.

(2) *Constraints on the actions of a director.* In recent years, certain well-published actions by directors, although not illegal, have met with wide public disapproval, and there is now a general acceptance that the law requires tightening up in a number of respects. The most important of these currently concerns the question of employees (not just directors) using the knowledge of privileged company information for their own gain — known as "insider dealing." For various reasons, immediate legislation is unlikely, but strong effective sanctions might be brought to bear on an offender by other means.

Composition and Organization of the Board

Data about the composition and organization of the boards of U.K. companies have been drawn from 70 of that country's largest manufacturing firms, representing 10 industry groupings, and 24 of its major nonmanufacturing companies, both financial and nonfinancial, in three industry groupings. None of the firms is nationalized, and none is an insurance company.

The stature of these companies can be gleaned from the following figures (which exclude data from three clearing banks, since they would distort the figures):

	Range	Average
Sales (millions of £)	160 - Over 8,000	735
Assets (millions of £)	40 - Over 5,000	525

Board Size

The basic statistics regarding board sizes follow:

Industry	Board Sizes (Number of Directors)	
	Range	Median
Manufacturing	6-25	15
Nonmanufacturing	7-24	20

Board Composition and Election

In contrast to the situation in most other countries surveyed, where outside or nonmanagement directors predominate, 70 percent of the manufacturing companies and 75 percent of the nonmanufacturing companies in the U.K. sampling have a majority of employee directors. All of these employee directors are executives; no nonmanagement workers or union representatives are reported.

The most common sources for outside board members on the participating U.K. boards, in terms of business or profession and ranked by frequency of mention, are:

Manufacturing Boards:

Executives of manufacturing firms
Major shareholders or their agents
Merchant bankers
Miscellaneous*

Nonmanufacturing Boards:

Miscellaneous*
Merchant bankers
Executives of manufacturing firms
Lawyers

Some other facts about board composition and election in the participating U.K. companies:

• One or more former (retired) employees serve on the boards of 39 percent of the manufacturers and 63 percent of the nonmanufacturers.

*Includes stockbrokers and others in financial community, insurance brokers, economists, consultants, and foreign or EEC industrialists.

• Women are so far a rarity on U.K. company boards; three manufacturers and one nonmanufacturer report having women directors.

• Under the Companies Act of 1948, directors are elected by vote of the shareholders, and this usually takes place at the annual general meeting. But the great majority of the directors of the firms in the sample are *nominated* by the board.

• Under common British practice, directors serve terms of either three or four years and then "retire," but customarily offer themselves for reelection. When a director reaches 70 years of age, he is customarily obliged to resign, but he may be reelected.

• The average board age reported is 54 years for manufacturers; 56 years for nonmanufacturers. The ranges of average board ages are 47-65 and 43-63, respectively.

• Exactly half of the full sample of 94 firms require (in their Articles of Association) directors to own shares, but the stipulated holding is minimal: 100 to 150 shares. In the United Kingdom there is no legal requirement for directors to be shareholders of the companies on whose boards they sit.

Committees

Although about 90 percent of the participating companies report having at least one board committee, U.K. boards by and large do not have an articulated or formal committee structure such as one finds in the United States and Canada. In fact, board "committees" may simply be informal board meetings held at short notice. The infrequency of board (directors only) committees may also be attributed in part to the majority of employee directors on most boards; since these directors can convene whenever the need arises, formal committees with fixed responsibilities and a predetermined meeting schedule might well be superfluous.

The Board Today and Tomorrow: Perspectives from the United Kingdom

The Principal Role of the Board

The Companies Acts in Britain leave a great deal of latitude when it comes to the role of the board of directors (pages 48-49). Not surprisingly, therefore, the role that the board plays is found to vary considerably from one company to the next.

The British board, like its counterparts elsewhere, has a basic responsibility to safeguard the interests of the company's shareholders. Its role in carrying out this responsibility is seen essentially as (1) protecting and enhancing the assets of shareholders, (2) seeing that the company is well managed within the law, and (3) determining distribution of profits (dividends) to shareholders, subject to their approval. But these basic requirements are only a starting point in an inquiry as to what boards themselves — or, rather, what those who serve on them — actually do, what their role is from day to day or month to month.

What has been sought principally for this report is the views of directors and chairmen on what the principal role of a board of directors is — or, more accurately, what it should be, since the board's performance as an institution is not without its critics (see page 56). Comments on the board's principal role have been gathered both through interviews and through a lengthy questionnaire.

What follows is an analysis of written responses from 15 thoughtful British business leaders to the question: "How would you describe the principal role that a board of directors plays, as you have seen it in your own experience?" The answers are examined from two points of view: (1) The degree to which the board's role is described as an active or direct one. (2) The areas of activity in which the board is expected to be involved. Comments were solicited specifically for private-sector, not government-owned, companies.

Almost every executive, in citing the role a board plays, lists at least one board function — and most refer to several functions — in terms of playing a direct or active part, as distinguished from a consultative or indirect one. In this category are tasks in which the board should *act, initiate, establish, set, determine, define, appoint, elect,* and the like. No executive describes every board function in such terms, however, although a few come close to doing so. Here are some examples of these board roles:

- Determine broad policy;
- Set corporate objectives;
- Define the broad strategy for the company;
- Decide the broad basis of allocation of the company's resources;
- Decide the appropriate capitalization of the company and decide its dividend policy;
- Set financial targets;
- Take the main financial decisions;
- Appoint the company's senior executives;
- Decide the remuneration of chairman and chief executive and other executive directors;

- Elect its own chairman;
- Act as the supreme management of the company.

This conception of the board's role as a relatively active one is not typical of other countries covered in this survey. Few North American boards, for example, are expected to play so direct a part. Even though the matters with which they concern themselves are essentially the same, their role is more one of approval and monitoring than of direct action. The German supervisory board, while it takes direct action in executive selection and in certain financial decisions, also serves more of a monitoring function than that outlined by these British executives.

The relatively direct involvement of the British board suggested in these responses is in keeping with, and perhaps a reflection of, the traditional makeup of boards in that country. Full-time company executives are in a majority on most British boards. It would seem inevitable· that a predominantly inside board would operate on a level of *deciding* and *establishing* to a greater degree than a board composed mostly of outsiders — prevalent in Canada, the United States, and Sweden — with a necessarily limited knowledge of company details.

A second category for descriptions of a board's role is called here "indirect but specific." Into this category have been placed board functions given in terms of *monitoring, controlling, approving, ensuring* or *confirming,* and where a specified area or concern is named. Some examples of "indirect but specific" board roles:

- Control (and be accountable for) corporate policy;
- Keep long-range objectives under review;
- Approve broad strategies necessary to achieve objectives;
- Confirm recommendations on policies from executive management;
- Ensure that management is conducted in accordance with principles laid down in broad policies;
- Approve major capital expenditures, investment and investment projects;
- Approve accounts;
- Control the executive management;
- Ensure that the chief executive and his senior colleagues provide effective day-to-day management;
- Ensure that the executive management provides regular information on operations;
- Approve corporate plans;
- Give "specialist" advice.

The list of indirect but specific roles for the board is somewhat longer than that of active or direct roles. It can be seen that the board's position here is one of making sure that management is doing its job, rather than that of telling management what to do. This posture is the chief characteristic of boards in most other countries included in this report. It appears that this is also the part of a board's contribution that is most suitable to the outside director, the man or woman who is not affiliated with the company and whose presence gives the board the objectivity it needs to provide a discipline for management.

Certain other descriptions of roles for the board of directors are very general and do not fit into either the "active" or "indirect but specific" modes. Examples:

• Create a successful future for the company;

• Promote the interest of the business as a whole, its shareholders, employees and customers;

• Ensure that the company remains a viable concern. This kind of role for the board was mentioned least often.

Decisions Boards Must Make or Approve

British executives were asked to specify what kinds of decisions a board of directors *must* either make or approve in order to carry out its responsibilities. Three types or categories of decision stand clearly above others.

Every executive names financial decisions as a must for the board, if financial matters are taken in a broad sense so as to include acquisitions and mergers. Important decisions of a financial nature mentioned are:

• Acquisition or disposal of corporate assets;
• Establishment and maintenance of an appropriate capitalization structure:
  • Approval of major capital expenditures;
  • Raising new capital;
  • Seeing that there is adequate overall financial control;
  • Distribution of dividends;
  • Investments.

A few of these executives place some of these financial decisions in the framework of allocating the company's resources (a term also applied to manpower as well as financial resources). Three put capitalization and dividend decisions in the context of relationship with shareholders, and all three give this relationship first priority in terms of board decisions.

Not only does every executive name financial decisions as being essential board matters, but fully half of them also place financial matters first in priority for board consideration. This combination places financial decisions clearly ahead of all others in importance among those named.

For example, all but one participant in this exercise names the area of management, and in particular the selection of the chief executive or managing director, as one involving decisions that a board of directors must reserve to itself. Yet only one of these executives gives such matters first priority where the board is concerned.

All of the following decisions in the area of management succession, organization or performance are named as essential considerations:

• Appointment or dismissal of the chief executive or managing director;

• Senior staff appointments;

• Ensuring that management succession for key posts is provided for; and

• Monitoring executive performance.

Two of these British commentators extend the board's role in this area downward to broad manpower planning in one case, and, in the other, to decisions on employment policies. But one takes the opposite approach and points out that the board must decide not only management questions, but also questions concerning the board itself — its own composition and performance. As he sees it, the board must ensure that the company is governed at all times by a board that fulfills its responsibilities, and that is led by a competent chairman.

Why is the subject of top management staffing and performance, although considered important, not rated more often as the first priority? One reason may be that British boards have a high proportion of members who are corporate executives (compared with boards in most other countries). Perhaps there is a feeling that when executives constitute a majority of the board, management performance is under routine scrutiny at the board level. It might also be noted that when a company runs into management trouble the board of directors almost inevitably gives first priority to this area, whatever its usual ranking on the priority list.

The last of the three groups of decisions considered most important for the board by British executives includes those that deal with policies, objectives and strategies. Just half of the respondents cite decisions in these areas as matters the board must reserve to itself — but in all but one instance they place it first in priority. In some cases the board's role is seen as being two-fold: The board should *set* or *establish* the policies (objectives, strategies), and it should also *monitor* or *review* performance to ensure that they are being met. Some representative statements of the board's involvement in this area:

"Read the environment, set objectives, and work out a macro plan."

"Crystallize commercial and operational objectives. Establish a broad plan by which objectives will be achieved."

"Decide the long-term objectives of the company and keep these under review. Approve the broad strategies necessary to achieve these objectives."

The last statement illustrates the fact that the board's involvement in this kind of decision isn't necessarily one of initiating or establishing. This particular chairman has distinguished between objectives — which, in his view, the board should initiate — and strategies, which are part of management's responsibility but subject to board approval.

Other decision "musts" for the board besides these dominant three (financial, top management selection and monitoring, and broad policies and objectives) include:

• Ensuring an appropriate organizational structure for achieving company goals;

• Seeing that there is clear delegation of authority;

• Approving operating units' plans;

• Making major decisions on product research and development policy;

• Overseeing industrial relations and employment policies.

• Supervising relationships with outside auditors.

• Arbitrating claims of various "stakeholders."

The range covered by these expressions of the decisions a board of directors must make or approve reflects the company-by-company nature of the role that boards of directors play. What one board *must* decide on may be quite different from what another board puts in the must category. Among the factors that contribute to this spread:

The composition and personal chemistry of the board itself;

The leadership and convictions of the board chairman;

The outside directors' confidence in the company's senior management;

The company's state of health and direction; and even the industry the company is in.

This variation in board priorities also reflects, as noted, the latitude under the Companies Acts as to the role boards can play, a flexibility found in varying degrees in most of the countries considered for this report. West Germany has left far less latitude for its supervisory board, whose priorities are prescribed to a large degree by law.

The board of a nationalized company in Britain may at times confront priorities that are quite different from those just described. Some of the most basic financial decisions may be made within government, for example. And other priority matters for the board's consideration may be decided on at the ministry level and handed to the board to carry through. (See page 48 for a discussion of nationalized industries.)

Whose Interests Does an Outside Director Represent?

When an executive or other prominent citizen in Britain is asked to serve on a board of directors, how does he see his obligation in terms of whose interests he is there to represent as a nonexecutive director?

Almost all study participants name the shareholders. About a third, in fact, believe that they should represent *only* the shareholders in serving as outside directors. But a majority extend the outside director's obligations beyond the owners of the company, with employees, customers and society (and/or the community) named about equally often. Suppliers get one mention, as does "the taxpayer," in connection with a nationalized company, where the public is the owner of the firm. One executive feels that he owes his obligation as an outside director to the long-term interests of the company itself as an ongoing entity, which he sees as distinct from the body of shareholders, which is constantly fluctuating.

These expressions of a broadened sense of obligation for board members — one going beyond the owners' interests — corresponds to the broadened sense of responsibility for the company now often articulated in Britain (and in other countries). The term "stakeholders" is commonly used in this context to convey the fact that others besides shareholders have an interest in the conduct and the success of the British company. (See box on pages 58-59.) But the responses to this survey show that the "stakeholder" concept is not universally accepted.

It is important to know whether the director's accountability is one that can be enforced. That is, by what means can those whose interests an outside director is obligated to represent hold that director — or the board — to account for performance (or nonperformance), and how effectively can they do so?

As to the means available, the most obvious one, and the one mentioned most often, is to see that a director who is not performing or not properly looking after the interests of shareholders (and other stakeholders) is removed from the board. Apparently the dismissal of a director during a term of office is rare, so that removal really means removing him from the slate at the next annual meeting for which he would otherwise be nominated for reelection.

But even this is more easily said than done. Shareholders of most major British companies, like their counterparts in the United States and Canada, are scattered and passive and not likely to take such a concerted action against a director, although they have the opportunity to do so through the annual general meeting. If action against a director is to come about it will probably be at the instigation of the chairman, according to these executives, often with the backing of the rest of the board, or of the other outside directors (sometimes just one or two of the most influential directors can be support enough). It *is* possible for public opinion, expressed through letters or in the media, to create enough pressure to unseat a director, but this is unusual. A few commentators hold that there is no practical or effective system for holding outside directors accountable.

One government-appointed director of a nationalized-industry firm points out that he is subject to a more direct, and potentially more effective, means of accountability than that just described for private industry: He can be dismissed from his position as a director by the appropriate government official.

One well-placed British executive, experienced both in public service and in private industry, believes that to consider the accountability of a British nonexecutive director only in terms of his "constituency," or of the company's stakeholders, leaves out a form of pressure that may be even more important. In his view, the code of honor that operates among peers at the level of those who make up the boards of major British companies is a subtle but quite powerful regulator of behavior. He feels that British boards have acquitted themselves quite well, and with a minimum of scandal, despite the apparent freedom from outside-enforced accountability.

Overall Effectiveness of British Boards

How effectively does the board system work on the whole in the United Kingdom? About half of the British executives answering this question feel that, in general, boards in their country work reasonably well. A typical comment to this effect: "[The board system] works well. Failures are publicized and give the impression that the system works less well than it does in practice." One commentator believes that British boards have improved steadily over the past 20 years.

But even the executives who feel essentially positive about the board's role in general usually suggest that there is room for improvement. One feels that the structure is too hierarchic, and that privileges are too jealously guarded at all levels in the organization. Another suggests that the system is weakened when the chairman is also the chief executive officer.

A small but evidently concerned minority of co-operators cite these board shortcomings:

• A failure by boards to define their role;

• A failure to respond in a timely and effective way to changing political, economic and social requirements;

• A tendency to get too involved with management matters.

The strongest indictment of board performance comes from a chairman who says: "Much of the poor management and inadequate performance in the United Kingdom can be traced to ineffectual boards."

Most of the executives who expressed their opinions of the effectiveness of the British board system also cited changes that they believe *should* be made to improve it. The list of these recommendations for improvement is both extensive and specific:

• Place more emphasis on the outside director. Make the presence of nonexecutive or part-time directors a statutory requirement, perhaps with a specified minimum (two or three) on the board of any large publicly owned company. Increase the proportion of such directors on boards, perhaps to one-third or even one-half.

• Strengthen the statutory responsibility of directors. Broaden their responsibility to include the interests of employees, and even the consumer and the public at large.

• Require that the chairman and the chief executive be different individuals.

• Make directors subject to reelection more frequently — annually or every two years (three years is now common).

• Require retirement from board services at some specified age, now an uncommon practice in U.K. companies.

• Tighten restrictions on "insider dealing" by directors on the basis of privileged company information.

• Get financial institution shareholders to take stronger action in the event of poor company performance.

• Limit the number of directorships a person may hold simultaneously.

The British Chairman

In Britain the position of chairman (not usually "of the board" as in U.S. practice) ranges from a full-time job to a part-time one. In a British Institute of Management publication, *The Effective Board, A Chairman's View* (Occasional Paper — New Series OPN 15, 1975), John G. Beevor gives four variants on the British chairman's role:

(1) The chairman is full time and is also the company's chief executive. The author says of this arrangement: "... I believe it to be unsound in principle, though it often works well in practice. This pattern means that two roles are combined in one man, who as chairman of the board is responsible for supervising, appraising and criticizing the performance of himself as chief executive. It is neither logical nor, in human terms, realistic." (Similar arguments have begun to appear in the United States, where the chairman-CEO position is now the favored one in large companies. Swedish law prevents this practice; under West German law it is not possible; but in France it has been traditional in the position of président-directeur-général, or P.D.G.)

(2) The chairman is full time and has certain executive functions, but there is a separate chief executive.

(3) The chairman devotes a substantial part of his time to his duties as chairman but probably not full time; he is not CEO.

(4) The chairman is nonexecutive and part time.

On the Chairman's Position and Role in Britain
(Excerpts from "The Responsibilities of The British Public Company," 1973, Confederation of British Industry)

99. Election of the chairman is the responsibility of the board; the whole tone of the company and its public image must be set by the board and, in particular, by positive leadership by the chairman. No company can be successful unless the chairman is of a caliber to provide this leadership and to represent the company properly to the outside world.

100. It follows that the board has the responsibility not only of electing the chairman, but also of ensuring that he continues to carry out satisfactorily the duties of his office; for this reason we are strongly of the opinion that the period of appointment of the chairman should not be long and that he should not be given too much security of office.

101. We . . . recommend that the chairman should be appointed for a period not to exceed five years, and that it should be left to each individual company to decide what period of appointment not exceeding five years is appropriate to its case. Appointment of the chairman for the chosen fixed period would be subject to termination within that period in the same way that the chairman's appointment is subject to termination at present. At the end of the fixed period the chairman, if of suitable age, would be eligible for reappointment.

102. The chairman has all the responsibilities which are held by other members of the board, but to a greater extent than any other director he is responsible for the performance of the board as a whole and of each member of it. He has the primary responsibility for ensuring appropriate membership of the board, for making necessary changes in board membership, for setting an example to all his colleagues in all matters affecting the company, for acting as spokesman for the board both inside and outside the company, and for promoting the position of the company in such a way as to strengthen the principle of private enterprise, the desirability of commercial risk taking, and the whole concept of entrepreneurism.

103. It is the function of the chairman to see that policies are initiated, to secure the agreement and approval of his board for what they consider to be the right policies, and to ensure by appropriate instructions and continuous monitoring that the policies are put into effect by those with executive responsibility.

104. There must be a clear distinction between responsibilities as chairman and responsibilities as chief executive; it is our view that the two functions should not normally be combined in one person; but experience in a wide range of companies shows that this is a matter in which some flexibility is essential. What is necessary in a substantial company is that if the chairman has executive functions, he should have with him, on an equal or near equal level, one or more colleagues who will share with him the executive responsibility and thus avoid too much concentration of power. We have been informed that in many cases of failure in management concentration of too much power in the hands of the chairman was a contributory cause.

Even when the chairman devotes only part of his time to his duties in that role and has no executive authority, his role is an important one, at least potentially. He is expected to provide leadership for the board; to see that part-time or outside directors contribute and represent an effective counterbalance to management; and to ensure that the organizational aspects of the board — proper membership, committee structure if any, scheduling and agendas for meetings. Often he is the company's spokesman to the outside world.

British executives questioned on board practices tend to emphasize the chairman's important, and in some cases unique, role when it comes to evaluating how well the board is doing its job, and in particular in judging the contributions made by individual part-time nonexecutive directors.

The British chairman position would appear to be one in which the incumbent's personal character and persuasiveness — especially when the position does not have formal executive authority — can be an essential ingredient in how well the job is done.

Excerpts from Statement of Board Policies, Chloride Group

1. CORPORATE RESPONSIBILITIES

1.1 The main board is responsible to the shareholders for the achievement of group objectives and for making the most effective economic use of its financial and human resources.

1.2 The main board recognizes that it has a responsibility to all stakeholders whose lives are affected by its business activity and have a claim on the business — employees (including pensioners), shareholders, customers, suppliers, local and national communities.

1.3 The main board will take into account the interests of all its stakeholders when formulating business policy, endeavoring to strike a fair balance when there are conflicting interests.

1.4 The main board will appoint the chief executive of the group (so delegating operational responsibility for its trusteeship of stakeholders' interests) and will ensure that the management of the group is conducted in accordance with the principles laid down in this policy statement.

* * *

7. SOCIAL RESPONSIBILITIES

7.1 *Responsibilities to all Stakeholders*

7.1.1 The group recognizes that it is an essential prerequisite to the fulfillment of board policies for the group to trade profitably and use its resources effectively in order to discharge satisfactorily its obligations to all of its stakeholders.

7.1.2 The group will not take a narrow or static view of its responsibilities to the stakeholders but will endeavor to anticipate where possible and be responsive to the movement of representative public opinion across the spectrum of social interests and issues.

7.1.3 The group will always act within the laws of the countries in which it operates.

7.1.4 The ability to take account of political and social changes and its consequences will be an integral part of the group's corporate planning activity.

7.2 *Responsibilities to Shareholders*

7.2.1 The group will take into account the long-term interests of the shareholders:

(a) by providing an adequate return on shareholders' capital, achieving a growth in earnings per share above the average for UK manufacturing industry with the aim of maintaining the optimum share market price.

(b) by continuing to develop communications with them, keeping them fully informed (so far as is commercially practicable) of all major decisions and policies, and providing meaningful information on performance and results in its Annual Report and Accounts.

7.3 *Responsibilities to Employees*

7.3.1 The group has a responsibility for the welfare of its employees and pensioners at all levels.

7.3.2 The group will be a progressive employer in respect of pay, retirement and other benefits, recognizing the principle that the employee should be given the opportunity of earning an improving standard of living, and will review its standards regularly.

7.3.3 The group will ensure that its operations do not render a known hazard to the health or safety of its employees and they will adhere strictly to the Chloride manual of standard health and to other codes of practice.

7.3.4 The group will actively seek to increase the satisfaction which its employees derive from their work, and encourage the reduction of unsatisfying jobs.

7.3.5 While good industrial relations are the responsibility of all concerned at all levels in industry, the group will, for its part, endeavor actively to maintain a climate of equable cooperation with all its employees, including trade union and other nominated representatives. There will be a progressive increase in the involvement of employees in the formulation of strategic decisions which affect them.

7.3.6 The group will provide its employees with adequate information for them to understand the aims and plans of the company for which they work. They will be informed at the earliest practicable time of the expected effects of investments, acquisitions, takeovers and divestments on company plans and their own futures and will be consulted as far as possible.

7.3.7 The group will maintain high standards of management practice and performance with a regularly revised program for employee development, deployment and succession. Methods of selection and training will be maintained which will provide for the most effective use of individual skills and aptitudes. The development of good caliber managers from within the organization, balanced by recruitment of a limited number from outside, will ensure that the group's overall objectives and individual aspirations are met.

7.3.8 Recognizing that the group operates in many different environments, the group will use its best endeavors to avoid and discourage discrimination as to sex, race, religion, color, disability or age when recruiting, developing or rewarding employees.

7.4 Responsibilities to its Customers

7.4.I The group will work always to provide its customers with goods which represent value for money and with a standard of customer sales service above average for their market sectors.

7.4.2 The group will always provide goods which are safe when used for their correct purpose.

7.4.3 All communications describing the group's products will be informative and true as to quality, reliability and performance. Terms of sale will state clearly and unambiguously the true amount of money customers are paying for the goods and the terms of guarantees.

7.5 Responsibilities to its Suppliers

7.5.1 The group will not abuse its economic power vis-à-vis suppliers.

7.5.2 The group will not encourage its suppliers to commit their resources for long-term demands unless there are reasonable guarantees that these demands will not be terminated prematurely.

7.6 Responsibilities to the Community

7.6.1 The group will pay proper regard to the environmental and social consequences of its business activities. It will conserve material resources and maintain standards of hygiene and environmental control at least as high as those likely to be established by central or local governments.

7.6.2 The group accepts that it has an obligation to contribute to the welfare of the national and local communities within which it operates. Local managements are therefore encouraged to take positive action in order to influence favorably the industrial patterns of the countries in which they operate. It will adopt a positive approach to the needs of charities, both social and cultural.

7.6.3 The group sees itself as a multinational company which seeks to operate profitably and to the benefit of the local community. In all territories it will be sensitive to local social, economic and political conditions.

7.6.4 In overseas territories, the group will ideally and wherever practicable employ local management which has some international experience, with the inclusion of at least one nonnational to avoid parochialism. Outside nonexecutive directors will be appointed to broaden and improve the quality of decision making.

Measuring Board Performance

The concept of accountability of directors (as well as the question of a board's effectiveness) leads to the need for performance standards and an appropriate means of measurement. In Britain, as in most of the countries surveyed, the measurement of board performance is felt to be lacking. The chairman of a large manufacturing group states the situation this way:

"In theory, the performance of a board is measured by the shareholders. In practice, boards are not sufficiently stimulated by the stakeholders — in particular by the shareholders themselves. The 'institutions' (the pension funds, insurance companies, and so on) tend to be even more passive than the individual shareholders."

If shareholders do not judge the performance of their boards, who does? The answer given most often in this survey was that the stock market and the financial press are the gauges of how well boards are doing their jobs in particular companies. One executive points to a drawback in this standard of measurement, in that it is based as much on the company's prospects — what *might* happen — as on actual performance.

Also mentioned as an appraiser of board performance is the board chairman — or, in a few cases, the nonexecutive directors themselves (in one case, a board committee). The chairman's role in this process is described by one executive, himself a board chairman:

"There is a responsibility for the chairman to assess, and to encourage the board to assess, performance both through measures such as profit performance and market share that reflects the quality of its decisions, and through analysis and discussion of the process it uses to reach decisions."

Two situations are cited that lead to an appraisal of the board and its performance, even where such appraisal might otherwise be nonexistent; a severe company crisis, which can get even passive shareholders involved, and a merger or takeover proposal.

This comment on board performance appraisal comes from the board chairman of a major concern:

"The very idea that boards are or could be subject to any form of evaluation or performance appraisal is virtually unheard of in the United Kingdom. But it is coming."

A somewhat different question is the extent to which individual nonexecutive or outside directors are appraised. The feeling seems to be that individual directors are evaluated to a greater extent, and on more specific standards of measurement, than are boards as a whole in Britain. Yet, says one banking group chairman: "If a director falls short of the standards expected of him, it is often quite difficult to make a change."

The performance of the outside director is subject to appraisal from three sources: his fellow directors (cited most often, and usually described as the *only* appraisers of the outside director); the board chairman (and any deputy or vice chairmen); and senior management in general.

Several measuring sticks are available for use in assessing the contribution of the nonexecutive director, but his contribution to boardroom debate is probably the primary one. A bank chairman comments: "The value of a director's contribution to the board's discussions is generally evident in the discernible extent of his influence . . . on the rest of the board, including executive directors and other senior directors."

Other criteria of performance by which an outside director is judged are his ability or willingness to:

- Stimulate and challenge top executives;
- Identify with corporate aims;
- Contribute to the corporate identity;
- Contribute special expertise;
- Share responsibility for decisions taken;
- Attend meetings regularly;
- Take his own line and, in extremis, to resign.

Legal Risks for British Directors

Contrary to the situation that has developed in the United States, serving on a board as an outside director in Britain does not entail great legal risk, at least according to those consulted on this question. Almost all say that legal risk is not a matter of concern for directors, and one of those who feels there is significant potential risk says that it does not deter candidates from accepting a directorship, so long as the company is a sound one. One kind of action in which directors do expose themselves to potential legal challenge is that of raising capital from the public; the wording of a prospectus for the sale of securities, for example, must be carefully attended to.

One executive makes this comment on risk for directors: "There is a legal risk in that there could be proceedings against, or damage to the reputation of, a director if there was found to have been fraudulent practice in managing a company's affairs, or if there has been action against the shareholders' interests." But another commentator feels that such risk as exists is satisfactorily defined by statute, and in most public companies individual financial liability is limited.

The Dual Role of the Employee Director

As has been stated, the British board usually has a preponderance of company executives in its membership, with outside, independent directors being in the minority. This has changed somewhat for certain large companies, it would appear, where size, complexity and an international scale of operations have resulted in boards composed largely of knowledgeable outsiders. Still, the British pattern on the whole is an inside-dominated board. (Any legislation that might ensue from the Bullock Report could conceivably impose a quite different structure on boards of major companies, of course; see page 64.)

With executives in a controlling position on the board, the question is sometimes asked whether it is not difficult for such directors to distinguish between their two roles — as managers with well-defined responsibilities within the company, and as board members with an obligation to consider broader issues and act in the interests of the shareholders and others. This same need to wear two hats applies to officer-directors in any country, of course, but is of particular importance in Britain, given its traditional board structure.

The opinion expressed most often by the group of British business leaders who were consulted for this survey is that the dual role generally does not pose a significant problem, although some indicate that it *can* be a problem in particular instances.

As one chairman explains, outside of board meetings an executive director is responsible for his "line" authority (and should account for it) to the chief executive. But the director should attend board meetings in a "staff" capacity; to perform the board role it is absolutely necessary to be objective and "nonexecutive" in attitude. A bank chairman characterizes the difference as between "Executive Director" and "Executive *and* Director."

Two conditions are cited as being important for ensuring that executive directors are successful in making the transition between their two roles:

• Those chosen for board membership should be selected in part for their perceived ability to function as directors.

• The outside members of the board, in their quantity and also their quality, should provide an influence that encourages the executive directors to participate as board members rather than as managers.

On the importance of selection, here is the comment of one chairman: "I do not believe that an individual should be appointed to the board simply because of his executive position or status. He should be made a director only if the board considers that he is capable of taking the detached and objective view and attitude required to meet the board's responsibilities."

And another similar comment, from a chairman in the banking industry:

"The choice of an inside director must not depend entirely upon his qualities and standing as a senior member of the management. It must include the capacity to carry on the director's responsibilities and a readiness to speak with a general objectivity on major issues which come before the board. He must be able to do this regardless of his relationship with the Managing Director, who is his superior outside the board meetings."

One executive suggests that executives who are chosen for board membership tend to rise to the occasion: "The change of status is of itself a great stimulant of a changed attitude."

Here is one chairman's comment on the pros and cons of inside and outside directors, and the solution as he sees it:

"While there is argument that insiders are less able to be objective about their own proposals to the board and that they are less likely to critize other directors in case their own projects are attacked later, there is, conversely, the argument that boards without insiders can have only limited knowledge of the company they direct. We believe that the best solution for the moment is to have a board with an appropriate proportion of insiders and outsiders who together will naturally produce a 'balanced view.'"

Perhaps the most pessimistic of the group on this important issue is the board chairman who says:

"It is never easy for executive inside directors to recognize their two roles and to act appropriately in each, although some do it successfully. Some never even try to do so, which explains why so many U.K. boards do not act like boards at all, but more like management committees."

More Outside Directors?

The preceding section, and particularly the last comment, suggest that perhaps there is some feeling for enlarging the proportion of outside directors on British boards so as to strengthen the independent view and its influence on board decisions. Executives consulted for this report were specifically asked whether they felt changes in the proportion of outside or nonexecutive directors on boards would be advantageous. A majority do stress the importance of independent outside members, and several put forward what they feel is a desirable number or proportion of outsiders, but only about a third appear to feel that a change to a greater number of outsiders is needed.

Four participants suggest a minimum of two nonexecutive directors; and one of these executives would prefer at least three for the large multinational companies. A minimum of three such directors for any company is felt necessary by one banking group chairman, while another financial executive believes there should be at least four.

Others convey their ideas of a desirable outside board representation in terms of proportions: one-third in three cases; as much as one-half of the board in three other cases; one-fifth in another case.

One of the advocates for having half the board selected from outside the company says it would provide more opportunity for independent assessment and appraisal of management. Another explains: "In our company we keep the number of insiders and outsiders about equal so that a balance is maintained and no one group dominates the other."

One chairman of a major manufacturing company, who believes that the balance of insiders and outsiders should vary according to the nature of the business and the people involved, points out that the need should be kept in mind of making it possible for a reasonable number of top full-time executives to achieve board status. But a bank chairman expresses his belief that the important thing is not the number or proportion of outside directors; what really counts is whether, by their number or their caliber, they have the ability to change the chairman and principal executives should this be necessary.

It should be pointed out here that none of these British executives who are arguing the case for strong outside representation is suggesting they be in the

majority. They are not taking as a model the Swedish or North American pattern, in other words.

Boards of Government-owned Enterprises

In Britain, as in most countries included in this report, the national government is a substantial participant in business through ownership (sometimes 100 percent, but sometimes considerably less) of major companies. In a report entitled *A Study of UK Nationalized Industries, Their Role In the Economy and Control In the Future,* published in 1976 by the National Economic Development Office (NEDO) — which is not a government agency — the important role of government-owned industry was summarized:

"By any standards the nationalized industries occupy a central role in our economy. Together they account for more than a tenth of the national product and nearly a fifth of total fixed investment. The four largest employers in the country (after central government) are nationalized industries. As suppliers they occupy a dominant position in energy, communications, steel and transport. They account for about a third of all the plant and equipment bought by British industry and for several sectors of industry they are the sole domestic customer." (page 7. This and the other quotations from this report are reproduced by permission of Her Majesty's Stationery Office.)

This description is based on 1975 figures. Since then the government has brought the aircraft and shipbuilding industries into the nationalized fold, after a struggle that began in 1974, and has been an active participant in the development of North Sea oil. (The instrument for this last step has been the British National Oil Corporation, a government-owned company.) British Petroleum Company, the country's biggest industrial firm in terms of turnover or sales, is not a nationalized company, even though the government at present owns directly about 31 percent of its stock and the Bank of England, which is a public (government) corporation, owns another 20 percent. The government has made some of its more recent investments in corporations in order to prevent these companies from failing; British Leyland and Rolls-Royce are two well-publicized examples.

The complex pattern of ownership and control of British publicly owned corporations is not the subject of this report and no attempt will be made to analyze it here. (The varieties of ownership are described on page 48.) The point should be made, however, that the poor profit performance of government-owned industry in recent years has become a matter of serious concern. (There are also critics of the proliferation of such companies, especially in the Conservative party.) One result is the NEDO report, just quoted, which enumerates a number of problems in the control and management of nationalized companies and suggests major changes aimed at correcting them.

An aspect of the publicly owned enterprise that *is* appropriate to this report, of course, is the board of directors; each such company has one. To quote the NEDO report:

"The nationalization statutes set out certain specific duties of boards and powers and duties of Ministers [heads of various government departments having jurisdiction over publicly owned enterprises]. Parliament creates the corporations and vests the assets in them. By implication, the boards are required to account to Parliament for the stewardship of those assets and for their efficient use in pursuit of statutory obligations. The statutes specify that the boards should present annual reports and accounts to Ministers who should in turn place them before Parliament. . . . . Ministers are given the power to appoint the boards and have a range of other statutory powers and duties, including the duty to approve programmes of capital expenditure, the power to approve loans and to require information from the corporations."

The NEDO report concludes that: "There is in practice considerable ambiguity about the accountability of boards of nationalized industries — to whom they are responsible, for what functions and dimensions of performance, and over what time scale. Ministerial responsibility for nationalized industries is correspondingly ill-defined. The resulting confusion leads to a situation in which boards are not effectively required to account for their performance in a systematic or objective manner. . . ."

To solve these problems, the report recommends establishing a body, a Policy Council, between the company's board (which would be a management board) and government. This council would monitor company performance and have specific approval power; it would also shield the company's management from direct government interference. (Government civil servants would sit on the council, but as a minority.)

The prospects for action on this proposal cannot be accurately judged at this writing. But the need for change found by the NEDO study team and advisers is reflected, if indirectly, in comments from British executives. Specifically, these cooperators were asked whether the principal role of the board of directors of a nationalized company differs from that of a private-sector firm, and, if so, in what way. Most say that there *should* be no difference in the essential role of the nationalized industry board, but as a practical matter there is a difference. Five contributing factors to this reality are spelled out:

(1) Some policy decisions are made in the government and handed down to the board for implementation. In such cases, one of the primary areas of responsibility and decision making of the private-sector board is taken out of the directors' hands.

(2) Capitalization decisions are also made in government in some cases. In private business, this would ordinarily be the board of directors' job, or at least the approval power would be theirs.

(3) Where the nationalized company has a monopoly position, which some but not all do, the company does not face the need to be competitive — a driving force in most companies and, therefore, a primary concern of the board of directors. The decision-making process can be quite different in a noncompetitive atmosphere.

(4) Board members, including the chairman, and top executives are paid what the government says they will get. There have been complaints that compensation levels in the nationalized industries are too low, with the result that the best people are not attracted to their managements and boards, and with the further result that there is diminished incentive to perform.

(5) Board members of nationalized companies must consider the potential social and political consequences of their decisions to a greater extent than is necessary in the private-sector boardroom.

The difficulty of this last problem is emphasized by one chairman, who points out that where decisions with long-term consequences are concerned, the board must not only take into account the policies of the government in power but must also try to interpret the attitude of future governments.

Two problems affecting boards of nationalized industries are especially singled out:

(1) The government's power (and, some say, its propensity) to interfere in company matters, which detracts from the role and the authority of the board;

(2) The political motivation for the government's decisions, which therefore tend to be short-range

oriented and to make long-range decision making difficult for the board.

One chairman links these problems when he says: "The time horizons of the boards of nationalized industries are artificially shortened by political intervention, which completely prevents long-term commitments on policy, investment and planning."

Changes could lie ahead for the boards of publicly owned British companies. The proposals in the NEDO report have already been mentioned, but there is another direction from which change could come. While the Bullock Committee's investigation and report have been widely publicized, to date little attention has been paid to a parallel investigation by another committee on the introduction of industrial democracy into the publicly owned companies. It has also been suggested that the drastic changes called for should be tried first in government-owned companies.

The Bullock Report

Easily the most important, and controversial, development concerning boards of directors in the United Kingdom is the appointment of a Committee of Inquiry on Industrial Democracy by the Secretary of State for Trade at the end of 1975, and the radical proposals put forward in the Committee's Report, which was published in January of 1977 after a year of inquiry in the United Kingdom and abroad. One reason for the importance of the committee, and for the storm of controversy that greeted its findings, is that the Labour Party was committed to putting through new legislation based on what the Committee proposed. At this writing it appears that the widespread criticism of the Committee's proposals and the vehement objections of employers to the Committee's recommendations may have succeeded in postponing any legislation until the next session of Parliament.

Chairman of the Committee was Sir Alan (now Lord) Bullock, Master of St. Catherine's College, Oxford. There were nine additional members (after one resigned to become Director-General of the Confederation of British Industry), of whom three were labor leaders, three were prominent businessmen, two were academicians, and one was an attorney. The members could not agree on recommendations. The three industrialists did not sign the majority report but drafted their own minority report. The attorney signed the majority report, but wrote a Note of Dissent on some of its key provisions.

The majority report's essential proposal, which would apply to (but not be mandatory for) major companies, is to add nonmanagement employees to the board of directors in numbers equal to representatives of shareholders. A third, smaller group of outsiders acceptable to both the above groups would also be added to the board. This change, and the procedure recommended for bringing it about, would have a number of results — but at least three major ones can be stated with some certainty:

(1) The structure of the boards of major British companies would be very radically altered from traditional patterns.

(2) The power and influence of the trade unions in the companies affected would be significantly increased.

(3) The traditional ultimate control of owners of these companies — the shareholders — over the use of their funds would be lost.

Apart from these changes, proponents and critics both cite other changes that might be hoped for or presumed to follow from such a restructuring of British boards. Results predicted range from the salvation of British industry and the economy on one hand to the destruction of private enterprise on the other. Some of these issues will be dealt with later.

What the Report Proposes

The following summarizes the specific recommendations of the majority report of the Bullock Committee and how they would be implemented:

(1) Companies affected would be those having at least 2,000 full-time employees working in the United Kingdom — or about 1,800 individual companies making up over 700 industrial groups, the Committee estimates.

(2) The addition of employees to the board would not be mandatory; it would take place only if (a) a union or unions representing at least 20 percent of the company's employees demanded a vote on the issue, the vote to be a secret ballot of *all* employees (union and nonunion), and (b) a majority of those voting, but not less than one-third of all employees, voted in favor of employee board representation.

(3) In the event of a favorable vote, the company's trade unions would have both the control of and the responsibility for the process of selecting the employees who are to serve on the board.

(4) A Joint Representation Committee would be formed, of representatives from *all* unions recognized by the company.

(5) This Committee would (a) negotiate with the existing board what the size of the new board would be, and (b) decide how employee directors would be selected.

(6) Board size would not be mandated but each board arrived at through the Committee's suggested process would have to meet the proportions mentioned above: 2X+Y, or equal "X" groups of employees and of shareholder representatives, plus a third group — smaller than either and with no connection with either — and agreeable to both sides. A board size suggested as a fall-back minimum in case of a deadlock between the outgoing board and the Joint Representation Committee, for companies with 25,000 employees or more, is 19 — two "X" groups of 7, and a "Y" group of 5. Appropriate fall-back minimum board sizes are also suggested for smaller companies.

(7) There would be only one board, not a German-style two-tier system, and all directors would have the same duties and responsibilities, with the requirement that the interests of employees as well as shareholders would have to be considered.

(8) The chairman would be chosen by the shareholder representatives on the board, at least initially.

(9) An independent Industrial Democracy Commission would be formed to implement and monitor the system and to interpret its provisions and arbitrate where necessary.

(10) A new concept of ownership would be codified in legislation, as well as reflected in the makeup of the board; the rights of shareholders would be reduced and a "new concept of a partnership between capital and labor in the control of companies" would replace traditional supremacy of the rights of ownership.

This is only a partial list of the features of the Bullock Committee's majority report proposals, but it describes in essence what the report calls for, including the recommendations that have aroused the strongest feelings. Essentially, the report has endorsed the program recommended by the Trades Union Congress (TUC) in a 1974 report, a starting point from which the Labour Government picked up the banner and created the Bullock group to look into the merits of such a program and how it might be implemented.

In the 1974 report, the TUC turned away from its traditional position that board representation for workers would compromise labor's adversary negotiating position to management. After its report, it changed sides on another point and backed the single-board structure instead of its original two-tier proposal; the Bullock Report, of course, also rejects the two-tier board.

The Pros and Cons

The debate surrounding the Bullock proposals has been so extensive — and intensive — that it is difficult even to summarize the arguments. It is perhaps easier to state the Committee's arguments in favor of the major changes it proposes before dealing with the objections they have raised. The Committee said, in part, that:

(1) Important changes have moved society in Britain (and elsewhere) toward industrial democracy in the sense of greater employee participation in decision making. The report cites industrial and economic change, social change, trade union and legislative developments in labor relations, and developments in Europe. One comment in the report: "The coming of age in our society is a process that inevitably affects the whole of people's lives; it cannot be excluded from the workplace."

(2) The economic difficulties of Britain require major changes in how companies are run so that greater efficiency and output can be achieved.

(3) The role of the employee as a partner in the enterprise, or company, along with the shareholders must be recognized.

(4) Board membership for nonmanagement employees is logical, given the premise that labor is in partnership with capital; and it has proved sound in Europe.

(5) Anything less than full parity of membership on the board for employees would still leave shareholders in control on every issue, which would mean that essentially nothing would have changed from present practice.

(6) A two-tier board, which many groups and individuals consulted had urged if there were to be employee representation, would not be appropriate for Britain. The two-tier system involves a strict separation of the supervision and management functions that would be inconsistent with the U.K. tradition of flexibility in company laws and in practice.

(7) Trade union machinery — in its internal form, the shop steward system — should be used to implement an employee board membership system. The

trade union movement is a highly developed system in the U.K.; unions represent about 70 percent of the employees of the large companies contemplated in the proposals; works councils and other consultative machinery outside the union structure have been declining in importance and thus would not be the proper vehicles for making board representation work; and union resistance if its mechanism were bypassed would probably make board representation impractical.

The criticisms of the Bullock proposals and attacks on the arguments for them have been numerous. Some have emphasized the inappropriateness of these proposals to the British situation in particular; others have found fault on more general terms. The resistance by the capital-employer segment of society has been organized and effective to date, with the emphasis on three issues on which the Confederation of British Industry (CBI) has said it will not yield:

• Any legislation considered must not *mandate* the addition of union-nominated directors to boards (CBI favors greater employee participation — with emphasis below the board level — but insists that companies must be allowed flexibility in implementing it).
• Employee directors must not have parity with shareholder representatives on the board.
• Unions must not be given a monopoly in the choice of employee directors.

Those groups and individuals who object to the Bullock plan because it does not suit the U.K. situation stress the following points:

• Unlike West Germany, in particular, the United Kingdom does not have a comprehensive system of consultative procedure (such as works councils) for implementing employee participation in the plant. Unless participation is established first at this level it will not work at the board level, it is argued.
• The United Kingdom does not have anything like the German system of labor law and courts that have been instrumental in resolving disputes under codetermination in that country.
• The British labor situation — again by comparison with Germany's — does not provide a stable platform on which to build employee board participation as envisioned by the report. The great number of unions (over 100 are affiliated with the TUC), their lack of cohesion, differences among them (some of the major

unions in the TUC are *against* board membership), and their traditional anti-management attitude would mean disruption and chaos for boards under the Bullock plan.
• British industry desperately needs to become more efficient and more competitive. The Bullock proposals, if put into effect, would complicate and slow down the decision-making process in industry and hinder efforts to improve industrial performance.

More generalized criticisms, some of them voiced from the Continent, include alarm that the Bullock program would be going much too far too soon, in three respects. It would create a massive disruption of boards without a trial period (such as Sweden had) and place large numbers of employees in positions for which they are untrained and unprepared. It would give unprecedented power to organized labor; it would give employees parity of representation in a one-board system, not on a supervisory board with limited authority; the unions would be full partners on the body that has absolute authority over company affairs. And the traditional rights of ownership would be seriously diminished since shareholder representatives would be only a minority on the board.

Some of the other objections raised:

• Nonunion employees and overseas employees would have little participation;
• The position of managers in the company hierarchy would be diminished;
• British industry would become less attractive as an investment;
• The boardroom would become a new high-level battleground for collective bargaining;
• The Bullock Committee and its investigation were anything but impartial; its membership and its narrowly defined mission were loaded.

The outcome of the report and the controversy it has caused cannot be predicted at this moment. It is a very political document and is not given much chance of survival as a basis for legislation if there should be a change in government. And the EEC could eventually move to mandate some form of employee board participation that might prevail in Britain if action on the Bullock program is delayed a long time. If the Committee's proposals are adopted, some Continental observers fear their labor movements will be tempted to press for similar innovations in their countries.

Chapter 6
France

The French Context

Government Control of and Involvement in Business

Consonant with the long-standing tradition of French society, the Fifth Republic is a highly centralized polity. It is the National Assembly and the Senate, the Cabinet and Ministries, that provide the legal framework and regulations for business and other institutions of French society. The administrative regions and administrative departments, functioning chiefly as subdivisions of the national government, have but modest influence, though a regional council may levy taxes on property.

The national government is intimately involved in business organization and governance. For one thing, it participates significantly in economic endeavors. Public enterprises — either nationalized companies or agencies of the government — have monopolies in the railroad, electricity and gas, coal mining, and tobacco industries. Such enterprises also compete with or complement private enterprises in the field of air transport, aircraft

Working under the supervision of the Institut de l'Entreprise, M. J.P. Leguay, Chairman of MANORGA S.A., and his partners gathered the information on which the sections on composition and organization of boards and on the perspectives of French directors are based. The context section derives from interviews of several French industrialists conducted by Mr. Bacon and a variety of written material, notably Dr. Walter Kolvenbach, Workers' Participation in Europe, Kluwer, Deventer, The Netherlands, 1977; Price Waterhouse & Co., Doing Business in France, September, 1975; and Business International Corp., Investing, Licensing, and Trading Conditions Abroad, December, 1974.

and automobile manufacture, petroleum refining, banking and insurance. Finally, the state participates in sociétés d'économie mixte — companies in which it is but one of several shareholders but for which it often appoints managers (typically civil servants) and exercises continuing supervision. In some of the industries where private, public and mixed enterprises are found, furthermore, the government has assumed overall direction by pressing for consolidation or rationalization, controlling entry, or prescribing market shares of the constituent firms.

The government also has much to say about the industrial employment practices of the private sector. Through laws and administrative decrees, it sets rules about the workweek, overtime compensation, and paid vacations (four weeks a year is the well-nigh universal period), and it requires employers of a certain size to provide medical and social services. Under a 1967 ordinance, enterprises employing more than 100 persons must set aside annually an amount for a profit-sharing plan. In the United States and Canada, by contrast, such matters are generally reserved to the discretion of corporate management or, if unions are involved, to negotiations between management and unions.

The government also influences private companies by providing financing, bestowing tax concessions, and rendering other forms of assistance in order to carry out its general economic plans and policies. Many businessmen believe that the burden of government regulations is constantly becoming heavier, that the outlook is for more and more restrictions on corporate governance. But note must be taken of a contrary force: the laws and regulations affecting business are not strictly enforced, according to some informed observers of the French scene. Thus it is claimed that many companies have failed to establish the Works Committee (Comité d'Entreprise) required of most enterprises.

The Board and Management

The two most common types of native business enterprises in France are the private limited company or S.A.R.L. (Société à Responsabilité Limitée) and the corporation or S.A. (Société Anonyme). Requiring capital of only 20,000 French francs, permitted a maximum of only 50 shareholders, and lacking a board of directors, the S.A.R.L. is not of concern here.

The S.A. has a minimum capitalization of 500,000 French francs if "quoted" (publicly owned), or 100,000 French francs if privately held. Most S.A.'s have a single board of directors (Conseil d'Administration) elected by shareholders. They are either individuals or corporate shareholder representatives. The board can have no fewer than three and, apart from holding companies, no more than 12 members; no more than one-third of the board may be salaried employees of the corporation; and only salaried employees with at least two years' service are eligible for appointment to the board. Another restriction placed on individuals who serve as directors is that, with certain exceptions, no one can be a member of more than eight boards. Each director is required to own a number of the company's shares — "actions de garantie" — fixed by company bylaws. Except for petroleum companies, there are no restrictions as to the nationality or residence of directors. Under the single-board arrangement there is an elected president (président-directeur-général or PDG) who is chosen from the individual board members and is responsible for the operational management of the company.

There is an alternative two-tier arrangement called the Directorate and Supervisory Council (Directoire et Conseil de Surveillance). Except in S.A.'s with capital of less than 250,000 French francs, the directorate has from two to five members, who are appointed for a four-year term by the supervisory council (three to twelve members), but are not members of it. They have virtually full power to conduct the affairs of the corporation; they vote by majority, and the one among them designated as president represents the firm in relations with outsiders. Like the directors in the Board of Directors-President arrangement, members of a Supervisory Council must own shares of company stock — the number is fixed in the bylaws — and no

member can serve on more than eight boards, with the same exceptions that prevail for a member of a Conseil d'Administration.

One estimate is that about a thousand companies have availed themselves of the Directorate and Supervisory Council option. The chief merits attributed to this option are that (1) it establishes a sharper distinction between the supervisory role of the board and the management function; (2) it is better designed for the effective use of professional management; and (3) it removes what some French commentators believe to be the excessive power of a single individual, the PDG, under the single-board arrangement.

Several other legal strictures are placed on both the Conseil d'Administration and the Conseil de Surveillance. As a rule, government employees and officials, whether appointed or elected, may not serve as directors of private corporations. Unless an exception is explicitly made in the bylaws, no more than one-third of the board members can be over 70 years of age. As will be explained more fully, at least two representatives of employees are entitled to attend board meetings, but only in an advisory capacity.

Although French boards under law have authority to act for the company under any circumstances, traditionally they have not exercised their full powers and, in effect, management dominates corporate governance. The managerial system is patterned after the military, with senior executives accustomed to a high degree of authority. Their attitudes are said to be, on the whole, paternalist and authoritarian; middle managers are rarely consulted about significant decisions, which has led to feelings of anomie, even bitterness, among them, and has perhaps been a force in many of them becoming unionized. Furthermore, French executives, some of their number point out, are not subject to the discipline on their performance provided by the powerful stock market and the well-developed financial reporting systems found in the United States. Finally, the pool of top managerial talent in France is relatively small, so skilled executives often cannot be readily replaced. All this reenforces management's position of primacy in corporate affairs.

Organization of Public Enterprises

The salient feature of public enterprise is the dominant role of the government. Its ministers or other service officials appoint both directors and the senior executives. And by law civil servants — a strong interest group in France — must be represented on these boards. They tend to remain on boards for a long time, gaining influence through continuity of service.

In a few industries, however, the overwhelming influence of government has been contained because only members of management are sufficiently familiar with the complexities of the business to assume initiative in policy making.

Management-Labor Relationships

About 25 percent of the work force in France is organized. Unions are organized more on ideological than on industry lines, and there is considerable difference in their viewpoints, as a brief profile of the four major unions indicates:

• The Communist-dominated Confédération Générale du Travail (CGT) has representation on many industries. This, by far the largest union, is dedicated to eventual collective control of the means of production.

• The Confédération Française Democratique du Travail (CFDT). Concentrated in the metals industries and among clerical and other nonindustrial workers, the CFDT also does not acquiesce in capitalism, but its prime concern is to ensure for its members maximum freedom against constraints imposed by companies, government and other institutions.

• The Force Ouvrière (FO) is made up mostly of workers in the public sector — notably civil servants and post office personnel. This union is Socialist but anti-Communist in outlook.

• The Confédération Générale de Cadres (CGC) is a unions of technicians, middle managers, foremen and sales persons and has a nonideological cast. According to some observers, this powerful union would like to see worker representation on the board of directors.

Wage bargaining does not take place at the national level — this usually occurs at the industry or individual company level — but other agreements involving conditions of employment and work are sometimes determined nationally. The government sometimes extends collective bargaining agreements to firms that have not been involved in reaching them.

Whether or not they negotiate with a union or unions, all companies employing 50 workers or more are obliged to form a Comité d'Entreprise, or Works Committee. The chairman of the company is an ex-officio member, as well as chairman of the committee. The other members (the number depends on the size of the work force) are elected by employees; in addition, each principal union can appoint one non-voting member. These committees, which are supposed to meet at least once a month, are entitled to be informed about the state of the company's business, investment proposals, and matters that may affect employment. And they must be consulted about planned reductions in the work force, work rule changes, training programs, and pay schedules. But the consensus is that Works Committees have little impact.

The Comité d'Entreprise has the right to have two members (in certain companies, four members) attend official meetings of the board of directors or the supervisory board of companies that have adopted this form. These individuals enter into the deliberations of these bodies, but are not official members of the board and specifically do not have the right to vote. One of them represents senior executives and middle management; the other, lower ranking employees. It is said to be not uncommon for boards to meet away from company offices in order to avoid discussing sensitive matters with workers' representatives.

The Sudreau Committee

In 1974, the government created a "Commission for the Study of the Reform of the Enterprise," which came to be known as the Sudreau Committee, after the name of its chairman. After soliciting the views of representatives of management, labor and outside authorities, it issued a report *(Rapport du Comité d'Etude pour la Reforme de l'Entreprise)* that contained some broad suggestions for reform, among them to reserve one-third of the seats on corporate boards of major firms for employee representatives, though it was not indicated how they were to be selected. It has been pointed out that this change would fall short of co-management, would rather create a kind of co-supervision, which would be more acceptable to employers. And it would also be consonant with the reluctance of French unions to undertake management responsibilities.

According to one commentator: "The Sudreau commission came to the conclusion that today's France is not suitable for the Mitbestimmung as it is exercised in the Federal Republic of Germany. Therefore, in the opinion of the commission, participation of the employees should result only in better information and control, but must not create any conflicts with the principles of uniform management and responsibility."[1]

[1] Kolvenbach (p. 31), see page 67.

The implementation of this proposal is far from certain — is, indeed, improbable for some time. A bill has been drafted to *authorize* boards of companies with more than 2,000 employees to appoint employee representatives as directors, but boards would retain discretion as to whether they would take this step. But important management groups and the CGT and CFDT, the two largest unions that negotiate with private-sector enterprises, have declared themselves opposed to it: management because of the fear of ensuing paralysis of the board; the unions because of a wish to remain entirely independent of management and a predilection for confrontation over cooperation. As for the government, it seems preoccupied with the country's economic problems (inflation, unemployment) and with putting its house in order pending the national elections scheduled for next spring. Similarly, the opposition (an uneasy coalition of Socialists and Communists) has not been pressing for this or other recommendations of the Sudreau Committee.

Composition and Organization of the Board

The information for this section of the report was gathered from 68 major French companies — all of them S.A.'s with a single board of directors or Conseil d'Administration: 41 of them manufacturers and 27 nonmanufacturing concerns.

Table 6-1 offers data on the age, term of office, and retirement practices of these boards. Other key statistics:

- The average board of directors has ten members, including the chairman.
- Of the 20 percent of board members who are presently full-time employees of the company (including the chairman), nearly all are members of management.
- Of the 80 percent of board members who are outside directors — that is, not presently employees of the company — 7 percent are former employees (mostly members of management); and there is just one woman outside director in all the companies surveyed.
- Ownership interests are well represented in this sample of firms. The proportion of outstanding company stock held by board members varies between 0.0001 and 100 percent; an average figure would therefore be misleading. But in over two-fifths of the companies the directors own 50 percent or more of the stock.
- Manufacturing company executives constitute the largest group of outside directors. Next in frequency

Table 6-1: Age, Term of Office and Retirement

	Range	Average
Average board age	47-66	58
Term of office[1]	1-6 years	5 years
Retirement age[2]	65-85	72

[1] In practice directors are reelected almost automatically.

[2] For two-thirds of the companies the retirement age is that fixed by law. In the rest, it is established in company bylaws. *Employee* directors, however, can serve on the boards of their companies after retiring from their executive responsibilities in almost four-fifths of the companies.

are bankers; then come merchandising or trading company executives, representatives of other financial institutions, and independent businessmen.

- The number of board meetings during the year ranges from one to twelve, with five the average.

Committees

Committees composed exclusively of directors are evidently a rarity in France. Only about a tenth of this group of companies have such committees, which usually deal with decisions about diversification, changes in corporate structure, and general policies.

Committees made up of management representatives and directors are more commonly encountered. Almost two-fifths of the companies hold management committee meetings which outside directors attend. The average number of meetings for such a committee is 16 a year; the average size of the committee is 8 members (the range is 4-14); and the outside director representation averages 25 percent of the committee's membership.

In a third of the firms surveyed, special committees — including corporate executives and outside directors — have been constituted to deal with particular issues. In decreasing order of incidence these are:

- General policies, strategy and diversification
- Finance and financial commitments
- Investments
- Financial results and declaration of dividends
- Forecasts and budgets

The Board Today and Tomorrow: Perspectives from France

Executives and directors of the 68 French companies whose practices regarding the composition and organization of their boards were described in the previous section, plus two other directors who were queried separately, have offered their views about the role of the board of directors.

Analysis of these views reveals two seemingly contradictory opinions:

(1) On the one hand, involvement in the determination of long-term policies is seen as the principal responsibility of the board by more respondents than any other function (see box). This traditional role is underscored by these opinions of a majority of the French study participants:

• The responsibilities that boards perform *best* concern financial and investment matters and general planning.
• Responsibilities handled less well are decisions about technical matters or sales, labor relations, and day-to-day supervision of the company business.

(2) On the other hand, 95 percent of respondents feel that general management has more influence over long-term policies than the board. This is so because of general management's direct, day-to-day handling of the corporation's business. Generally speaking, it is more competent than the board in the company's field of activity, in the assessment of constraints affecting this field, and in the awareness of existing and future development problems. Thus general management takes the initiative in matters concerning the future of the company; the board's role is to bestow (or withhold) approval.

For issues other than finance or long-term policy, the board is at a disadvantage because it has insufficient knowledge of the company and its businesses, cannot spare enough time, or cannot get adequate information prior to board meetings.

The respondents believe that the board is *most useful* in three domains:

• Selecting general management
• Counseling with general management on major decisions to be reached. At such times, it acts as a "council of wise men."
• Taking over in case of a serious crisis such as conflicts that may jeopardize management continuity.

Even though regular board meetings often are purely formal events, several respondents stress the importance of these occasions as proof of the company's self-discipline: Managers are impelled to review major

---

Responsibilities of the Board (listed in order of number of mentions)

Long-term general policies
Selection of management
Investments
Financial policy
Budgetary control and control of operating results
Company strategy (manufacturing and sales)
Approval of financial statements
Disposal of assets
Declaration of dividends
Solving power structure crisis
Personnel administration and labor relations
Changes in corporate structure
Relations with subsidiaries
Ethical conduct

---

problems in greater depth and to analyze the reports to be presented to the board to a greater extent than they would in the absence of meetings.

In summary, board life does not always stick to the rules and regulations governing the responsibilities of the board. Responses to the survey indicate that the board is often seen as a body of experienced men, a safeguard for the shareholders, an opening to the world outside the corporation, and an instrument of control. But, most often, even in the domain of long-term policy, it is not a decision-making authority or a source of initiative and leadership.

Outside and Inside Directors

By law, at least two-thirds of French boards must be outside directors. All but a few respondents endorse this requirement, and some say the portion of outside directors should be increased, despite the problems of availability of qualified persons and their remuneration.

Yet this view does not imply criticism of inside directors. The executive serving on the board of his own company is not considered by most French directors to have an irreconcilable conflict between his directorial and managerial responsibilities. Thus the board chairmen in the sample think it possible to reconcile the differing interests of management and shareholders for the company's welfare.

But about a fifth of the respondents disapprove of the overlap in the respective roles of manager and inside director. For example, in the matter of profit distribution, as a representative of the stockholders, he would recommend payment of dividends; in his capacity of managing executive, however, he would favor reinvesting the profits into the company. Another problem with the inside director, these critics say, is that he cannot be uncommitted on a board whose chairman also happens to be the executive officer to whom he reports.

Overall Effectiveness

Most French directors are by and large satisfied with the effectiveness of the corporate board, as the tabulation below shows:

	Percent of Respondents Endorsing This Statement
The board system is effective	47
The board system is more or less effective	33
The board system is not effective . .	20

A number point out that board effectiveness largely depends on the quality of its members and their communication process. Personality (expertise, sense of responsibility, authority), is also said to contribute to effectiveness. It is also claimed that directors feel more committed to their work if they represent major shareholders. Only a few respondents express preference for the "Directoire" type of corporation (described in "The French Context").

Nonmanagement Workers as Board Members?

As "The French Context" points out, representatives of the Comité d'Entreprise (Works Council) attend board meetings but do not vote. Their presence is now part of the board's normal working procedure. Though they tend not to be active participants, the French executives questioned believe that, through them, personnel have better awareness of the company's problems, while board members keep posted about current labor relations problems.

Most respondents, however, do not think it desirable to implement the recommendation of the Sudreau Committee that nonmanagement workers be represented on corporate boards as full members, with voting rights — especially if these representatives were to come exclusively from unions. Their two principal objections:

(1) French unions are, on the whole, opposed to capitalism and so are uncooperative with management.

(2) The differing viewpoints of shareholders and management on the one hand, and unions on the other, concerning company objectives would freeze any talks or, in the opinion of some respondents, would focus discussions on exclusively labor problems.

Having union members on the board would, according to some, cause further problems:

— The confidential aspect of some policymaking decisions could not be safeguarded.

— The position of a union member director would be ambiguous. How could he simultaneously protect the company's and the individual worker's interests? How could he step from board member to company employee? What would be his legal responsibility?

— The board would be forced to handle problems so far considered as part of general management's responsibility in carrying out the day-to-day operations of the corporation.

A few respondents believe that this innovation would permit a useful permanent dialogue at board level among workers, managers and directors, a fruitful discussion of conflicts within the company, and the establishment of realistic labor relations policies. But others insist that this dialogue already exists within present company organizations and need not entail appointment of worker board representatives.

Changes Advocated

Here are suggestions of changes in board organization voiced by the French study participants. They are listed in decreasing order of mention:

— To limit the age of directors more strictly (70 years is the retirement age cited most often).

— To renew board members more frequently (for example, by setting the maximum number of terms of office at two or three).

— To improve information supplied to directors (in particular, items on the agenda for board meetings).

— To have fewer members on most boards. Regardless of company size, large groups tend to be less effective.

— To have the smaller shareholders better represented in the case of large companies, where they often own a substantial amount of stock.

— To facilitate the operating processes of subsidiaries' boards. In many instances, these boards duplicate existing organization structures of management committees.

Chapter 7
Turkey

The Turkish Context

Government Control of and Involvement in Business

Administratively, Turkey is organized into 67 provinces, which are the local administrative divisions of the central government. This administrative arrangement is similar to the political organization of France. Each province includes several municipalities. Turkey's population of 41 million is distributed unevenly among the provinces.

The Ministry of Commerce of the central government incorporates business and other private organizations and spells out the duties and responsibilities of their officers and directors in accordance with prescribed rules and regulations stated in the Turkish Commercial Code. In spite of recent efforts to introduce securities and disclosure laws and regulations, codification has not yet been realized in these areas.

Government enterprises are a major factor in Turkish commerce, including such natural monopoly industries as electric power and rail and other forms of mass transportation — as well as those other industries that produce basic goods and services. Both the central government and local authorities participate in competitive industries as owners and investors. Industrial and

Dr. Mustafa A. Aysan of the School of Business Administration of Istanbul University wrote the context section of this chapter and gathered the information on which the section on composition of boards is based. His work was arranged and supervised by The Economic and Social Conference Board (Ekonomik ve Sosyal Etüdler Konferans Heyeti) in Istanbul.

commercial government enterprises — called State Economic Enterprises (SEE's) — produce approximately 15 percent of the GNP and employ about 40 percent of the nonagricultural workers of the country. The State Economic Enterprises Code (Law No. 440) is the basic law affecting SEE's.

Business functions under stronger governmental constraints in Turkey than in other countries. There is comprehensive national planning. Government-owned (public sector) firms must, of course, comply with the plan; but it is considered to be an overall guideline for private business firms as well. Furthermore, extensive economic policies related to price controls and the encouragement of investment are utilized to give definite direction to private enterprise. For government-owned firms, legislation requires that nonmanagement workers participate in company decision making and be represented on the board of directors. For private businesses, there is no law requiring participation of workers in decision making. However, two of the largest labor union confederations are presently campaigning for worker participation in management in general, and representation of workers on the board of directors, in particular.

As the Turkish Commercial Code is applicable to all foreign and domestic business firms in Turkey, there are no differences as to the nationality of business firms in this respect. Subsidiaries of foreign private business firms are subject to the Foreign Investment Encouragement Law (No. 6224), which is considered to be one of the most liberal of its kind in the world. Although the law has been in effect for the last 25 years, foreign investment has not reached major proportions in Turkey due to other economic and political reasons.

Major Laws Affecting the Board of Directors

Corporations constitute the major proportion of all business enterprises of significant size. Of seven possible forms of business organization, only corporations and cooperative companies must have boards of directors.

A corporation is formed under the provisions of the Turkish Commercial Code of 1957.

Two types of business corporations — the Limited (Liability) Company and the "Anonim Company" — offer limited liability to investors. The Anonim Co. (A.S.) is similar to the German Aktiengesellshaft (A.G.) or a French Société Anonyme (S.A.), or a U.S. corporation. The Limited Co. (Ltd. Ş.) is similar to the German GmbH or the French S.A.R.L. The cooperative company is similar to the French Cooperative Society, which has limitations on dominant share ownership.

The Turkish Commercial Code grants the control and authority over a corporation's affairs to a single board of directors. The law requires the directors "to manage the business and affairs of the corporation" with almost unlimited powers between stockholders' meetings — except for powers to distribute profits. The dividend decision is reserved for the stockholders' meeting.

Since the separation of ownership from management is not fully developed, in many limited liability companies directors get involved in day-to-day decisions and operations. In many companies there are executive directors, or "managing directors," as they are called in the U.K., to whom authority to manage the firm is delegated. In fact, major shareholders are frequently represented on the corporate boards. In government-owned companies, according to the State Economic Enterprises Code, the president and two of the vice-presidents of the SEE's are also board members.

The Turkish Commercial Code grants authority to boards of directors in very general terms. But directors have two important duties under the law:

(1) The duty of care: This requires directors to act with that degree of diligence, care and skill which an ordinary prudent man would exercise under similar circumstances in like positions.

(2) The duty of loyalty: A director is considered a fiduciary to whom stockholders have entrusted the welfare of the corporation. Therefore, a director is not permitted to take advantage of the corporation for his personal gain.

A board of directors is considered to have authority only as a group; directors as individuals have no legal power, except for that delegated to them by the board. On the other hand, directors can be held liable as individuals for their actions, or failure to act, as board members.

Directors of private-sector companies are elected by shareholders, and are required by the Turkish Commercial Code to own shares. If the person is not a shareholder when elected, he cannot start working as a board member until he owns shares equal to one percent of paid-in capital or 5,000 Turkish liras in nominal value.

There are virtually no legal restrictions on the election of directors in private-sector corporations. (Even electing foreigners does not require government permission.) Outside directors in the European and North American sense of the term — persons who are not employed by the company and who are not major shareholders — are rarely seen on the board. Since there is a high concentration of shares in certain hands (individuals or families) in the private sector, many boards are identified with certain large shareowners. There are no laws limiting the number of boards on which a person may serve simultaneously.

In government-owned corporations, board members are appointed by the government, directly or indirectly, except for the nonmanagement employee serving on each such board.

Most private-sector corporations elect directors for one-year terms, but large companies usually have longer terms. This is true for the majority of the 30 corporations that contributed information about their board practices for this study. According to the Commercial Code, if there is no specific reference in the corporation's by-laws, board members may serve for as long as three years. Directors are forbidden from engaging in other businesses directly or indirectly related to the company's field.

Corporate directors have to act in the best interest of the owners they represent in accordance with the Commercial Code, the tax laws, civil law, the Law of Obligations, and related regulations. In this capacity, they are responsible for reporting significant financial information to the shareholders. The Turkish Commercial Code does not require periodic public disclosure of financial information to the public at large, since Turkey does not have public disclosure laws, although there have been intensified efforts for introducing such laws for the last 15 years.

A parliamentary bill has been prepared for bringing compulsory public disclosure for corporations having more than 50 shareholders. "Corporate auditors," stipulated by the Turkish Commercial Code, are elected by, and responsible to, the shareholders. Although the

Commercial Code has assigned major auditing responsibilities to the legal corporate auditors, their activities are not similar to those of independent auditors such as the certified public accountants in the United States and the chartered accountants in the United Kingdom. Turkish auditors have no public responsibility or professional requirements. Financial reporting to the shareholders is the responsibility of the board of directors, the auditor's report being appended to the annual report. Such reporting must, by law, be made available to shareholders two weeks before the stockholders' meeting. Directors cannot use the knowledge of privileged company information to take unfair advantage of buyers or sellers of the company's stock who lack the same information. They are also forbidden from disclosing confidential company information.

Management-Labor Relations and Unionization

In the private sector the choice of corporate directors and function of the board might appear to be insulated from management-labor relations. However, since executive directors to whom the managing authority is delegated play an important role in the company's day-to-day decisions, the board frequently gets involved in management-labor relations in the private sector. Since the management of a government-owned firm is on the board and the management is appointed by the government, government involvement in management-labor relations is frequently observed in the public sector.

About one-fourth of the industrial work force (nongovernment and nonagricultural employment) is unionized. The industrial relations system of the country is subject to Laws No. 274 and 275 of 1963, which allow for multiple labor confederations within the country. Hence, there is no single nationwide organization. There are three confederations of unions. The biggest one, which has about 1.2 million members, is the Confederation of Turkish Labor Unions (Türkiye İşçi Sendikaları Konfederasyonu-Türkiş, or Türk-İş), and it seems to be dominant in the sense of acting as a national coordinator or spokesman in collective bargaining. The stance of Türk-İş is to the left of center.

The second biggest confederation, having about 500,000 members, is the Confederation of Reformist Labor Unions (Devrimci İşçi Sendikaları Konfederasyonu — DISK) and represents views farther to the left of Türk-İş. The third union, with about 100,000 members, is the Confederation of Nationalist Labor Unions (Milliyetçi İşçi Sendikaları Konfederasyonu — MISK) and it represents rightist views. Unions can negotiate labor contracts with companies individually or on the industry level. In order to negotiate with the company, a union must have a majority of the workers of that company as its members.

Major unions in Turkey have traditionally focused on negotiating wages, benefits and working conditions with company managements; they have not sought a *direct* political role and have not formed a political party. Yet the two largest confederations are thinking of such a role. However, they differ in views on method. DISK advocates forming a political party and playing a direct role in politics. Türk-İş is discussing whether to form a political party or to support a major existing party. It is worth noting that the president of Türk-İş is a Senator appointed by the President of Turkey. Meanwhile the unions do take positions on legislation and keep track of the voting records of politicians, and union leaders have influence among politicians because of the number of potential votes they represent.

Public-sector enterprises are required to have one worker representative on the board. In private companies, there are some committees having workers as members at lower levels of organization, and they deal mainly with technical matters. There is no two-tier board system such as found in German corporations (A.G.'s).

Ownership of Corporations and Control of the Board

Most major Turkish corporations are owned either by a small number of shareholders — single individuals or families — or by the government. However, in recent years, there has been a tendency among private-sector corporations "to go public"; i.e., selling some minority share to the public, keeping a sufficient amount of shares to preserve the control of the firm for the dominant family or the dominant individual. Commercial banks make equity investments, but are limited to keeping their equity investments at a reasonable ratio to their own equity.

A recent development is the increasing dominance of pension funds in the ownership of major corporations. Notably, 35 percent of the equity capital of the largest commercial bank is owned by the pension fund of the same bank, and the Army Pension Fund has major holdings in large corporations.

As owners, the shareholders have the power to elect directors at the required annual shareholders' meeting. They do this in most cases largely by proxy vote. But management almost always proposes a slate of directors and only rarely is a candidate of management defeated.

Since major shareholders are also managers in many corporations, this mechanism works easily. Shareholders also have the power to remove directors but such action is extremely unusual.

Other actions that are generally reserved for the owners — and require their approval before management can carry them out — include major changes in the corporation's size or organization, including mergers and acquisitions; the issuance of new securities; and, as already noted, the decision about the amounts of profits to be distributed. Any changes in the registered capital must also be approved by the shareholders.

The concept of "authorized capital" as observed in the United States is not recognized in the Turkish Commercial Code, and hence a shareholders' meeting is required for increasing the equity capitalization of the corporation. In this respect, the Turkish system is almost similar to the French and German systems. (In fact, the Turkish Commercial Code is influenced by the Commercial Codes of the latter two countries.)

The agenda of the annual meeting is determined by the board of directors. In some cases, stockholders representing one-tenth of the shares can add new items to the agenda. In addition, company auditors, elected at the shareholders' meeting from among the shareholders, can also add items to the agenda. Otherwise, minority stockholders are virtually powerless in exercising control over the affairs of the corporation. Since in almost all corporations shares are concentrated in certain hands — wealthy individuals and families, pension funds, holding companies, or the government — minority shareholders are essentially passive. And although one-tenth of the shares may call for a shareholders' meeting, minority shareholders are primarily concerned with the profitability of their investments in a company rather than with the stewardship of directors or the actions of management. When minority shareholders become dissatisfied, they prefer to sell their shares rather than to call directors or management to account. But the absence of an organized capital market makes it difficult for a dissatisfied minority shareholder to sell his shares profitably on short notice.

In the private sector, management traditionally has controlled the board of directors, because the two almost always consist of the same persons. In the SEE's, the senior members of management are also directors. Therefore, the management strongly influences, and in some cases controls, the board. The boards of these companies are also influenced — in makeup as well as point of view — by the political party or parties forming the government.

Recent Changes

Recently, there have been changes in two directions which are financially motivated and affect boards of directors:

— The first is the tendency of some of the large family corporations to sell shares to the public; since 1970, these public offerings have indeed been phenomenal. They have been made to take advantage of the lower cost of equity financing as compared to bonds, but debate on the possible encouragement of corporations that are more open to the public has also been a motivating factor. The issuance of share has, in turn, led to more use of outside board members as a means of getting the confidence of the public.

— The second change is in the direction of creating holding companies. Although some loopholes in the tax laws have encouraged this development, forming holding companies has made it easier for corporations to diversify and to take advantage of pyramiding, i.e., managing large companies with relatively small equity capital.

The use of the holding company structure has increased the number of directors needed compared with other business forms, because of subsidiary boards and because parent boards of holding companies are larger. Members of management in many corporations became directors of the newly formed subsidiary companies, although certain individuals or families kept equity control.

Following a period of rapid change in the above tendencies between 1970 and 1973, public offerings have been reduced to minimal with hyper-inflation (at the rate of 20 percent per annum) prevailing during 1974-1976. However, the tendency of large private corporations for increasing the number of outside directors continues to prevail. More pronounced changes are yet to occur: enactment of some basic disclosure laws and the development of better accounting and auditing standards. But many private corporations are still dominated by one or two members of the family holding a majority of the equities.

Current Concerns

The main concerns of Turkish directors today appear to be:

(1) Specifying the proper role of the board and its relationship with management. The relationships be-

tween the owner(s) and the board, between the board and management, and between the directors from inside and outside the company require a clear understanding about the authority and responsibility of the parties involved, and the process of decision making at the board level.

(2) Introducing legal recognition of the attest function (i.e., the auditing profession), development of a financial press, formulating methods for better representation of minority shareholders on the boards, and creating public consciousness for ensuring that corporate assets are used to the best interests of all the share owners, including the minority share owners.

(3) Introducing rules enforcing public disclosure of financial information.

(4) Developing better auditing and accounting standards.

(5) Coping with an ever-growing public sector producing and pricing almost all of the basic raw and intermediary materials such as energy, primary minerals and iron and steel, transportation facilities, fertilizers and other basic chemicals which, in fact, constitute the inputs for lighter industries and other sectors of the economy.

(6) Coping with pressures for greater government control of the board in public and private corporations.

(7) Coping with increasing political influence and interference on the board and the management of the government-owned corporations and with the decreasing influence of market conditions on decisions at the board level.

(8) Coping with increased demands from one of the major political parties for employee representation on the board.

Composition and Organization of the Board[1]

As noted in "The Turkish Context," both government and private enterprises are involved in commerce and industry in Turkey. Government businesses produce about 15 percent of the GNP and employ about 40 percent of the nonagricultural workers of the country.

The boards of directors of both private and public enterprises bear certain similarities to one another. Their composition is influenced significantly by national law: the Turkish Commercial Code for businesses in the

[1] This section is based on a survey of 30 firms on the Istanbul Chamber of Industry's list of "Turkey's 100 largest firms of 1975." Twenty-three of these firms are privately owned (businesses in private sector, or BPS's); seven are owned by the government (state economic enterprises, or SEE's).

private sector (BPS's) and the State Economic Enterprises Code (Law Number 440) for state economic enterprises (SEE's). The two types of boards are similar in:

— The average age of board members (47 and 48, respectively; the median age for both BPS and SEE board members is 50), which is somewhat younger than the average ages of board members in other countries included in this study.

— The term of office (typically three years).

— The paucity of board committees (only three BPS's have them; no SEE has a committee).

But in other important respects the boards of directors of businesses in the private sector differ significantly from those of state economic enterprises.

Private Sector

In terms of board composition, the Turkish Commercial Code requires that a board of directors must have at least three members. Seven members is both the median and by far the most common board size for the firms participating in the survey (Table 7-1). There is no requirement that nonmanagement employees be represented on the board. The code does require that each board member should own or pledge stock equal to one percent of the paid-in capital or to 5,000 Turkish liras. This requirement can usually be met with 10 shares. If a person who is not a shareholder is elected to a board,

Table 7-1: Size of Boards

Number of Board Members	Number of Companies	
	BPS	SEE
3	1	-
4	2	1a
5	2	-
6	1	6
7	11	-
8	1	-
9	4	-
11	1	-
Total	23	7

Notes: Median and modal board size: 7 for BPS's, 6 for SEE's.
According to the Turkish Commercial Code, a board of directors should have a minimum of 3 members (Article 312).
SEE boards of directors consist of six members according to the State Economic Enterprises Code (Law Number 440).

a Company subject to different law from other six.

Table 7-2: Number of Full-time Employee Directors

Number of Full-time Employee Directors	Number of Companies BPS	Number of Companies SEE
None	4	-
1	9	-
2	6	1[a]
3	3	6
4	-	-
5	-	-
6	-	-
7	1	-
Total	23	7

Notes: Median and modal numbers: 1 for BPS's, 3 for SEE's.
According to the State Economic Enterprises Code, the President and Vice-Presidents of an SEE are members of the board of directors. There are three board members as insiders.
No BPS has a nonmanagement employee on the board. On the other hand, according to Law Number 440, the board of directors of each SEE must have one worker representative. This worker representative is elected from among the workers of the SEE by the management of the union. He is considered to be on leave during his term of service on the board, hence is not counted as a full-time employee director in the table. When he completes this term, he returns to his former job.

[a] Company subject to different law from other six.

another shareholder may pledge stock on his behalf to the company.

Within this legislative framework, the characteristics of BPS boards are:

— Ownership and management are not distinctly separated in Turkey. The great majority of board members are also major shareholders. Furthermore, the common management post of executive director (which corresponds to managing director in the United Kingdom) makes it easy for a major stockholder to manage the firm.

— All private-sector firms contributing to this study have boards on which a majority of members are *not* full-time executives of the company. In the seven SEE's in our sample, 50 percent of the board members are full-time executives of the company (Table 7-2). By far the largest class of nonemployee directors (76 percent of all such directors in the companies surveyed) consists of principal owners or shareholders of a company, or their agents (see Table 7-3).

— A BPS is free to set a director's term of office for up to three years (Table 7-5).

— It is unusual for BPS's to fix an age at which directors must retire. Only two of the 23 such firms

Table 7-3: Principal Occupation of Outside (Not Full-time Employee) Directors of 23 BPS's

Occupation	Number of Outside Directors
Principal owners or shareholders of company, or their agents	90
Owners or executives of manufacturing firms	6
Bank executives	8
Executives of public utilities or transportation firms	2
Owners or executives of merchandising or trading companies	3
Attorneys	1
Independent businessmen, financiers, consultants	3
Educators	3
Other	3
Total outside directors	119

Note: Of the 14 outside directors of SEE's, 13 are government officials and the other is an attorney.

contributing to this survey have done so. For outside directors this is no doubt because so many of them are also major shareholders. And private-sector businesses do not, as a rule, require full-time employees — including those who are board members — to retire at a specified age. There are just six retired company executives sitting on the boards of the 23 BPS's surveyed.

— The sharp discrepancy in the number of board meetings per year held by BPS's and SEE's — the median figures are 16.5 and 52, respectively (Table 7-4) —

Table 7-4: Number of Regular Board Meetings Per Year[1]

Number of Meetings	Number of Companies BPS	Number of Companies SEE
6	1	-
10	3	-
12	5	-
15	2	-
18	2	-
20	4	-
24	5	-
50	1	2
52	-	2
55	-	1
64	-	1
80	-	1
Total	23	7

Note: Median number of meetings: 16.5 for BPS's, 52 for SEE's.
[1] Does not count committee meetings.

reflects important managerial philosophy and practice differences in the two sectors. In the SEE, management is highly centralized and almost all problems, including technical and day-to-day decisions, are examined and decided on by the board. In the BPS, by contrast, management has more authority and can exercise more initiative than can the management of an SEE.

— The three BPS's with board committees have four such committees in all, as shown in the tabulation:

Name	Number of Board Members	Number of Outside Directors	Number of Meetings Annually
Consulting-Auditing Committee	3	--	35
Executive and Coordination Committee	8	--	35
Executive Committee	5	4	not specified
Advisory Committee	3	2	not specified

These committees are essentially advisory rather than decision-making bodies. The small number of board committees among BPS's is attributed to the fact that major shareholders in the BPS often are executive directors of these firms and, therefore, are fully knowledgeable about company affairs.

State Economic Enterprises

The State Economic Enterprises Code sets forth these stipulations about the composition of SEE boards:

— An SEE board must have six members: The president and two vice presidents of the enterprise, who are civil servants; two members appointed by the government; and a nonexecutive employee who is elected by the board of the union that represents employees of that enterprise. In practice, therefore, the

Table 7-5: Terms of Office for Directors

Term of Office	Number of Companies BPS[1]	SEE
1 year	7	-
2 years	3	-
3 years	13	7[a]
Total	23	7

[1] According to the Turkish Commercial Code, if there is no specific reference in the corporation statutes to the term of office, the board members may serve on the board for as long as three years.

[a] For government and employee representatives only. Management directors — presidents and vice presidents — serve on board for as long as they hold those positions.

government, or the appropriate minister, controls the board. This means that political considerations play an important role not only in board appointments but also in the decision-making process of the enterprise.

— The term of office for the two official government representatives and the employee representative is fixed at three years. The other three directors — the president and two vice presidents — have no specified term; they continue to serve as directors while they occupy these posts.

— There is no fixed retirement age for the three outside directors. The management directors, however, as civil servants must retire from their executive positions when they attain 30 years' service or 65 years of age, and cannot continue to serve on the board of these enterprises after retiring as managers.

The absence of committees in SEE's is attributed to legal requirements which concentrate all powers in the board with no room for delegating such powers to committees. In fact, the frequency of board meetings plus the composition of the boards of these enterprises make the effective working of board committees almost impossible.

Chapter 8
United States

The United States Context

Government Control of and Involvement in Business

In the United States there is a division of powers between the national (federal) government and regional or local governments: the 50 states and such jurisdictions as the District of Columbia and the Commonwealth of Puerto Rico.

Unlike the situation in the U.K., Western Europe, Turkey and Japan or Venezuela, the U.S. Federal Government does not incorporate businesses or other private organizations or spell out the duties and responsibilities of their officers or directors; that is left to the states. The Federal Government is involved with corporate directors chiefly through enforcement of (1) securities laws, and (2) antitrust or restraint of trade laws.

Although there are some substantial government enterprises in industries commonly described as natural monopolies — notably, electric power and rail and other forms of mass transportation — practically all the production of goods and services in the United States is accomplished through private enterprise. Neither the Federal nor the state governments participate in competitive industries as owners or investors.

On the whole, business functions with fewer governmental constraints in the United States than it does in the other countries surveyed. There is no comprehensive national planning to which business firms must comply, for example. Neither the Federal Government nor any state government has passed legislation that would require nonmanagement employee participation in company decision making or employee representation on the board of directors. And, probably because there are relatively few U.S. subsidiaries of foreign-owned corporations, there is no law, or pressure for a law, that would reserve a portion of the seats on the boards of such subsidiaries for U.S. citizens.

State Laws Affecting the Board of Directors

Virtually all business enterprises of any size are corporations, and, of the three major forms of business organizations, a corporation alone must have a board of directors.[1] A company is free to incorporate under the laws of any state.

There is only one type of business corporation: a limited liability share capital or stock ownership organization similar to a German Aktiengesellschaft (AG) or a French Société Anonyme (S.A.). The United States does not have the equivalent of the Gesellschaft mit beschränkter Haftung (GmbH) in Germany or the Société à Responsabilité Limitée (S.A.R.L.) in France.

Although each state has its own laws of incorporation, and although these laws vary in detail from one state to another, all states grant the control and authority over a corporation's affairs to a single board of directors. (There is no provision for a two-tier board.) Most state statutes require the directors to "manage the business and affairs of the corporation," but in practice boards do not — and, it is widely maintained, cannot — manage in the sense of direct supervision of the company's day-to-day decisions and operations. Manage-

---

[1] The other two are sole proprietorships and partnerships. The partnership form is favored by professionals like lawyers and accountants who work together.

ment in this sense is delegated to full-time executives who are engaged for this purpose.

State corporation laws grant authority to boards of directors in very general — and permissive, some critics assert — terms, with the result that the role played by the board is somewhat unique to the situation in each company, the product of interplay between the directors and management. But directors have two important duties under consistent interpretation of the various laws:

(1) The duty of due care. This requires directors to act with that degree of diligence, care and skill which an ordinarily prudent man would exercise under similar circumstances in like positions.

(2) The duty of loyalty. This arises from the concept that the director is a fiduciary to whom stockholders have entrusted the welfare of the corporation. It follows that a director is not permitted to take advantage of the corporation for his personal gain.

A board of directors is considered to have authority only as a group; directors as individuals have no legal power, except for that delegated to them by the board. On the other hand, directors can be held liable as individuals for their actions, or failure to act, as board members.

Directors are elected by owners (shareholders) but are not generally required by law to be shareholders themselves. However, it is common for companies to require that directors own stock. There are virtually no legal restrictions on the selection of directors.[2] Most major corporations have a majority of so-called outside directors — persons who are not employed by the company — on their boards but there are also inside directors who are members of management. The bulk of outside directors traditionally have been recruited from the ranks of business and financial management and the legal profession.

There are no laws such as one finds in other countries that limit the number of boards on which a person may serve simultaneously. Most corporations elect directors for one-year terms; three-year terms are fairly common in the insurance industry.

Federal Laws Affecting Corporate Directors

Although directors function primarily under state law

in dealing with corporate affairs, they are subject to federal laws in two important areas:

— Federal laws governing the issuance and trading of securities require that shareholders and the investing public receive full and fair disclosure of significant information on company conditions and developments. These laws apply to the content and to the timing of various reports and of statements made to the public. Directors have responsibility for seeing that the company complies with these requirements. Also, directors are forbidden from personally using the knowledge of privileged company information to take unfair advantage of buyers or sellers of the company's stock who lack the same information.

— There are federal laws to ensure competition and prevent restraint of trade ("antitrust" laws) that affect directors. For example, a director (or officer) of one company may not sit on the board of a competitor. The government's definition of "competing" companies and industries has broadened in recent years, which has forced the resignation of directors from several prominent companies.

Management-Labor Relations and Unionization

In the United States, the choice of corporate directors and functioning of the board are essentially insulated from management-labor relations, which are quite different from those in most of the other countries surveyed. Only about a fourth of the nongovernment and nonagricultural work force belongs to unions. Though several unions have memberships numbering in the millions, no single union is dominant in the sense of acting as a national coordinator or spokesman; there is no overarching organization of unions comparable to the German Federation of Labor (DGB) or the Swedish Confederation of Trade Unions (LO). (Similarly, one does not find in the United States a predominant national organization dedicated to the management side of management-labor relations.) Rather, each union sets and pursues its own goals. Indeed, there is considerable rivalry, and in some cases personal animosity, among leaders of prominent unions.

Management-labor agreements take the form of legal contracts, and these contracts are negotiated and administered without, as a rule, any intervention by the Federal or state governments. Nor does either party normally want such intervention unless a deadlock develops.

Major unions in the United States have traditionally focused on negotiating wages, benefits and working conditions with company managements; they have not

---

[2] In certain industries (intercoastal shipping is an example) there are federal or state laws that forbid or limit board membership by noncitizens.

sought a *direct* political role and have not formed a major political party such as the Labour Party in the United Kingdom. To be sure, unions do take positions on legislation and keep track of the voting records of politicians, and union leaders have influence among politicians because of the number of potential votes they represent.

A consequence of the limited, adversary role unions have conceived for themselves is lack of interest in negotiating with companies for, or pressing for legislation that would require, representation of nonmanagement employees on corporate boards of directors. Indeed, a number of labor leaders have asserted that to do so would be to compromise their effectiveness in carrying out their essential mission. The concept of employee participation in decisions affecting their jobs is practiced by some companies but entirely on their own managements' initiative. It has not been among the demands of unions to date. There are no "works councils" like those found in several other countries covered in this report.

Ownership of Corporations and Control of the Board

Most major U.S. corporations are owned by a large number of shareholders — individuals and institutions like mutual funds and pension funds — with no single individual, family or other owner holding more than a small percentage of the corporation's stock. Unlike the practice in a few of the other countries surveyed, though, commercial banks do not make equity investments in corporations for their own account.

As owners, the shareholders have the power to elect directors, which they do, largely by mail proxy vote, at the required annual shareholders' meeting. But almost invariably it is management that proposes a slate of directors, and only rarely is a candidate of management defeated. Shareholders also have the power to remove directors, but such action is extremely unusual.

Other acts that are generally reserved for the owners, and therefore require their approval before management can carry them out, include major changes in the corporation's size or organization, including mergers or acquisitions. But these changes much more often than not are approved as a matter of course by shareholders following management's recommendation.

Management's control of the proxy machinery, enabling it to determine what issues will be considered at the annual meeting, is frequently cited as the chief reason why stockholders are virtually powerless in exercising control over the affairs of the corporation —

or control of their elected representatives, the board of directors. Also contributing to these ends is the wide dispersion of stock ownership alluded to above. Furthermore, the great majority of shareholders, both individual and institutional, many observers of the business scene maintain, are essentially passive, being primarily concerned with the profitability of their investments in a company rather than the stewardship of directors or the actions of management. When stockholders become dissatisfied, they simply sell their shares rather than call directors or management to account.

The net of all this is that except in crises management traditionally has controlled the board of directors, rather than the other way around, as both the law and management theory have it. Some commentators indeed have insisted the board is really an anachronism that survives only to satisfy legal formalities.

Recent Changes

In the last few years there have been signs of greater independence and initiative by corporate boards. Reasons for this development are: (1) well-publicized instances of management incompetence or malfeasance which directors should have detected sooner than they did; (2) increased awareness, occasioned by suits brought against corporate directors, of directors with regard to the legal liability of their position; and (3) pressures on corporate managements and boards from outside groups seeking more responsible boards of directors.

Manifestations of this development include: (1) a steadily increasing number of boards in which outside directors outnumber inside directors; (2) the growing use of audit committees of the board, which committees are generally made up entirely of outside directors and are empowered to work independently of corporate management with the company's financial staff and its outside auditors to make sure that corporate reporting and accounting are entirely adequate and proper; and (3) greater diversity in board membership: specifically, the election of blacks and other minority-group representatives, women and professional directors — that is, individuals who spend full time serving as outside directors of a number of major corporations — to directorships of prominent corporations.

Current Concerns

The principal concerns of U.S. directors today are:

(1) Defining the proper role of the board and its relationship with management. Clearly the board cannot

manage the affairs of a large company, but just as clearly the board can and should be more vigorous than it traditionally has been. One frequently mentioned area for improvement: better controls to ensure ethical conduct by management.

(2) Clarifying whose interests directors should represent.

(3) Resolving, in a matter satisfactory to shareholders, management, directors and the interest of public policy, the vexing problems surrounding the director's legal liability.

(4) Seeing that outside directors have adequate, accurate and timely information about the corporations they serve.

(5) Coping with pressures for greater federal control of the board and the corporation — for example, the proposal of the influential consumer activist Ralph Nader for federal incorporation of major corporations, and the heightened efforts of the government to eliminate conflict-of-interest situations.

Neither required by law nor sought by labor unions, employee representation on the board is *not* a significant concern for U.S. directors.

Composition and Organization of the Board

A total of 248 U.S. companies (167 manufacturing, 81 nonmanufacturing) contributed information about the composition and organization of their boards as of 1976. All but five of these companies are large ($200 million or more in assets); more than half (55 percent) have assets or sales of at least $1 billion, with 70 being in the $3 billion-or-more size range. The following tabulation summarizes information about company industry and size:

Industry and Size of Companies	Number and Percent of Firms in Each Category	
	Number	Percent
Manufacturing (by assets):		
Under $200 million	4	2%
$200-499 million	41	25
$500-999 million	39	23
$1 to 2 billion	48	29
$3 billion and over	35	21
Total	167	100%
Nonmanufacturing (by sales):		
Under $200 million	1	1%
$200-499 million	14	17
$500-999 million	12	15
$1 to 2 billion	19	24
$3 billion and over	35	43
Total	81	100%

Board Size

The basic statistics regarding board sizes are:

Industry	Board Sizes (Number of Directors)	
	Range	Median
Manufacturing	7-33	13
Nonmanufacturing	8-27	15

Board sizes in the manufacturing companies tend to correlate closely with company size (larger companies have larger boards). This correlation is not quite as regular in the nonmanufacturing industries. The following tabulation shows board size (medians) related to company size in the two types of industries:

Company Size Categories (assets for manufacturing, sales for nonmanufacturing)	Median Board Size	
	Manufacturing	Nonmanufacturing
$200-349 million	11	12
$350-499 million	12	11
$500-749 million	12	15
$750-999 million	14	16
$1 to under 2 billion	14	15
$2 to under 3 billion	15	15
$3 billion and over	15	18
(Overall medians)	(13)	(15)

Banks and bank holding companies account for about half the nonmanufacturing companies included, and their median board sizes are considerably larger (21 and 22 directors, respectively) than the other industries. Median board sizes in the other nonmanufacturing industries (retail merchandising, transportation, utilities and miscellaneous services) are 15, 15, 13 and 12, respectively.

Board Composition and Election

Most of the companies surveyed have boards on which outside directors — defined in the broadest sense as persons not presently employed by the company, and therefore including former or retired employees — are in the majority. The figures are:

Industry	Companies Whose Boards Have Outside Director Majority	
	Number	Percent
Manufacturing	138	83%
Nonmanufacturing	70	86%
All companies	208	84%

If the above tabulation is done on the assumption that former or retired employees on the board should *not* be considered outsiders, a different picture emerges, particularly for manufacturing companies:

| Industry | Companies Whose Boards Have Outside Director Majority (former employees counted as insiders) | |
	Number	Percent
Manufacturing	99	60%
Nonmanufacturing . . .	64	80%
All companies	163	66%

This second tabulation reflects the fact that almost two-thirds (63 percent) of the U.S. company boards surveyed have former employees as members, and that in almost half of these cases there are two or more such directors.

Some other facts concerning board composition and election in the participating U.S. companies:

• Women are found on 28 percent of the manufacturing industry boards and on 41 percent of the nonmanufacturing industry boards, a far greater prevalence than that in any other country. Since only about nine percent of the companies having women directors say that their presence on the board reflects substantial stock ownership, most women directors in the sampling have been selected on the basis of their business or professional experience or reputation.

• Black directors are found on 17 percent of the manufacturing industry boards and 32 percent of the nonmanufacturing boards. The presence of black directors in such numbers, like that of women, also appears to be a practice limited to the United States among the countries surveyed.

• Most participants (82 percent of manufacturers, 89 percent of nonmanufacturers) require outside directors to retire from the board at a predetermined age. The two principal ages specified under such policies are:

| Outside Director Retirement Age | Percent of Companies with Retirement Policies Reporting Each Age | |
	Manufacturing	Nonmanufacturing
70	55%	49%
72	29%	38%

These figures indicate that nonmanufacturing companies tend to allow directors to serve to an older age

than do manufacturing companies. Yet the median ages of boards in the two kinds of industries are very close — 58 for manufacturing, 59 for nonmanufacturing.

• Directors serve one-year terms in close to 90 percent of these companies; there is an industry difference (93 percent of nonmanufacturing companies have one-year terms, while 84 percent of the manufacturing firms do).

• Ownership of company stock is not generally required of directors, especially in manufacturing companies, where only 14 percent of them require it; for nonmanufacturing companies, the figure is somewhat higher (25 percent).

Meeting Frequency

The basic figures for the annual frequency of regular board meetings in the U.S. companies are the same in both types of industry:

| Industry | Number of Regular Board Meetings Per Year | |
	Range	Median
Manufacturing	4-13	10
Nonmanufacturing	4-13	10

Meeting frequency is related to size, so that the largest companies meet most often: A median of 11 meetings for manufacturing companies with assets of $750 million or more, a median of 12 for nonmanufacturing companies with sales of $2 billion or more. The single most common board meeting frequency for all companies combined is 12, which is reported by a fourth of all companies. None of these figures includes committee meetings.

Committees

Almost every company has at least one board committee, and in fact almost all have each of the three most common committees, as shown in the tabulation below. The relative frequency of these committees is all but identical in the two types of industry:

| Name of Committee | Percent of Companies Reporting | |
	Manufacturing	Nonmanufacturing
Audit	93%	94%
Executive compensation/ salary and bonus	90%	89%
Executive	87%	88%

Other committees of significance or special interest reported in the United States are:

Name of Committee	Percent of Companies Reporting, All Industries
Stock option	40%
Finance	31%
Nominating	23%
Pension and retirement benefits	22%
Social or public responsibility	11%

There are only slight differences between the two kinds of industries in how large the three most common committees are and how often they meet. The following two tabulations make this clear:

Name of Committee	Median Number of Directors on Committee	
	Manufacturing	Nonmanufacturing
Audit	4	4
Executive compensation/salary and bonus	4	5
Executive	6	6

Name of Committee	Median Number of Committee Meetings per Year	
	Manufacturing	Nonmanufacturing
Audit	3	4
Executive compensation/salary and bonus	4	3
Executive	6	7

The Board Today and Tomorrow: Perspectives from the United States

This discussion is based on (1) The Conference Board's continuing program of directorship research, including several of its recent publications, and (2) interviews conducted with a number of prominent U.S. directors during the latter half of 1976 to examine and illuminate issues of current concern to directors not only in that country but also, in most cases, other countries represented in this study.

Before embarking on an examination of U.S. board practice, it seems appropriate to repeat several salient characteristics of most boards of large, publicly owned U.S. corporations:

— The majority of board members are outside directors — persons who are not members of the firm's

management. This provides at least a symbolic indication of the board's independence from management.

— Most outside directors have other occupations that command most of their time. In order of incidence these occupations predominate: executives of other corporations; practicing attorneys; and representatives of financial institutions — commercial banks, investment banking firms, insurance companies.

— The chairman of the board is almost always one of the two senior executives of the company — and more often than not he is the top one, or chief executive officer, in U.S. parlance.

— There is a well-articulated board committee system. Audit committees (dominated by outside directors), executive compensation/salary and bonus committees (made up, again, predominantly or exclusively of outside directors) and executive committees (which either act for the full board between its meetings or make recommendations to the full board) are well nigh universal. Less frequently encountered committees are stock option, pension and retirement benefits, finance and nominating. In addition, special committees are constituted on an ad hoc basis by a number of companies — a recent example has been the committees that have uncovered facts about illegal corporate payments to political figures.

The Board's Role

A 1975 Conference Board study of U.S. corporate boards included these essential findings about the role of the board.[3]

• Despite their legal mandate, boards of directors in no significant sense manage the business and affairs of a corporation — nor can they.[4]

• The areas of major concern to boards of directors are: corporate objectives, policies, strategies and plans; corporate capitalization, resource allocation, and the like; diversification, merger, acquisitions and divestitures; executive compensation; and management appraisal, development and succession.

[3] Jeremy Bacon and James K. Brown, *Corporate Directorship Practices: Role, Selection and Legal Status of the Board.* Conference Board Report No. 646. Hereafter called *Role, Selection and Legal Status.*

[4] The law on this point seems to be changing. "During 1974, both the general corporation law of Delaware and the influential Model Business Corporation act were amended...whereas both laws previously provided for a corporation's business affairs to be 'managed by a board of directors,' each now provides for management 'under the direction of a board of directors.'" Bryan F. Smith, *Directorship,* January, 1976, p.3.

• The accountability of directors — to whom, for what, and how accountability is enforced — is a thorny, complicated — and in important respects highly ambiguous — issue. In different senses, and to varying degrees, corporate boards are accountable not merely to present shareholders, but also to future shareholders; to Federal and state governments; to other "stakeholders" — customers, suppliers, employees, the public at large; and, although the law and management theory have it the other way around, to management.

• As distinct from the areas of major concern to the board, its special contributions to the well-being of the corporation are two: giving management advice and keeping management on its toes.

• In making these contributions or in dealing with areas of major concern, a board has essentially three roles to play: It can initiate or determine. It can evaluate and influence. Or, it can simply monitor.

• What posture a board adopts, and how effective it will be whatever its posture, depends upon the competence and diligence of the directors; the adequacy of information available to them or obtainable by them; the committee structure of the board; and, above all, the receptivity and interest of the chief executive in the work of the board.

• A powerful weapon of the board, one that can be used informally as well as formally, is that of bestowing or witholding approval of proposals made by management.

• Within any board there is marked variation in the effectiveness of individual directors — which, of course, is true of any group that works together.

Against this backdrop can be placed the salient comments of the contributors to the present study about the role of the board.

• In a number of companies, an effort is emerging to define anew the role of the board and its relationship with its management. This has led to such statements as those shown in the inserts on pages 89 and 91. Some companies have prepared fully detailed "job descriptions" for their directors, which parallel those covering management positions. Others have assembled manuals for their outside directors, which documents include prominently what is expected of them.

• The proper roles of directors and management in any particular firm and the proper relationships between them are, in several senses, unique. For one thing, these roles and relationships are influenced by the size and the situation of the company — by its prospects and problems. Does management need advice (a much more

likely need in a smaller than a larger firm)? Is there a crisis situation — for example, a threat of an unwanted takeover bid? Are major investments contemplated?

Another factor contributing to uniqueness in these roles and relationships is the singular dynamics of the individuals making up the board. A recurrent comment made by study participants: "Each board I'm on is different in its interests, in the interaction among the people on it, in its role, and in its relations with management."

• Whatever the group dynamics of the individual board, it is essential that management and the board reach a consensus on all key issues, although it is perfectly proper — and indeed sometimes necessary — for a director to record a minority vote. Fundamental disagreements cannot but impair the effectiveness of the board and of management.

• There is perhaps less hesitancy about dismissing the chief executive and other members of senior management than there used to be. There have been a number of such dismissals prominently reported in the last few years, not merely for management activities in connection with questionable payments either in this country or abroad, but also for the classic reason of unsatisfactory performance.

• Similarly there seems to be much more collaboration between management and the board in the appraisal of management and in management succession. Incidentally, practically every contributor emphasized that management succession is very much a shared responsibility of the board and senior executives, but these executives must take the initiative by bringing to the board's attention those individuals it considers worthy of promotion to the top jobs in the company.

• One can discern that the boards on which study participants sit are being more fully consulted on objectives, strategies and policies than they used to be. In this realm, too, management must initiate; the board's role is to evaluate and influence, and, later, to monitor.

• Whether influenced by concern over possible liability, the criticism of boards voiced by academic and other commentators, the rash of illegal payments that have come to light in the last few years, or whatever, directors are asking more searching and pointed questions of management — as indeed virtually every participant agrees they should.

• Yet boards tend to make comparatively few major decisions — one chief executive thinks a good batting average is "once a year." He looks to his board to offer what he terms "institutionalized oversight" of the company.

The Director's Role and Responsibility: Comments by U.S. Directors

"The role of the director is changing. But the impetus for change is not illegal payments, slush funds, and such. Rather the impetus is coming from the courts and from the greater liability being placed on the outside director.

"In the past, pressures were presumed to be greater on the inside director. Today the outside director must be more sensitive to what is happening in the company. He needs to be more involved in the management of the company. As a result, board meetings are longer, and directors ask more pointed questions than they used to.

"The responsibilities of the director haven't changed; there is just a greater need for management to recognize these responsibilities."

— College president who serves
as outside director of
several corporations

*   *   *

"The single job I consider most important as a director? Using my head."

— Executive director of a foundation
who serves as outside director of
seven corporations

*   *   *

"A board makes no more than one significant decision a year; its ongoing role is oversight. So far

as decision making is concerned, the only way a company can live up to the legal charge that the board of directors will manage the affairs of the corporation is to hire professional management and delegate to it most of the managerial chores. But to fulfill its responsibility, the board must continually oversee management: Measuring performance against objectives and standards; making sure that management is forthcoming with objectives, policies and strategies; assuming responsibility for management succession.

"Major decisions [my] board has made in recent years are: The decision to go from a one-product company to a diversified company, and the subsidiary decision to pursue diversification by means of acquisitions; the decision to appoint a separate person as president following some years in which [I] served both as chairman and as president; the approval of major acquisitions and other major commitments and risks (actions that could affect the company for good or ill ten years hence); the decision to go into business overseas."

— Chairman of a multibillion-dollar,
multinational industrial corporation and
outside director of three other companies

• The board is having a greater say in the choice of directors — particularly outsiders — than it used to. Formerly, director selection was almost exclusively a prerogative of management (again, despite the law and management theory); but in a considerable number of companies board members and top executives are jointly discussing the kinds of persons it would be desirable to recruit to fill vacancies or new seats. Some firms have appointed board committees to make recommendations about board membership and functions.

• With regard to accountability, the director's primary allegiance is to stockholders — and this means all stockholders, and not any particular group of them — but he or she must see to it that all the company's stakeholders have their interests properly taken into account.

• One responsibility, perhaps not new, that has gained prominence in the last couple of years is that of monitoring the ethics of the company and its executives. The mechanism for this is often the audit committee.

Another procedure, followed by many companies, is to have an annual review by the full board of statements submitted by senior executives reporting that they do not have conflicts of interests and listing their outside activities and interests.

Relations with Shareholders

One can discern in recent years greater shareholder activity in challenging management and corporate boards. Either through shareholder resolutions or the threat of them, company policies and practices on such matters as doing business in South Africa, product distribution and quality, and equal employment opportunities have been altered. Shareholders have successfully mounted lawsuits to change the membership of certain boards that have run afoul of the law or have been guilty of unethical conduct. In a few cases, the suing shareholders have actually named new directors. Compared with the situation of 10 or 20 years ago, more

The Jewel Board of Directors

The Jewel board of directors is legally and morally responsible to watch over and represent the long-term interests of Jewel shareholders. It is responsible for the selection and performance of Jewel's management — as distinguished from the responsibility for managing Jewel. To fill such a role, the work of the Jewel board has been structured to acquaint independent outsiders with the inside plans, programs, successes and failures of the company.

The fact that 8 of the 14 Jewel directors have never been members of Jewel's management is no accident. We strongly believe that a majority of our directors should be outside directors so that an independent overview of Jewel management is always present. As we admire a system of checks and balances in our political system, we look for it, too, in our corporate system.

The Jewel board works to fulfill its responsibilities by concentrating its attention on certain key aspects of the company.

- Monitoring management's performance against plans and forecasts;
- Reviewing the objectives and strategies of the business;
- Reviewing and approving the company's three-year investment and growth plans and related financial goals;
- Determining how the proceeds of the business will be shared between our two forms of profit sharing — dividends for shareholders and retirement programs for Jewel people;
- Monitoring the ethics of the company;
- Monitoring the strength, diversity and attitudes of Jewel human resources;
- Maintaining a close contact with Jewel's external and internal auditors to assure the maintenance of adequate financial controls and the authenticity of Jewel's financial statements; and
- Determining the compensation of Jewel's senior levels of management.

Source: 1975 Annual Report, Jewel Companies.

shareholders are disposed to bring class action or derivative suits against directors and officers for acts of commission and omission. But shareholders in most companies still exert little or no influence on corporate affairs, management or the board of directors.

The last statement is corroborated by the experience of the great majority of U.S. contributors to this study. In their capacities as outside directors, they find that shareholders, both individual and institutional, are by and large a passive lot.

They have little contact with individual shareholders of the companies they serve as directors. One of them notes that this is probably as it should be because "all that investors want from an outside director is inside information." Another director makes the point that the amount of criticism a director gets from shareholders depends on the particular board(s) of which the director is a member. In her case, she observes, none of her three companies does business in South Africa; if any of them did, doubtless she would get some criticism about company involvement there. Others use a different illustration to underscore the same point: companies of which they are directors have had fine profit records, have done well by their shareholders.

In explaining why he has had little challenge from shareholders, the chief executive of a large, diversified firm serving industrial markets in this country and abroad states that many of his company's individual shareholders have held their stock for a long time. Some, for example, have gotten it through an employee stock purchase plan; others, through acquisitions the company has made; still others, through inheritance. This association with the firm, coupled with its growth in sales and earnings, makes for a by-and-large contented shareholder body. To be sure, he gets occasional letters from shareholders complaining that the dividend is too low, or that he and his fellow officers are being paid too much, but these are insignificant in volume. Another director deplores that there is not more interaction between shareholders and outside directors than in fact there is.

Institutional Shareholders

It is a widely remarked phenomenon that the incidence of institutional (pension funds, mutual funds, and so on, holdings of common stock is rising while the incidence of holdings by individuals is falling. What about the institutions? Do they voice approbation or disapproval of management?

In the experience of most of the U.S. directors surveyed, the answer is "no." Most institutions simply buy or sell stock, and do not get involved with management. Yet the institutions do have an indirect influence on management, one director suggests, because if several of them should sell large numbers of shares abruptly, this could lead to a reshuffling of management. He adds that management must have a good idea of what, in his term, "interested institutions" are thinking. To that end, he notes that some proposals or programs never see the light of day simply because management discerns that these institutions have looked askance at these proposals or programs.

Another director opines that the trend toward greater institutional ownership of common stock conceivably could yield a more disciplined shareholder review of company operations because the representatives of institutions tend to be more knowledgeable than individual shareholders. She also believes that should this trend continue there will be more emphasis by management on "looking good for the short term," and both management and the company itself will be more vulnerable because of greater volatility in stock performance associated with increased institutional ownership. Finally, continuation of the trend might create an appearance of greater "elitism" in corporate ownership and thus invite more government interference in business.

An outside director, who used to be chief operating officer of a large manufacturer and whose principal occupation is now as dean of a prominent graduate school of business, would welcome more "input" by institutional holders, thinking that they could contribute valuable insights and opinion to management. He believes that institutional shareholders will be more influential with respect to the conduct of company affairs in the future.

Some Special Groups — and Some Exceptions

Most of the directors interviewed mention one or another special groups of shareholders. Most of these groups have raised protesting voices, in one way or another, about the companies in which they hold stock. A few of them, it appears, each have acquired small holdings in major corporations chiefly to gain a forum in which to vent their complaints about business and to press for the particular remedies they espouse. Some groups do not become shareholders but attempt to exert influence in other ways (see box).

"Professional" Stockholders. These well-known corporate gadflys concerned with corporate governance, and, more specifically, the role and organization of the board — notably, the Gilbert brothers, Wilma Soss,

Evelyn Davis — continue their long-standing practices of framing resolutions and speaking out at annual meetings. The Gilberts are considered responsible, indeed constructive, by some; the last two, irresponsible — in fact disruptive.

Women's Groups. As a whole organized women's groups have not been active as shareholders, in the experience of both men and women directors contributing to this report. A couple of the latter have spoken of "little old ladies" who come up to them after annual meetings and tell them how glad they are that representatives of their sex are serving on the boards of prominent companies.

Social Action Groups. Churches, followers of Caesar Chavez — the saint or devil, depending on one's viewpoint, who was the first successfully to organize farm workers in California — and educational institutions that hold common shares each have challenged directors and management by asking hostile questions at annual meetings and by proposing resolutions that, if adopted, would change company practices. (On one occasion, some Chavez adherents, concerned that a retail food chain was selling grapes that had been picked by nonunion workers, acquired a few shares of company stock and put forward an entirely new slate of directors at the annual meeting.) Thus far, these groups have not been accomplishing their diverse aims, although there are signs that they may be becoming more effective.

At the least, however, stockholders who speak up in person — or by resolution — force directors to think

Black Groups

Two of the black directors surveyed indicate that black groups have approached them in their capacity as directors, asking them for better employment opportunities or support for black suppliers or, more generally, for their companies "to do more" for blacks. But these requests cannot be characterized as pressure, according to these directors. One makes the point that she cannot do more for blacks in her role as director and tells anyone making such a request just that. (She adds that as a black she believes she looks at company affirmative action programs more closely than other directors, but this is the product of her own concern and conscience, and in any case all the companies on whose boards she sits are working rather hard at affirmative action.)

anew of their accountability. To whom are they accountable? When a shareholder, or a group of shareholders, insists upon a point, a director must consider the likely views and interests of other shareholders. Nor is this all. For many of this fellowship maintain a director should strive to balance fairly the interests of all the company's *stakeholders;* not just shareholders, but also employees, suppliers, customers and society at large. Stockholder activism can usefully remind him or her of this obligation.[5]

Composition of the Board

U.S. participants in this study have strong, and in some respects varied, views about the proper composition of the board of directors of publicly owned corporations. First, some points of general agreement.

• Every board should spend time thinking about how it *ought to be* comprised — what interests, skills and viewpoints should be represented in its membership.

• The election of new directors should be a consultative process between the board and top management aimed at eventually achieving the desired composition.

• The board should have a majority of outside directors — persons who are not members of management. Indeed, a number of these participants maintain they would not serve on a board in which outsiders were not a majority. Only in this way can a board properly carry out its responsibilities and maintain its necessary independence of management. Some contributors feel that insiders should number no more than two — the chief executive officer and the chief operating officer, or, if that distinction is not made by a company, the top man and his heir apparent. Others think that there should be other insiders as well, so that the outside directors can be intimately exposed to them in the areas of business they oversee. One chief executive warns, though, that it is not a good idea to have as inside directors heads of the major profit centers or divisions of the company; their presence on the board will, he believes, promote constituency representation, which he deplores.

Another chief executive who believes that outsiders should form a majority notes a possible adverse consequence if the increasing incidence of outside directors

[5] In his capacity as a professional director, one study contributor has, from time to time, met with dissident shareholder groups intending to put in proxy statements, or bring up at the annual meeting, resolutions not favored by management in an effort to reconcile the differences between these groups and management.

Role of the Board

The board of directors of [the company] is, on behalf of the stockholders, the guardian of the interests of those who have a stake in the health of the enterprise. In addition to stockholders, these include customers, employees, suppliers, the communities in which it operates, and society as a whole.

The board's function is to ensure that:

(a) The enterprise has acceptable purpose, direction and plan;

(b) Management is managing effectively in accordance with such purpose, direction and plan and in accordance with legal and regulatory requirements; and

(c) The future health of the enterprise is not jeopardized by the risks to which its financial resources, human resources, and public image are exposed.

Its method is to appoint the management, reach agreement with management on major policies and objectives, approve major transactions recommended by management, inspect and evaluate management's work, determine the nature and extent of management's rewards, and change the management from time to time as necessary.

It will normally spend most of its time in inspection and evaluation but must be able to shift readily into the other functions when it desires. It must organize itself accordingly. It must also maintain control of its own organization and processes, since it can expect to be held accountable for prudence and diligence in the performance of its functions.

— *An insurance company*

---

should continue. It will remove the incentive of younger executives to achieve board seats in their own companies, or at least dampen it; and this incentive presumably will have to be replaced by another.

• For multinational corporations it is fitting to appoint as outside directors citizens of foreign countries in which the corporation has extensive interests. The chief executive whose board includes both a Canadian and an Italian explains it this way: When the strategic decision was made that the company would do business overseas, both through local facilities and through exports from the United States, the policy was established that to manage its affairs abroad the company would hire residents of the countries where it did business and teach them company procedures and techniques, rather than send abroad United States managers who had mastered these procedures and techniques. It was simply a logical extension of this policy that foreigners have been added to this board.[6]

• The professional director — a person whose principal occupation is to serve as outside director of a number of large corporations and who spends more time on the affairs of each corporation he serves than do other outside directors, for which he receives additional compensation — is widely regarded as a useful innovation.

• The appearance of "new faces" on corporate boards — women, blacks, academics and others whose background differs markedly in one or another respect from that of white male directors drawn from the ranks of business, finance or the law — is regarded as a healthy development. One chief executive officer puts the matter this way: business needs a broadened base of directors; for the broader the base of those crucially involved in business affairs, the more likely it is that the United States enterprise system will survive.

But the new faces do not mean, study contributors insist, that there should be constituency representation on the board; that is, it would be entirely inappropriate for these new faces to regard themselves or to act as spokesmen for or as representatives of women's interests, black interests, and so on. For if they did, they would impair the board's devotion to the well-being of the entire shareholder body. By raising issues of interest to these constituencies but not perhaps of vital concern to the corporation, they would inhibit the board from the effective performance of its duties.

• Whatever the merit of professional and "new faces" directors, most of the U.S. directors interviewed are equally firm in asserting that no board should be without chief executive officers of other firms. More than one chief executive has found these individuals to

---

[6]*Role, Selection and Legal Status* had this to say about foreign directors. "[The foreign director] can bring to the board insights and views deriving from his nationality. . . .In addition, a foreign director can, in many cases, open doors and otherwise get things done for a company in his home country. For these directors typically are men of preeminent stature in their native lands and such people are likely to have more clout with national governments and their administrative and regulatory bodies than the U.S. business executive has with corresponding groups in this country." But the report noted that as an alternative some U.S. firms have constituted councils of foreign advisors to give management and the board informed opinions about developments in foreign countries. See page 35 of that study.

Toward More Effective Boards

Following are three resolutions defining the responsibilities of board committees concerned with the functions and membership of the full board.

Board Nominating and Review Committee

_____ are designated the Board Nominating and Review Committee, _____ to act as Chairman of such Committee, and which shall review, advise and make recommendations to the board with respect to: (1) the general responsibilities, functions, liabilities, talents and compensation of the board and its members; (2) the organization, structure, size and composition of the board; (3) nominations for board membership; (4) operations and procedures for board meetings; and (5) approval of long-range corporate objectives and strategies, and any proposed changes.

(A chemical company)

* * *

RESOLVED that pursuant to Section 141(c) of the General Corporation Law of the State of Delaware and Section 6 of Article IV of the By-laws, [4 outside directors named] be, and they hereby are, designated as a *Committee on Directors* of the Board of Directors, with the following responsibilities:

To make recommendations to the board with respect to the size, composition, and functions of the board of directors, the qualifications of directors, candidates for election as directors, and the compensation of directors;

and that _____ be, and he hereby is, appointed Chairman of the Committee on Directors;

(A merchandising company)

* * *

Board Policy Committee: Under the powers delegated to it by the Board of Directors (1) to assess and recommend timely changes in the role, composition and structure of the board; (2) to formulate criteria and initiate rules to be adopted by the board governing and regulating its affairs; and (3) to work with the Chief Executive Officer in developing plans for the orderly succession of principal corporate executives.

(A petroleum company)

be far and away the most effective outside directors on his own company's board.

• The practice, legally required in several European countries, of appointing nonmanagement employees or labor union officials to the board, would not be a healthy innovation in the United States.

• The presence of suppliers of services to the company on its board — specifically, its commercial bankers, its investment banker(s), and its outside legal counsel — is coming to be recognized as unsuitable — for symbolic reasons if nothing else.[7]

The reasons given for their unsuitability as outside directors are the same as those mentioned by contributors to *Role, Selection and Legal Status:* (1) As representatives of institutions that do business with the company, they are inevitably in a conflict-of-interest situation, because they will acquire inside information (e.g., when the company will need financing) that could benefit their institutions, and because, sooner or later, they will have to choose between the best interest of the company and the best interest of their institutions; and (2) it is difficult to withdraw business from a supplier represented on the board. (For an elaboration of these reasons and opposing views, see *Role, Selection and Legal Status,* pages 44-47.) A few companies, wishing to add the contributions of independent attorneys, commercial bankers, or investment bankers to the deliberations of their boards, but concerned about the problems just described, have appointed to their boards such persons who are not associated with the law firms, commercial banks, or investment banking firms with which these companies regularly do business.

The United States study contributors offer more complete perspectives about three types of directors (one of them still hypothetical in that country): professional directors, women and nonmanagement employees or union officials.

Professional Directors

Some contributors to *Role, Selection and Legal Status* foresaw that the professional or extra-time director — a seasoned business executive, financier or attorney whose chief occupation is to serve as outside director of six or eight, ten or even more corporations — would become an increasingly common presence in the United States boardroom. Although the professional

director is by no means ubiquitous, it is certain that there are more professional directors on the boards of United States corporations than there were two or three years ago.

The United States contributors to the present study recognize about the same merits in the position that the contributors to the other earlier study did. A professional director is able to spend ample time and devote ample interest and attention to directorial responsibilities, undistracted by the commitments of a nearly full-time job as a corporation executive or in some other calling. Thus he can achieve that degree of knowledge of the firm earnestly urged on outside directors by both supporters and critics of boards of directors. One person who functions in this capacity observes that the six boards on which he serves take up to 50 hours a week.

One director, whose chief occupation is academic economist, urges a greater use of professional directors:

"Expand the use of professional directors. The ideal board member is an intelligent generalist with strong financial, economic or accounting background, with ample time to devote to the 'business of business.' These qualifications are not developed casually; they must be honed by the kind of professionalism and experience which comes from full-time devotion to the effort. Thus, directors who are too busy running their own businesses, directors who really cannot participate intelligently in financial discussions — which dominate virtually every agenda — directors whose specialty is too narrow for modern boardroom problems can do little except take up space at the table. I firmly believe they should be replaced with individuals who offer professional qualifications."

In more specific terms, a professional director is said to be able to make committees more effective, since he can assume the burden of preparing for their meetings and do much of the follow-up work. In addition, in the words of one professional director: "He can be the implementer who organizes the work of the board."

Another professional director cites some tasks he has performed that ordinarily fall outside the purview of an outside director. When one of his companies was involved in controversy about questionable payments overseas, he accompanied the company's counsel to testify before the SEC; he has also testified before Congress; and he has met with dissident shareholders who have wanted to include, both in the company's proxy statement and in the business taken up at the annual meeting, resolutions management would prefer

---

[7]A number of law firms and investment banking firms have established policies, or are considering policies, that would enjoin their partners and other professionals from serving on the boards of clients.

not to have included. He notes that the groups before which he has appeared have been pleasantly surprised by his being on hand.

Other perspectives on the professional director offered by study participants:

— No board should be composed entirely of professional directors, or indeed of a majority of them.

— The professional director must be particularly careful not to infringe upon the prerogatives or functions of management.

— For the chief executive officer of a company, a professional director can be very helpful because the chief executive can call upon him for advice, for a special assignment, and so on, in good conscience — recognizing that this individual is receiving greater compensation than other outside directors — and thus can avoid overburdening other outside directors whose principal occupations have the major call on their time.

As suggested earlier, professional directors are compensated much more generously than regular outside directors in recognition of the greater amounts of time they devote to board business. The general feeling is that from his service on all the boards of which he is a member, a professional director's total line of compensation should approximate that of a chief executive officer. One figure that is referred to more than occasionally in conversations with members of this breed is $100,000 a year.

Joseph W. Barr, a former Secretary of the Treasury and for several years a professional director, in 1976 conducted a survey of 200 senior executives in industry, finance and government about professional directors. The results of his survey were published in the May-June, 1976, *Harvard Business Review*. The chief matters of concern expressed by the 160 respondents were:

(1) Widespread dislike for the term "professional director."

(2) Almost as much support for the view that the contributions of chief executive officers of other publicly held corporations, busy as they are, made invaluable contributions to the boards which they served as outside directors.

(3) A deep concern that a professional director might tend to blur the line between management's responsibility to manage and the responsibility of directors to oversee and evaluate management. "They were worried that a professional director could not keep his hands off day-to-day operations."

(4) Disquiet that a professional director would want his own staff, which staff would have the potential for creating confusion and discord.

(5) The extra compensation paid to a professional director for his added time and responsibility might imperil his independence.

Women

When a woman is appointed to a board, it is generally agreed that it ought to be because of competence and diligence and not because of her sex. She should not be a token — a symbol of corporate guilt that in the United States business has been a for-men-only career.[8] She should be, to recast a distinction familiar in the United States, a director who happens to be a woman rather than a woman director. But several study respondents — both men and women — express the belief that women have a unique contribution to make to the board: They are more sensitive to consumer issues — product quality, reliability and safety, for instance — and to other social issues that impinge upon the corporation.

In terms of qualification, it appears that, virtually without exception, the women appointed to boards of major United States corporations have been persons of notable achievements — in law, in foundations, in academic life, in government service.[9] Of course, only a handful of women corporate chief executives have been elected outside directors, because very few women have become chief executives.

One chief executive disapproves of what he terms the "let's-have-a-woman-on-the-board" syndrome. He believes that if a company has but a single woman on the board, her fellow directors will crown her with the responsibility of "representing women" — and that she herself will assume this responsibility. This not only promotes the bad practice of constituency representation, but is degrading to the woman director. She may also feel ill at ease if she is the sole female in a group of 10 or 15.

[8]There are not a few token men directors, one woman director tartly observes: ". . .the actor or sports celebrity; the high visibility black; the occupant of the tit-for-tat seat on most boards — the 'you put me on your board and I'll put you on my board' arrangement that has kept so many boardrooms as sacrosanct as the men's locker room at the club."

[9]Not considered in this discussion are women directors who have large stock holdings in small- or medium-sized corporations that have relatively few shareholders — holdings they came by as a result of founding or co-founding the business or being the wife or descendant of one of the founders. Such corporations and their directors lie outside the scope of the present examination of United States directorship practices.

Thinking it desirable to have women represented in its membership because of their greater sensitivity to social issues, his board simultaneously elected two women directors, and he declares that the syndrome he finds distasteful has not appeared on his company's board. (One of these women directors serves on two other boards, on one of which she is the only woman. Her experience on this board makes her question the validity of the syndrome mentioned above, but she cautions against generalizing from her impressions.)

One concludes, then, that in their self-perceptions and the perceptions of their male fellow board members, women directors seem to occupy a somewhat ambiguous position. One of them recalls the advice she got from a soon-to-retire male director at her first meeting of the first board to which she was appointed: "We didn't appoint you because you are a woman, but don't ever forget that you are one."

Employee or Union Representation

As noted in the "United States Context," non-management employee or union representation on the board of directors is an issue of only academic interest in that country. (Indeed the same can be said of the larger issue of participative management — the involvement of workers in decisions affecting business plans and operations. Only a few U.S. firms have experimented with the practice, and in each such firm the practice has been introduced at management's initiative.) Labor union leaders have not manifested interest in electing union officials or employees their unions represent to corporate boards. Indeed, there have been no legislative proposals or even hearings by Congress on the question, unlike the situation with respect to federal chartering of corporations. Finally, the U.S. directors participating in this study all agree that employee representation on corporate boards is not likely to come to the United States soon — "certainly not during the tenure of the present labor leaders," one of them remarks. Although a few believe that this practice will eventually get a toehold in the United States, this is not a matter of either concern or serious discussion in the management circles of which they are a part.

Most U.S. directors surveyed are against the appointment of nonmanagement employees or union officers to corporate boards, because they fear the practice would produce some very undesirable results:

• It would lead to constituency representation in the form of internal self-interest groups competing with each other at the board level.

• An employee or union representative would have divided loyalties — to the interests of the corporation on the one hand, to the interests of his fellow workers or the union on the other. This would be difficult for him and a potential problem for the entire board.

• The traditional arm's-length adversary relationship of management and labor would be compromised or blurred, and thus a cornerstone of the free-enterprise system would be threatened.

• Vital or sensitive issues would not be discussed in the boardroom, but in private conversations involving only directors with a management viewpoint.

• The board would eventually become directly involved in labor negotiations, which should not be its function.

These negative predictions are based on conjecture, to some extent, but on the other hand many of these U.S. executives are familiar with the experience of European companies who have worker board members and are therefore reflecting their observations of what they deem to be an unsatisfactory arrangement. Some U.S. observers take a more positive view and say that having workers on a supervisory board does not really hamper management, that employee exposure to the problems of management and ownership probably makes unions more realistic about wage demands, and that employee representation on boards results in better communications and cooperation between management and the work force.

Some Key Issues in Organizing the Board's Work

With heightened concern about the board's fulfilling its responsibilities adequately has come stronger interest in how the board can function effectively and efficiently. Conversations with United States directors about this question tend to focus on three principal topics: the adequacy of information provided directors, especially outside directors; the audit committee; and the separation, of the jobs of board chairman and chief executive officer.

Adequacy of Information

The comments of United States directors about the adequacy of information separate into information about their responsibilities as directors and information about the companies they serve in this capacity.

At least one of these directors finds what she terms "director education" wanting, and urges corporations to do more in this area:

Guidelines Used by Northern Illinois Gas Company for Evaluating an Outside Director Candidate

1. Has outstanding business, administrative, or other valuable experience, proven ability, and significant accomplishment.

2. Holds position of high responsibility (preferably chief executive officer, currently or prospectively) with a major organization. If it is a business corporation, volume of business should not be too small in relation to NI-Gas 'and preferably should be greater (unless other compelling reasons override).

3. Has no present or visible potential for conflict of interest. Is not connected with any organization presently serving or that might serve the company, such as institutions engaged in commercial banking, investment banking, law, or management consulting. Is not an officer or director of any (a) major supplier to competitors of the company, (b) other sizeable Illinois utilities, or (c) rivals of companies represented on our board. Is not the CEO or a top administrator of an organization that has the NI-Gas CEO on its board.

4. Contributes to the collective experience of the board, so that a diversity of age, business, geographical location, area of endeavor, and view-

point is represented, all of which are significant to the company's opportunities and responsibilities.

5. Has shown a willingness and is connected with an organization that has shown a willingness to serve the community in civic, social, and charitable activities.

6. Possesses self-confidence and is at ease with persons of distinguished attainment.

7. Is articulate, but not garrulous, and commands respect from peers.

8. Possesses maturity, but also displays youthful initiative, enthusiasm, and a progressive attitude.

9. Is independent of recent past or present directors.

10. Is an existing or potential stockholder.

11. Is enthusiastic about the prospect of serving, and can devote the necessary time.

12. Is neither chosen nor excluded solely because of race, color, or sex.

Source: Marvin Chandler, "It's Time to Clean Up the Boardroom," *Harvard Business Review,* September-October, 1975, p. 78. Copyright © 1975 by the President and Fellows of Harvard College; all rights reserved.

"All directors, old and new, must be educated or reeducated to live up to legal and moral responsibilities to a degree not contemplated in the past. Unfortunately, many corporations will not take the task of director education seriously. They may feel it would be presumptuous to try to 'teach' successful adults something about positions they currently occupy and may have occupied for many years. Or, some corporations may assume their directors have picked up the nuances of new responsibilities 'in the street.' However, most of these same corporations would be appalled at how little directors do know about the specifics of new laws, court actions, and the like. And I am convinced that most directors would welcome a carefully prepared information packet that would bring them up to date and keep them current through periodic supplements. I am also convinced that most directors would welcome an agenda item that encourages discussion of the key elements. Such a discussion would serve a secondary but very important purpose of letting the directors know that management is aware of the responsibilities the directors bear and that management expects to be

responsive to the directors' need to know. Open communication on these subjects would clear the air and mark a new beginning for many boards that have long been moribund."

But most of the other directors interviewed believe they have been well enough informed about their responsibilities. For some, of course, their confidence arises from their backgrounds: as attorneys, as long-term directors, as senior executives of business concerns. Beyond that, a number of companies have developed indoctrination programs for new directors that cover their general responsibilities as well as board and committee routines and schedules, vital facts and figures about the company and issues confronting it. A few have prepared position guides or handbooks for their directors.

But there are other sources to which a director can turn. The company's or his personal legal counsel can be helpful. There are writings aplenty about the role and responsibilities of directors, of which The Conference Board has contributed not a few. Various universities,

management training organizations, professional associations, and other groups periodically offer seminars on
the role and functions of directors.

Information about Companies. Most of the surveyed
directors declare themselves well satisfied about the
information they get on the affairs of the firms of which
they are directors. The managements of these firms
evidently have succeeded in preparing and disseminating
adequate documentation to be studied before meetings,
and the meetings themselves do touch on all areas of
vital concern. Furthermore, as noted above, a number of
these companies indoctrinate each new director or about
the company, its industry, its markets, and so on. And
most firms have scheduled at least one visit a year for its
directors to production or distribution facilities away
from company headquarters. Directors find these visits
very useful in enlarging their understanding of and
familiarity with the company's business and people.
Perhaps most important of all, the managements of these
firms are solicitous about making sure the questions
raised by directors are adequately answered.

Other points made about information concerning the
company:

• The greater institutionalization of boardroom procedure has improved the flow of information to outside
directors, according to one chief executive, who himself
sits as outside director of three firms. For example,
twice a year there are scheduled reviews of his company's progress with respect to equal employment
opportunity, employee safety, and environmental protection programs.

• Audit committees are an invaluable source of
information to those directors who serve on them and
are a source of great assurance for those who do not that
the full board will eventually get all it needs to know
about the subjects the audit committee covers in its
meetings with the independent auditors and the internal
auditing staff.

• On the other hand, practically all these directors are
against the proposal advanced by former Supreme Court
Justice Arthur Goldberg in 1972, when he was on the
board of TWA, that outside directors have an independent staff to gather information for them. Such an
arrangement would be too costly, or would jeopardize
normal management prerogatives, or would create
friction between the staff and company managers.
Several directors voice a qualified approval of the more
recent suggestion of Robert Estes, formerly Vice
President, Counsel and Secretary of General Electric
Company and now practicing law independently, that

outside counsel be made available to outside directors
for guidance on problems with legal ramifications that
might be greater than appear at first blush.

• Not to be overlooked as an important source of
information is informal, private conversations with one's
fellow outside directors, some of whom may have had
greater training or more experience in particular areas of
the business than others.

• But in the end, despite conscientiousness on the
part of management in getting information directors
want and need to them, it is the director who has the
inescapable responsibility for asking the right questions
at the right moments.

Audit Committees

As mentioned earlier, the boards of large publicly
traded United States corporations are characterized by a
well-articulated committee structure. Of the several
common committees, the audit committee (or the
examining committee as it is often called in banks and
other financial institutions) is coming to be regarded as
the most vital one. This is underscored by the recent
ruling of the New York Stock Exchange that by
mid-1978 all domestic companies with common stock
listed on that exchange — there are about 1,200 such
companies — as a condition of continued listing of its
securities must establish an audit committee of the
board comprised solely of directors independent of
management. (When this ruling was adopted in January,
1977, it was estimated that 86 percent of the domestic
firms listed on the exchange had already established, or
had planned to establish, audit committees that would
conform to the ruling.)

Role, Selection and Legal Status had this to say about
the duties and responsibilities of audit committees:

"The most common functions of the audit committee, as described in board resolutions, are:

"(1) Selecting auditors or recommending auditors to
the board and/or stockholders.
"(2) Determining the scope of the audit.
"(3) Reviewing audit results.
"(4) Reviewing internal accounting procedures.

"Other activities assigned to audit committees include:

"• In banks, reviewing reports of examinations by
regulatory authorities prior to consideration of these
reports by the entire board.

"• Monitoring internal programs to ensure compliance with the law and avoidance of conflicts of interest.

"• Determining the duties and responsibilities of the internal auditing staff (although some companies delegate this to the outside auditors).

"• Approving recommendations of management for changes in the responsibilities of the controller or of the person holding that office, or proposing such changes on its own initiative.

"• Approving the annual compensation of independent outside auditors.

"This list of duties is really only a starting point; it does not convey the role that an effective audit committee can play, or even the purpose it serves. Essentially this committee is thought of as an independent check on the financial health of the corporation and on the reliability of its financial controls and of its financial reporting. . . ." (pp. 117-118)

Typically an audit committee, in keeping with its role as an independent check on top management, consists entirely of outside directors. It meets with the firm's outside auditors — usually privately, although some companies make it a practice to invite a member of management to attend these meetings. Some audit committees also meet with the internal auditing staffs as well, often without a top management representative present unless by invitation. One contributor to the present study describes an apparently not uncommon practice: His board's audit committee can ask internal auditors for any information it wants. There are, however, those who believe that senior management — particularly the chief financial officer — should not be bypassed in meetings or written communications be-

---

An Informed Board

We believe it essential to communicate regularly and frequently with Jewel directors. All directors receive a weekly newsletter designed to keep them and all officers of the Jewel operating companies informed of sales, personnel changes, operating policy changes, and other internal and external events influencing the company. Every four weeks these newsletters contain summary information relating to sales, earnings and return on investment for each division of the company. In addition, and in advance of each directors' meeting, a detailed *Management Report* is forwarded to each director. This includes separate reports prepared by the presidents of each operating division of Jewel which detail operating, merchandising, financial and administrative results of the preceding quarter. Thus, board members have a direct link with the presidents of our various companies. The report also includes comparisons of individual company and consolidated results for the latest quarter and year-to-date, with explanations of variances from plans and from the prior year. The report generally amounts to 100 or so pages and is valued by directors and by management as a highly useful communication vehicle.

Because our directors receive a continuous flow of information throughout the year, supplemented by not infrequent telephone contact, board meetings are not a management reporting session but are largely devoted to responding to observations and discerning questions of the outside directors relating to the business, social, ethical and legal conduct of Jewel and the environment in which it operates. On the day of each directors' meeting, the management of a major segment of the company typically makes a special in-depth presentation to the directors.

Annually, Jewel's Chairman and President meet alone with outside directors to review their thoughts on management succession. Discussions at this meeting center on both long-term succession plans and immediate succession strategies in the event of an unexpected development. This special meeting follows a similarly structured meeting of the Chairman and the President with the senior officers of the company.

An annual presentation for approval by the directors of Jewel relates to the growth program for the company for the following three years. This meeting is preceded by a special report forwarded to directors, which details projections of sales, earnings, resource allocation, financial position, sources and uses of funds, and return on investment for each Jewel company and in consolidation for each of the ensuing three years.

Source: 1975 Annual Report, Jewel Companies.

tween the audit committee and the company's internal auditing staff.

One task not explicitly mentioned in the 1975 study but which has been occupying quite a few audit committees in the past two years, has been investigation of illegal domestic political contributions and questionable payments overseas aimed at getting business. As several study participants put it, the role of the audit committee has been expanded to include ethical as well as financial questions. One gathers that this additional burden has fallen to the audit committee since it has seemed to be the best in-place mechanism to pursue such inquiries.

According to one study participant, an audit committee of which he is a member, in investigating unusual payments by company officials, over a six-month period prepared a lengthy questionnaire that was sent to 137 company employees, interviewed 83 employees, participated in a task force that went abroad for on-the-spot investigations, and made changes in the company's accounting practices to forestall improper payments in the future.

Another task, which apparently has fallen to audit committees recently, is reviewing and approving annual reports to shareholders (and in some companies quarterly reports as well).

Virtually every board of which U.S. contributors to this study are members have audit committees. All these individuals sit on at least one such committee; all believe that every board of a publicly held company should have an audit committee (though one commented that he did not like to have such a committee established by fiat, as the New York Stock Exchange ruling will do); and a number of these contributors volunteer the information that they would not sit on a board lacking such a committee. Finally, several who are board chairmen or presidents of their corporations said that they value the contribution of their firms' audit committees.

Here are other salient points these directors made about audit committees:

• Participation in their work is extremely time-consuming — in some cases routinely requiring as much time as regular board service. This is why, in boards that have them, professional directors are commonly appointed to audit committees. Four to six committee meetings a year seems to be typical.

• It is essential for audit committee members to know "the key people" in the company because it is more likely that these people, rather than investigations conducted by the committee, will bring to light any irregular practices.

• An audit committee member (excluding the chairman) does not have to be particularly well versed in accounting to serve effectively. As with other work of the outside director, the key is the ability and the proclivity to ask informed, searching questions.

• The charge, leveled by some critics, that the audit committee is a needless group created primarily for the benefit of the outside auditors — because in meeting with and responding to the committee they sharply increase their time charges — is preposterous.

• In the past few years there has been a change in the relationship between the audit committee and the outside auditors. Specifically, the audit committees are asking sharper questions of the auditors and insisting on broader accountability by them.

• Although most participants are satisfied that the audit committees on which they sit get, or can get, the information they need to fulfill their functions, several think that they can never be certain. "No institution or individual can do enough policing of the affairs of a major corporation to insure 100 percent honesty," one of them observes. And another points out a particular instance in which neither the audit committee nor the outside auditors had detected some questionable payments overseas — nor, in his view, could either group have done so. The sum involved, between $700,000 and $800,000, was dispersed over several years, and only four executives in the company knew about it. Not even with a staff could an audit committee have acquired knowledge about these payments until well after they had been made.

Separating the Jobs of Chairman and Chief Executive Officer

Role, Selection and Legal Status reported:

"It has become fairly common practice in large U.S. corporations to divide the responsibility of the chief executive between two people (sometimes more, but that is still exceptional). The chairman serves as chief executive officer, concentrating on policy, planning and external relations, and is responsible to the board; the president is the chief operating or administrative officer, concerned with day-to-day operations, and reports to the chairman. This top management structure prevails in most of the companies consulted for this report."

The advantage of this arrangement, from a management viewpoint, that report noted, is that it provides desirable flexibility, since the two men can split the chief executive's load according to their respective talents and vary their respective responsibilities with the requirements of specific situations. But, the report continued, the arrangement has its critics. "The argument against having the chairman of the board hold the title chief executive officer is that it gives him too much authority and, at the same time, it undercuts the independence of the board and its ability to call him to account." An alternative division of responsibilities between the chairman and president is preferred by these critics: " . . .the chairman should have authority over board functions, but should not run the company; the president should have the authority to do that as chief executive, but should be subordinate to the board."[10]

More recently, a prominent chairman emphasized enhanced board performance in arguing for the separation of these two positions:

" . . .Another fundamental question is whether or not the Chief Executive also should serve as Chairman of the Board, or whether it would be better to have an outsider serve as Chairman. Although there has been a trend since World War II to combine the two positions, the desirability of the trend must be examined. When the Chief Executive Officer is the Chairman, the Board's ability to organize itself for its important oversight and review functions is impaired. The executive role of management and the oversight role of the Board are blended, and the latter role is compromised. There needs to be a greater separation than exists today between the Chief Executive and the Board for a proper evaluation of the Chief Executive's performance. A Board Chairman who is not a member of management can organize the activities of the Board and thus permit it to achieve some independence in judgment and policy — something which is essential if the Board is to develop its role properly."[11]

In recent years a few United States companies have deliberately gone against the trend and made organizational changes that have clearly separated the functions of chairman and chief executive. Texas Instruments has done so, calling the chairman of the board the chief corporate officer, but only by virtue of his responsibilities as chairman of the board. As chief executive officer, the president does not report to the chairman but, rather, to the entire board. According to a company document, "this is to emphasize that, while the board headed by its chairman is responsible for company policies and performance, it has delegated to the company's executives, headed by the chief executive officer, responsibility for the detailed management of the corporation."[12]

More recently, the Connecticut General Insurance Co. has done likewise. The chairman explained this organizational change in the first quarter, 1976, report to stockholders:

"As part of a new organizational concept adopted by the directors, I have been elected chairman of the board. Under this concept the chairman organizes and leads the board in its work. The president is chief executive officer and is responsible to the board for the company's management.

"The essential elements of the new concept are the careful distinction between the role of the board and the role of management, the provision of each with its own leadership, and the maintenance of an effective working relationship between the two.

"The work of the board, put simply, is to make sure that the corporation has acceptable purpose, direction and plan; that management is pursuing these effectively and in accordance with legal and regulatory requirements; and that the future health of the corporation is not jeopardized by the risks to which its resources are exposed. Leading the board in that work is the job of its chairman.

"As chief executive officer, but not chairman of the board, the president has a job which differs from the one I have had in just two respects: he is not responsible to the board for organizing and leading it in the performance of its functions; and he works with a board that is more independent in the performance of its functions, since it has its own leadership structure. He reports directly to the board as a whole, not to the chairman of the board.

"Eventually, the president will be the only director who is also a member of management. One or more others may have had experience in the company's management but must have stepped completely out of the management ranks.

"We believe that this new concept will help to ensure the company's continued success. We believe, too, that

[10]*Role, Selection and Legal Status,* pp. 25-26.

[11]Arthur D. Lewis, Chairman, U.S. Railway Association, "The Changing Role of Directors in the 1970's," *Responsibilities, Relationships & Liabilities for Boards of Directors,* proceedings of a conference sponsored by the School of Business Administration of Southern Methodist University and Booz, Allen and Hamilton Inc., 1976, p. 23.

[12]For further details about the Texas Instruments board, see *Role, Selection and Legal Status,* pp. 37-39.

such self-imposed systems of checks and balances can help business organizations preserve their freedom to pursue their legitimate purposes. Such freedom of enterprise is vital to our country's future, as it has been to its past. We hope that arrangements such as we have adopted, or ones having similar objectives, will become more common among major business corporations."

One commentator has observed that this separation of the chairmanship from the post of chief executive officer "embodies several developments that are changing the relationship between the board and the CEO. It's changing not out of any distrust for the CEO, nor out of any desire to render top management less effective in its management of the corporation. Rather it's changing in order to make the board more effective."[13]

This chairman's position description and the relationship of the president to the board are set forth on pages 102-103.

Liability and Government Control

As the concluding part of "The United States Context" pointed out, two of the principal concerns of U.S. directors are the unsettled — and unsettling — problem of liability and the pressures for greater federal control of the board and the corporation. Liability is the more concrete concern at the moment.

Liability

One can hardly pick up a U.S. business periodical without coming across a story about a lawsuit mounted by a shareholder or someone else against the directors and officers of a business concern. A commonly held view is that potential liability makes qualified people refuse, or at least hesitate, to serve on corporate boards.

In recognition of directors' exposure to liability, practically all major companies indemnify them against losses sustained personally as a result of legal actions arising out of their activities as board members. Most offer protection for directors and the corporation alike through directors' and officers' (D&O) insurance, which typically (1) "reimburses the corporation for amounts it pays in indemnification of the directors," and (2) "covers the losses of directors not subject to indemnification."[14]

The U.S. directors contributing to this study hold a

wide range of opinions about liability. Some of them are personally concerned — "a sword of Damocles hanging over my and my fellow directors' heads," one of them says. A commonly cited problem is that not even the most astute lawyer knows where a director's liability begins and ends, save in the most flagrant circumstances of misconduct on his part; the body of law simply has not been developed sufficiently to make the matter clear. A related difficulty, one director observes, is that liability is inevitably proved "after the fact." At the time an act was committed — or there was a failure to act — reasonable people can and do differ as to whether the act or inaction was sound. Incidentally, all the members of one of this director's boards are being sued for manifesting what is alleged to have been poor business judgment in a major decision.

What about D&O insurance? The consensus view of the surveyed directors is that this affords at best limited protection: A settlement may be awarded to stockholders or others bringing an action that exceeds the maximum dollar limit of the policy, or the policy may not cover the actions or inactions of which the directors are accused.[15]

A second group of directors declare themselves not worried about liability. One of them observes that she is in a far riskier position in her day-to-day job as an executive than she is in her position as outside director of several corporations — but acknowledges that many of her fellow directors are deeply concerned about liability. Finally, several directors think that worry over liability has receded in the last few years; it was a far more troubling spectre when the Penn Central Railroad collapsed and its directors were sued, according to one. (This same study participant believes that insurance is adequate and that its cost has dropped because there have been few suits lost by directors.)

Consequences: Only a minority of the directors interviewed believe that the problem of liability has made it difficult to recruit qualified directors. But others suggest that there may be an indirect cause-and-effect: Because of the risk of being subject to multimillion dollar suits, boards are putting in more time and effort and this means that a conscientious, concerned director has to limit the number of boards he serves on more than he would have had to, say, ten years ago.

---

[13] Harold Stieglitz, "An Anachronism Comes to Life," *Across the Board*, April, 1977, p. 24.

[14] *Role, Selection and Legal Status*, p. 87.

[15] For more information on indemnification and D&O insurance, see *Role, Selection and Legal Status*, pp. 86-88. Another Conference Board report, by Jeremy Bacon, *Corporate Directorship Practices: Compensation 1975*, Report No. 678, offers data on the dollar limits of coverage of D&O insurance policies in that year. See page 69 of that report.

Function of the Chairman of the Board

The Chairman of the Board is responsible to the board for organizing and leading it in the performance of its role.

The Chairman of the Board maintains effective communication, and joint work as necessary, with the management in order to meet both the board's and the management's needs. In the process he keeps the board and himself out of the business of running management, and also out of defaulting to management the performance of the board's role.

The Chairman presides at meetings of the board, of those committees of the board of which he serves as chairman, and at meetings of stockholders.

Acting on behalf of the board and subject to its approval, he builds and maintains a board membership that meets agreed criteria for activity and diversification.

Subject to approval of the board, he establishes committees, defines their roles, and assigns chairmanships and memberships with due regard for individual preferences.

In coordination with the President, he

— develops meeting schedules and agenda for the board and its committees that meet the needs of the board and of management;

— organizes the work of the board so as to keep the demand on directors' time within acceptable limits and to concentrate the time available on the highest priority issues;

— ensures that the board gets all the information it needs to appraise and evaluate long-range issues and the longer term implications of current decisions;

— provides the board with such staff services as it requires.

Through the conduct of meetings and otherwise, he brings the board's full diversity of perceptions to bear on the discussion of issues. He facilitates clear communication and understanding between board and management in both directions. He causes the board to make its position on major issues sufficiently clear for the President to use in the performance of his duties. He ensures that the President is informed of the proceedings of any meeting of the board or of committees or of any segments thereof at which the President is not present.

He communicates to stockholders on behalf of the board as necessary.

He maintains with the President a mutually agreeable communication system to meet each other's job needs.

He identifies promptly to the President any material dissatisfaction he has with the manner in which he and the President are relating in practice to each other, and develops with the President a mutually agreeable solution, using such processes of conflict resolution, including mediation by the People Resources Committee, as may be necessary to ensure against continuing unresolved conflict. Jointly with the President, he reports regularly to the board on this work and recommends from time to time any desired changes in the formal statements of their duties or in the policy relating to contacts between directors and others in the organization.

*— Connecticut General
Insurance Company*

There are some positive consequences growing out of increased awareness of and concern about liability. Boards are insisting upon, and getting, more information; the greater time and effort they invest in their jobs mean that directors are fulfilling their functions better; and directors themselves are much better informed about their legal status than they were in the past.

Finally, from the point of view of the director himself, there is evidently more selectivity in deciding to accept invitations to join new boards. It is partly because of the risk of liability that many directors, including most of those contributing to this study, insist they will not join the board of a corporation unless three conditions are met: There is adequate D&O insurance; the majority of the board consists of outsiders; and the board has an audit committee of outsiders only.

Federal Chartering

Spurred in part by revelation of questionable — and, indeed, illegal — payments by corporations both at home and abroad for political and business-getting purposes, the idea of federal chartering of major U.S. corporations, which would entail an enlargement of stockholders' power and a corresponding diminution of management's and the board's, has gained widespread notice in the past few years. The well-known business critic Ralph Nader and his colleagues have published two books, *Constitutionalizing the Corporation: The Case for Federal Chartering,* and *Taming the Giant Corporation,* that, among other recommendations, advocate this radical departure from traditional practice for the largest corporations.

One prominent legal scholar, Donald Schwartz, Professor of Law at Georgetown University, has lent his endorsement. Professor William Carey of the Columbia Law School, and formerly chairman of the Securities and Exchange Commission, has proposed an alternative: Enactment of a federal minimum standards law that would impose minimum standards of fiduciary conduct on all corporations large enough to fall under its purview. Finally, during the summer of 1976, the Senate Commerce Committee held hearings on the behavior of business corporations, and several witnesses appearing at these hearings urged federal chartering. Although no bill has been introduced in either house of Congress, a few observers believe that Congress will consider federal chartering within a few years – indeed, perhaps in 1977.

The basic arguments advanced for these new forms of federal control of major corporations are:

(1) State charters do not effectively control corporations because, in an effort to win revenues from incorporation fees, states traditionally have competed to be the most permissive in their corporate laws. Delaware seems to have won the competition; over half the 500 leading U.S. manufacturing concerns, for example, are incorporated in this state.

Relationship of the President to the Board of Directors

The President is the Chief Executive Officer of the corporation. He is responsible to the board for leading the management in conducting the business of the corporation. He is the chief spokesman for the corporation.

His obligations to the board are to:

(1) Operate within legal and regulatory requirements, within corporate policy as established and understood between board and management, and within such requirements for prior approval by the board as have been expressly stated by the board.

(2) Maintain processes that regularly inform the board of the corporation's purpose, direction and plan, obtain the board's acceptance thereof and report progress thereon.

(3) Keep the board informed of major issues and developments that affect the corporation and of management's position and plans with regard to such issues.

(4) Use his resources to respond to board and committee requests for information. In addition, make provision for officers and employees to respond on their own behalf, as well as his, in accordance with a policy communicated to the organization.

(5) Serve as a director, attend board meetings, report his position on issues as appropriate.

(6) Serve as a member of the Investment Committee, attend meetings of all other committees, and in all cases report his position on issues as appropriate.

(7) Collaborate with the Chairman of the Board and committee chairmen to develop board and committee meeting schedules and agenda that meet the needs of the board and of management.

(8) Cause regular reports to stockholders to be prepared, reviewed by the Audit Committee of the board, and released.

(9) Maintain with the Chairman of the Board a mutually agreeable communication system to meet each other's job needs.

(10) Identify promptly to the Chairman of the Board any material dissatisfaction he has with the manner in which he and the Chairman of the Board are relating in practice to each other, and develop with the Chairman of the Board a mutually agreeable solution, using such processes of conflict resolution, including mediation by the People Resources Committee, as may be necessary to ensure against continuing unresolved conflict. Jointly with the Chairman of the Board, report regularly to the board on this work and recommend from time to time any desired changes in the formal statements of their duties or in the policy relating to contacts between directors and others in the organization. – *Connecticut General Insurance Company*

(2) Stockholders do not control major corporations, because they cannot enforce accountability on management or the board.

(3) Neither do directors. As "The United States Context" points out, despite signs of the exertion of greater independence by some boards, management has traditionally controlled the board rather than the other way around, as both state corporation law and management theory prescribe. More specifically, if directors are insiders, they are necessarily subservient to the chief executive; and if they are outsiders they are likely to be too busy or too sympathetic to management to exercise the control they should.

(4) The Federal Government does not now effectively control corporations because most regulatory agencies are too favorably disposed to the interests of the businesses they regulate, and those that are not do not have the resources for proper control. (The Securities and Exchange Commission is often excepted from the charge, but that agency is concerned primarily with investors and not the public at large.)

(5) The business corporation has changed markedly in the two centuries of this country's history. Multinational corporations make decisions and initiate actions that have not merely national but international implications. In Ralph Nader's phrase, they are "private governments." Only the Federal Government can effectively provide the necessary restraints on their power.

The Views of U.S. Directors. Several of the directors contributing to this study believe that federal chartering, and presumably tighter control by the Federal Government, particularly with respect to the role of directors, are — like nonmanagement worker representation on the board of directors — essentially a non-issue. That is to say, they do not find their colleagues in various boardrooms seriously concerned about it. One remarks that although the mere fact of a Senate committee's holding hearings on the subject might be regarded as a threat, the chairman of that committee is deeply opposed to federal chartering, and so no bill is likely to pass. But a consensus view would be that with an apparent Populist now serving as President of the United States, and with lopsided majorities of his party controlling both houses of Congress, this could be an idea whose time is about to come.

At any rate, these directors and others interviewed for the study have themselves worked out responses to the question of federal chartering — most of them negative.

The Case Against Federal Chartering. One of the most widely held beliefs of study participants is that federal chartering is simply a stalking horse or — to change the taxonomy — a camel aiming to get his nose under the tent of the conduct of business affairs. What is really at issue, what the advocates of federal chartering are seeking, is greater federal control of business. Here are some illustrative comments:

• "It would be damaging to innovation and free enterprise."

• "It would undoubtedly be only the first step in a series of unwanted changes culminating in burdensome federal interference with business."

• "It would lead to the government's telling business how to function, and forcing companies to have stockholders make decisions that should be made by management."

• "It would needlessly constrain business freedom and flexibility and inevitably place a significant cost burden on corporations, just as other forms of federal control have."

Several directors point out that the Federal Government already controls business in many ways. The Securities and Exchange Commission, the Federal Trade Commission, the Department of Justice, the Environmental Protection Agency and other bodies enforcing environmental-control laws, the 1970 Occupational Safety and Health Act, the 1973 Employee's Retirement and Insurance Safety Act, the strictures sometimes placed on overseas private investment — these laws and agencies and many others tightly control, not to say hamper, business corporations. Moreover the outlook is for more, rather than less, control from these sources.

The board chairman of a large multinational corporation makes a more philosophical point pertaining to the conduct of corporations overseas. Corporations are quite properly governed by laws. If a change in legislation is needed regarding business conduct overseas, it is Congress that should make the change following adequate exploration and debate in its committees and on the floors of the House and Senate. But with federal chartering, bureaucrats in the chartering agency could well assume unilateral and stifling control of business operations. Furthermore, this executive points out, when a business makes a mistake, "life goes on for the rest of us"; only the business' management and stockholders suffer. So there is a built-in element of automatic purification. But if a federal chartering agency — or any other federal agency — makes a mistake, usually it cannot readily be corrected. In his view, it is appropriate for the Federal Government or state governments to set, and if necessary, to improve, standards of business conduct and responsibility. But this power does not imply, and should not entail, arbitrary interference with the necessary freedom of action for businessmen in the production and distribution of products and services, which lies at the heart of the effective U.S. enterprise system. Such interference, along with increased costs for and lower performance by business, would be the inevitable accompaniment of federal chartering.

The Case for Federal Chartering. Among the directors surveyed, three arguments for federal chartering can be discerned. First is the argument-by-analogy which advocates of federal chartering have urged: Since large corporations do business in many countries in the world, it is the Federal Government that should provide their basic charters. It is simply anachronistic for a state to charter multinational companies especially when state regulation has historically been so ineffective.

The second argument is that federal chartering would clear the air and provide rather advantageous uniformity, if it enabled corporations to operate within the bounds of a single set of guidelines issued in Washington. Several contributors explicitly made the point that, as a quid pro quo for federal chartering, business should press for Congressional preemption of the field of corporate law, removing it from the purview of states. One bank director, who is against the idea of federal chartering in general, suggests that it might be salutary for banks which, he believes, are being whipsawed by state as well as federal regulatory agencies.

The third argument is that federal chartering might help legitimize the corporation, might raise it from its presently low level of public esteem.

FTC Challenges to Interlocking Directorships

As "The United States Context" noted, federal laws aimed at ensuring competition and preventing restraint of trade affect the board of directors — specifically by forbidding interlocking directorships on companies of a certain size. According to an official of the Federal Trade Commission, which enforces these statutes as they apply to interlocks:

"The two most basic proscriptions of interlocking relationships, at least for concerns which are not subject to federal regulatory schemes, are Section 8 of the Clayton Act, 15 U.S.C. Section 19, and Section 5 of the Federal Trade Commission Act, 15 U.S.C. Section 45. Section 8 proscribes interlocking directorates between

competing corporations if one of them has capital, surplus, and undivided profits aggregating more than $1,000,000, and if the elimination of competition by agreement between them would constitute a violation of any of the provisions of any of the antitrust laws. Section 5 of the Federal Trade Commission Act proscribes unfair methods of competition and unfair or deceptive acts or practices. Interlocking directorates were specific targets of Section 5. Of course, Section 5 has been broadly interpreted to prohibit all acts and practices which violate the letter or the basic policies of the other antitrust laws, and also those which harm consumers, regardless of their effect on competition. Section 5 would therefore prohibit every interlocking relationship proscribed by Section 8 of the Clayton Act and would proscribe interlocking relationships violating the basic policy of Section 8 as well. In addition, any interlocking relationship which is demonstrably conducive to anticompetitive conduct most likely would also be proscribed by Section 5. The outer limits of the sweep of Section 5 have not yet been defined.

"... interlocking directorates are viewed with suspicion because they may lead to conflicts of interest which will in turn lead to anticompetitive conduct. Proscriptions of interlocking directorates are therefore designed to prevent relationships which would tend to encourage anticompetitive conduct; they are 'incipiency' statutes. For example, Section 8 of the Clayton Act prohibits interlocking directorates between competing corporations whether or not the interlocking directorate is actually used to restrict competition. The only question to be answered is whether or not the corporations interlocked would be capable of committing a violation of 'any of the provisions of any of the antitrust laws,' such as price fixing, or an allocation of territories."[16]

The FTC has recently become extremely vigorous in challenging what it perceives to be interlocks. For example, it brought pressure on one director, through an action brought against two companies, to resign from the board of one or the other because the companies competed in a business that amounted to less than one percent of the total sales of each company. And it has called into question indirect interlocks — the situation in which two representatives of competing corporations (banks, say) sit on the board of a third corporation (a

---

[16]Owen M. Johnson, "Interlocking Directorates — A Government View," *Responsibilities, Relationships & Liabilities For Boards of Directors,* p. 8. Mr. Johnson is Director, Bureau of Competition, of the Federal Trade Commission.

manufacturing firm), the principal business of which is not related to the business in which the competitors are engaged.

Furthermore, the FTC's activism aside, as large corporations have diversified and industrial technologies have developed, firms that ten or even five years ago were in no sense competitors are now offering similar or functionally identical products to common customers. It would have been a bold seer in 1967 to prophesy that the International Business Machines Corporation and the American Telegraph and Telephone Company would one day be vying in the marketplace. Such changes in the competitive milieu have given a new facet to the hard stone of interlocking directorships.

Most of the U.S. directors surveyed for this study are sympathetic with the notion that interlocking directorships — at least direct interlocks — ought to be eliminated principally because they believe that competition is essential to the flourishing and public acceptance of an enterprise economy. Yet a good number believe that particular FTC interpretations of competition or interlocks have been extreme, and that the FTC, others in government, and the public need to understand that an interlock will not necessarily — indeed, is not likely to — lead to competitive restraint or conflict of interest.

More specific ideas advanced by study participants about interlocking directorships:

• It is important not to drive normal and inevitable relationships underground, or to pretend they can be eliminated by fiat. If, for example, two insurance executives from competing companies wish to discuss common interests or problems, they will do so, whether or not they both serve on the board of, say, a manufacturing company.

• There is a mistaken presumption underlying the FTC's program that competition will be reduced if interlocks continue. In fact, no director of proper moral stature would act to reduce competition; even if he were so disposed, peer pressure — from his fellow directors — or the possibility of a subsequent stockholders' suit would constrain him. As a practical matter, even an unscrupulous director rarely is in a position to reduce competition through board service. (Virtually all the directors they know, study participants say, recognize that they should comport themselves like Caesar's wife. Thus it is common practice, when an issue coming before a board might even appear to present a director with a conflict of interest, for that director either to abstain from voting or leave the meeting.)

• The FTC has on occasion conjured up farfetched visions of inhibited competition — for example, the previously mentioned two firms judged to be competitors because of their participation in a business of miniscule importance to each.

• There is a positive value to be gained from simultaneous service on boards of companies that are tangentially competitive. One director points out that four of the boards on which she sits — a commercial bank, a savings bank, a diversified financial institution, and an investment firm — have overlapping issues and problems to deal with, and she finds she is a better director on each of these boards as a result of her service on the other three. Similarly, the chairman of a bank says that it would be very helpful to have the perspective of an insurance company executive represented on his board.

• Finally, several respondents believe that there are more fundamental anti-competitive or conflict-of-interest forces represented on corporate boards than interlocking directorships — specifically, outside counsel, investment bankers, and commercial bankers.

Consequences. The FTC's program has already had one consequence for several surveyed directors: They are more sensitive than formerly about accepting new directorships. One of them, already a director of a firm that was predominantly a retail food chain, was dubious about accepting a seat on the board of a firm that manufactures food products until she was reassured by the latter company's management that the interlock issue had been looked into and the conclusion reached that the FTC would be very unlikely to object to her joining that firm's board. (Three years later, it has not.)

As for the future, it is the opinion that continued — excessive, some would term it — zeal by the FTC will make it reduce the population of available persons, or make it more difficult to recruit them, not only as directors for business boards, but also as trustees for foundations and universities. A bank chairman is a trustee of a university and a member of that board's finance committee. From time to time issues arise that could conceivably be interpreted as putting him into a conflict-of-interest position because of his role at the bank. He either abstains from voting on these issues or absents himself from the boardroom when they are discussed. He would think it unfortunate if, through the FTC or through widespread acceptance of its viewpoint about competition and conflicts of interest, otherwise qualified businessmen, financiers and professionals declined to accept seats on the boards of such pro bono publico institutions.

Limit Outside Directorships by Law?

Some critics of U.S. boardroom practices have suggested that a legislative limit be set on the number of outside directorships any individual may hold. This is the practice in several European countries. The theory underlying this proposal seems to be that it would help ensure that present directors would devote adequate attention to the firms they serve in that capacity, and that it would bring new talent into boardrooms.

The several study participants who have commented on this proposal all are opposed to it. Pointing out that the energy, competence and drive of different individuals vary greatly, one of their number observes that one person can be overwhelmed by serving as a director of two companies, whereas another can render distinguished service to ten firms in this capacity. Clearly, then, they consider this a poor subject for legislation.

Another shortcoming ascribed to the proposal is that it does not recognize the role a professional director can play. Having no other principal occupation, he or she can spend far more time in directorial work than can other directors. Therefore, it would seem appropriate for him or her to serve on more boards than, say, a chief executive who has to devote most of his time to running his company.

At the same time, practically all the surveyed directors — both part-time outside directors and professional directors — claim their board and attendant committee responsibilities demand considerable time and energy, and most maintain that for this reason they would not accept another board seat were one offered to them. A conscientious director will limit his boards to a number which he believes he can serve properly and competently; but it appears to be the consensus opinion that it should be his conscience — and not legal fiat — that fixes this number.

Changes Taking Place...

To sum up this review of U.S. board practices and the perceptions of a number of U.S. directors, here is a list of major changes these study contributors discern.

— Board service is becoming more demanding, more nearly professional. In many companies, both management and the board are taking steps to make the role of the board more nearly correspond to what the law and management theory says it should be — the supreme body of the corporation. And both in these firms and others as well, crucial decisions, including selection of directors, are more and more recognized as a shared responsibility of management and the board.

— In the pursuit of a more substantive role for the board, one discerns two major efforts:

(1) Improving board effectiveness; and
(2) Designing blueprints of an ideal board in terms of the talents and background of its members and then working toward this ideal as vacancies on the board are filled.

— Directors are spending more time in exercising their responsibilities not only because they are playing a larger role in company affairs than they used to, but also because of their concern over their liability, because of greater government involvement in corporate affairs, and because many businesses are bigger and more complex than they used to be.

— Directors are becoming more selective about accepting new board seats.

— In the last couple of years, many boards either have been significantly involved for the first time or have acted with unprecedented vigor in the area of corporate ethics. It seems likely, furthermore, that corporate ethics will remain high on board agenda.

— The audit committee, composed predominantly if not entirely of outside directors, seems destined to become ubiquitous and the preeminent board committee.

— New faces — women, blacks, persons with backgrounds other than the traditional ones of business, law and finance — are likely to be seen in greater numbers in boardrooms; and, in the view of the study participants, properly so.

— Although nonmanagement employee or union representation on the board is not likely to be legislated in the United States, and although it seems questionable whether federal chartering of corporations will soon be required, the Federal Government has had, and will continue to have, a mounting impact on corporate boards (and company managements as well) through such agencies as the Securities & Exchange Commission, the Department of Justice, The Federal Trade Commission, and through legislation affecting employee safety and health, pension funds, and equal employment opportunities. What the thrust or consequence of this impact will be remains far from clear; but it is certain that it will change the role and functions of the board.

...And a Pair of Quandaries

Two complex issues confront U.S. directors as they appraise their role in the governance of business enterprises. One is accountability — to what groups other than shareholders are directors accountable, for what, and how is accountability to be enforced? And to the extent that there is conflict in a director's several accountabilities, how should this conflict be resolved?

The second quandary is the liability of directors. What is needed, many directors insist, is a definitive resolution of its bounds, so that a director can be more nearly certain than he is now of what actions (or failures to act) on his part run significant risk of liability, and what do not.

The extent and direction for settling, or at least clarifying, these issues in the future will influence further changes in the U.S. boardroom.

Chapter 9
Canada

The Canadian Context

Government Control of and Involvement in Business

Canada is a federal state. The constitution divides political power between the central, or federal, government and ten provincial governments. A business may be incorporated under federal law or provincial law in accord with either the federal companies act or one of the ten companies acts of the provinces.

A company incorporated in one province can apply to other provinces for extra-provincial registration and so carry on business outside the province of its incorporation; but a provincial charter is usually preferred by companies which restrict their activities to one province, and a federal charter by companies which operate in more than one province. Federal incorporation ensures that a company can exercise the same powers in all provinces.

A few types of companies — mainly insurance companies, banks, trust companies, loan companies, and railways — and most crown corporations are created by Special Act of the Parliament of Canada or of the legislature of any one of the provinces. The powers and responsibilities of boards of directors, based either on the common law or statute, are similar in the various jurisdictions in Canada. The behavior of directors is also affected by securities laws.

The Conference Board in Canada, in particular Susan Peterson, Leslie Ferrari and Morris Heath, prepared the context material and gathered the information on which the remainder of the chapter is based.

A number of factors of both history and geography have produced in Canada an economy which is characterized by considerable public enterprise and public financing of private enterprise. Both the federal and the provincial governments have from time to time created "crown corporations," that is, companies owned by the government, with various objectives in mind: to provide services at a reasonable cost to a small population in a vast country; to control industries that are natural monopolies; to participate in joint ventures of otherwise prohibitive cost with private enterprise to develop natural resources; to avoid or decrease foreign ownership of Canadian industry; to establish substantial Canadian ownership in new industrial sectors. Frequently competing with private enterprise, crown corporations are active in railways, airlines, public utilities, uranium, oil and gas, potash, steel, atomic energy, telecommunications, insurance, some manufacturing, banking, broadcasting, liquor sales, and lotteries.

Notwithstanding this amount of governmental involvement, there is virtually no interest in Canada in large-scale nationalization of industry — with the possible exception of the recently elected Parti Québécois Government in the Province of Quebec, and actions of the Government of Saskatchewan in the direction of provincial ownership of the potash industry.[1] For its part, the federal government has

---

[1] Before its election on November 15, 1976, the Parti Québécois formulated an economic and political platform that proposed extensive nationalization and a downplaying of private enterprise in favor of cooperatives or government-private sector consortia. Since this party's unexpected electoral victory, the new premier has said forcefully that his Government is not bound by this platform and that the only likely candidate for nationalization is the asbestos industry.

recently stated that it will reduce the size of government and expand the range of opportunities for private enterprise by identifying governmental activities which can be transferred to the private sector without reducing the quality of service to the public.[2] The sections pertaining to boards of directors of the special legislation by which most crown corporations are created sometimes differ from those contained in the companies acts.

Canada, traditionally very receptive to foreign capital, has more recently become concerned about the extent of foreign ownership and control of its business and industry — particularly, ownership by U.S. companies. Approximately 75 percent of petroleum and natural gas, 57 percent of other mining and smelting, and 59 percent of manufacturing industries are foreign controlled. Demands for more self-conscious public policies relating to this have resulted most notably in the creation of a Foreign Investment Review Agency. The Agency scrutinizes the plans of foreign direct investors in Canada — otherwise the investment can be blocked. This concern is also reflected in recent changes to a number of the companies acts which require, usually, that a majority of directors of all companies that offer securities to the public be resident Canadians.

Laws Affecting the Board of Directors

Virtually all business enterprises of any size are corporations, and, as in the United States, of the three basic forms of business organization only a corporation must have a board of directors.

A company is free to incorporate under the laws of the federal government or of any of the provincial governments. All business corporations are limited liability share-capital or stock-ownership organizations. Although the terminology is changing, there has been a distinction drawn between public companies and private companies. Private companies, essentially, are those that have never sold shares to the public.

All companies acts in Canada grant the control and authority over a corporation's affairs to a single board of directors. (There is no provision for a two-tier board.) Most statutes require the directors to "manage (or "manage or supervise the management of") the affairs and business of the corporation." In practice, boards do not — and, it is widely maintained, cannot — manage in the sense of direct supervision of the company's day-to-day decisions and operations. In this sense, management is delegated to full-time executives who are employed for this purpose.

[2] Speech from the Throne, October 12, 1976.

Corporation laws grant authority to boards of directors in very general — and, some critics assert, permissive — terms. The result is that the role played by the board is somewhat unique to the situation in each company — the product of interplay between the directors and management. But directors have two important duties that have been largely established in common law and are now codified in the companies acts of Canada and in three of the ten provinces. (The remaining provinces will probably follow this lead in updating their statutes.)

(1) The duty to exercise the care, diligence and skill that a reasonably prudent person would exercise in comparable circumstances.

(2) The duty to act honestly and in good faith with a view to the best interest of the corporation. This arises from the concept that the director is a fiduciary, entrusted by the stockholders with the welfare of the corporation. Therefore, a director is not permitted to take advantage of the corporation for personal gain.

A board of directors is considered to have authority only as a group; individual directors have no legal power, except for that delegated to them by the board. On the other hand, directors can be held liable as individuals for their actions, or failures to act, as board members.

Directors are elected by owners (shareholders) but are not generally required by law to be shareholders themselves. The most notable exception is directors of banks; they are required by law to be fairly substantial shareholders. However, it is common for other companies to require that directors own stock.

There are some legal restrictions on the selection of directors. In addition to the traditional ones prohibiting persons who are of unsound mind, under 18 years of age, or bankrupt, some provinces and the federal authority now require that a majority of directors be resident Canadians. In some instances, the citizenship rules that apply to the board also apply to a quorum of the board and to any committees of the board. Some provinces further require that for corporations chartered there at least one director be resident in that province. Most corporations elect directors for one-year terms; but three-year terms are fairly common in the insurance industry.

Some statutes require that at least two of the directors of a company that sells securities to the public be neither officers nor employees of the company or any of its affiliates. Most major corporations in practice have a majority of these so-called outside directors on their boards. The other directors are members of management.

The bulk of outside directors traditionally have been recruited from the ranks of business and financial management and the legal profession.

There are no laws, such as one finds in other countries, limiting the number of boards on which a person may serve at any one time. While a director of a bank may not simultaneously be a director of another bank or of a trust or loan company, there is no general law preventing a person from sitting on the boards of competing companies. However, a director owes a fiduciary duty to each company and so walks a legal tightrope in any attempt to fulfill his obligations to both. In practice, most directors and boards of directors avoid such situations, although the understanding of what constitutes "competing" companies or industries does not seem to be as inclusive as that now in effect in the United States.

The report of a federal body (The Royal Commission on Corporate Concentration), appointed to study the facts and effects of "corporate concentration" in Canada, is expected imminently and is likely to comment on the power and potential conflicts of interest involved in multiple and interlocking board memberships. Also, the new Competition Act being considered by the federal parliament proposes that the Competition Board, which would administer competition policy, be empowered to prohibit a director or an officer of a company from being a director or officer of another nonaffiliated company where it finds that, as a result, competition is likely to be substantially lessened, or sources of supply or outlets for sale are likely to be foreclosed to competitors.

In Canada there is no federal regulation of the securities industry as there is in the United States, but the legislative provisions of the securities laws in the United States and Canadian provincial jurisdictions are now remarkably similar. Directors are generally responsible for the accuracy of statements contained in a prospectus or takeover bid circular; as "insiders" they are required to report transactions made by them in the company's securities; and they are forbidden from using any confidential information about the company for their own advantage or benefit if the information, if generally known, would affect the value of the company's securities.

Management-Labor Relations and Unionization

In Canada, as in the United States and in contrast to Europe, the choice of corporate directors and the functioning of boards of directors are essentially insulated from labor-management relations. Only approxi-mately 30 percent of the labor force, or approximately 37 percent of nonagricultural paid workers, belong to unions. In 1975, there were 571 unions; 14 had memberships of more than 50,000, with the largest having not quite 200,000 members. Collective bargaining is highly decentralized — collective agreements between a single company and a union are the rule rather than the exception — in contrast to most European countries. Collective agreements must be ratified by the membership.

Just over 70 percent of unionized workers are in unions affiliated with the Canadian Labour Congress. The purpose of this central body has been to broadly coordinate activities at the national level and to maintain relations with organized workers internationally. Its role has until recently been minimal because labor relations and most social security legislation are under the jurisdiction of the provinces, not the central government. The Canadian Labour Congress has recently taken an important new initiative in asking for a full partnership status with government and business in national planning on social issues. At present, however, most Canadian workers are not unionized, and the CLC does not have the power to commit even those workers who are members of affiliated unions. Neither is there in Canada an organization that can speak as the collective voice of Canadian business, although a federal task force has recently recommended that a permanent consultative mechanism between the federal government and business be established.

Management-labor agreements take the form of legal contracts. Strikes are prohibited during the period of time covered by a contract. As a rule, contracts are negotiated and administered without any intervention by the federal or provincial governments. Nor does either party normally want such intervention unless a deadlock develops. The recent past has been exceptional, however, with the introduction of compulsory wage and price controls as a part of the federal government's program to fight inflation. Wage settlements which exceed certain limits can be "rolled back" under the enabling legislation.

The labor movement in Canada has sought a direct voice in politics through support of the New Democratic Party. The NDP is the third of Canada's three national parties. It is the party in power in two provinces and is the official opposition in two others. The extent to which organized labor can count on the party to endorse its stands on public issues is unclear. The two provincial NDP governments failed to support the Canadian Labour Congress in its opposition to wage controls.

To date, unions have shown little interest in negotiating with companies for, or pressing for, legislation that would require representation of nonmanagement employees on corporate boards of directors. A number of labor and business leaders have stated that while it might be desirable to have the employees' point of view given expression in the boardroom, there would be an irreconcilable conflict of interest in having a director with a specific mandate to represent workers. The federal government, however, has stated that it will use its own operations to test new methods of improving labor-management relations. The president of Canadian National Railways, a federal crown corporation, has urged management to accept the European trend of having union representatives on boards.

Worker participation in decisions affecting their jobs is practiced by some companies but entirely on their own managements' initiative. It has not been among the demands of unions to date, but, again, the federal government is encouraging this. There are no "works councils" like those found in some other countries. In the near future, heightened interest in exploring the applicability of European models of management-labor relations to the Canadian situation can be anticipated as part of a search for methods of attenuating the adversarial character of labor-management relations and the economic effects of continuing labor strife.

Ownership of Corporations and Control of the Board

Most major Canadian corporations are owned, either indirectly through parent companies or directly, by a large number of shareholders — individuals and institutions like mutual funds and pension funds. Thus no single individual, family or other owner holds more than a small proportion of the corporation's stock. Unlike the practice in a few of the countries surveyed, though, banks are restricted in the amount of voting shares they can hold in corporations for their own account.[3]

The shareholders, as owners, have the power to elect directors at the required annual shareholders' meeting. They do this largely by mail proxy vote. Almost invariably it is management that proposes a slate of directors, and only rarely is a candidate of management

[3] The Bank Act of 1967 for the first time limited the power of banks to hold voting shares of other Canadian corporations. The Act prohibits a bank from holding more than 10 percent of the voting shares of a corporation except where the bank's investment is $5 million or less. In the latter case, the bank may hold up to 50 percent of the voting shares. It has been proposed that the new Act drop this exception and impose a uniform 10 percent rule.

defeated. Shareholders also have the power to remove directors, but such action is extremely unusual.

Other decisions that are generally reserved for the shareholders — and therefore require their approval before management can carry them out — pertain to major changes in the corporation's size or organization, including mergers or acquisitions, and the issuance of new securities. Much more often than not, these changes are approved as a matter of course by shareholders following management's recommendation.

Management's control of the proxy machinery, enabling it to determine what issues will be considered at the annual meeting, is frequently cited as the chief reason why stockholders are virtually powerless in exercising control over the affairs of the corporation — or control of their elected representatives, the board of directors. The wide dispersion of stock ownership, already mentioned, also contributes to these ends. Furthermore, the great majority of shareholders, both individual and institutional, are essentially passive, being primarily concerned with the profitability of their investments in a company rather than with the stewardship of directors or the detailed actions of management. When stockholders become dissatisfied, they usually show it by simply selling their shares.

The result is that, except in crises, management traditionally has controlled the board of directors, rather than the other way around, as both the law and management theory have it. Indeed, some commentators have argued the board is really an anachronism that survives only to satisfy legal formalities.

The significance of recent legislative changes in a number of jurisdictions to allow for derivative suits or "class actions" against directors for neglect of their duty of care to the company is not yet clear. Formerly, only the company itself could bring a legal action against directors. Because directors were ordinarily in control of the company, this never happened. It is now possible for shareholders to bring an action in the name and on behalf of the company, and to be granted interim funds to cover the cost of so doing, but only after having gained the permission of the court to do so. This qualification, and the additional one that a suit, once initiated, may be discontinued only with court approval, are designed as safeguards against "nuisance suits."

Current Concerns

It seems fair to say that challenges to, and feelings of need for change in, boards of directors have not been as strong in Canada as in the United States. Events and ideas in the business world in the United States invariably have effects in Canada both because of simple proximity and because of considerable U.S. ownership and control of Canadian industry. Moreover, it is not an unusual pattern for change or reform to get under way first in the United States and then to be adapted to the Canadian context after a time lag. But the impetus provided in the United States by well-publicized instances of management incompetence or malfeasance, by suits against directors, and by outside group pressures for reform of boards has not been matched in Canada.

There has been public and government concern about the following issues:

(1) Representation of the Canadian point of view on boards of foreign-owned or controlled companies;

(2) The effects on the public interest of the concentration of corporate power represented by interlocking and multiple directorships;

(3) The ability and willingness of boards of directors to give adequate consideration to the social responsibilities of corporations;

(4) The means of holding boards of directors to account for what they do or fail to do, especially the remedies available to dissatisfied shareholders;

(5) The paucity of women directors;

(6) The respective roles and responsibilities of boards of directors, management and the relevant government ministers for the conduct of the affairs of crown corporations.

In addition, the principal concerns of Canadian directors themselves appear to be these:

(1) The need for independence and effectiveness of boards of directors in their relations with managements — the value of outside directors and of audit committees is widely recognized;

(2) The growing amount of time and information required to do a good job as a director;

(3) The fear that the trend of class actions, and especially "nuisance" class actions, against directors might enter Canada;

(4) The pros and cons of opening up board membership to a more diverse group of people.

Composition and Organization of the Board

This section is based on a survey of 116 *Canadian-owned* corporations, of which 112 are private enterprises and 4 are crown corporations (owned by the federal or provincial governments). The distribution of these firms by industry and size is indicated in the tabulation below.

Industry and Asset Size (millions of Canadian $)	Number and Percent of Firms in Each Category	
	Number	Percent[1]
Manufacturing		
Small (up to $99)	16	14%
Medium ($100-$499)	18	16
Large ($500 and above)	8	7
Subtotal	42	37
Nonmanufacturing		
Small (up to $99)	19	16%
Medium ($100-$499)	23	20
Large ($500 and above)	32	27
Subtotal	74	63
All Companies		
Small (up to $99)	35	31%
Medium ($100-$499)	41	35
Large ($500 and above)	40	34
TOTAL	116	100%

[1] Details do not add to totals because of rounding.

Board Size

The next tabulation presents salient data on the size of the boards of these firms.

Industry	Number of Directors		
	Range	Median	Most Often Reported (Mode)
Manufacturing	5-18	12	10 and 14
Nonmanufacturing	5-53	13	12, 14 and 15

Profile

A simple profile of the boards of 116 Canadian-owned firms can be gleaned from an examination of the figures below:

	Percent of Companies by Type of Industry	
	Manufacturing	Nonmanufacturing
Have a majority of outside directors	88%	86%
Have former or retired employees on the board	10	8
Have women on the board .	4	20
Require board members to be company shareholders	45	55[a]

[a] Three companies did not respond to this question as they are mutual fund companies and, as such, do not require stock ownership.

Table 9-1: Terms of Office for Directors

Number of Years	Percent of Firms by Industry	
	Manufacturing	Nonmanufacturing
1	82%	74%
2	2	1
3	2	12
4	—	1
5	—	1
No response	14	11
Total	100%	100%

As Table 9-2 shows, practicing lawyer is the most common occupation of outside directors.

None of these firms has either a nonmanagement employee or a union representative on its board.

The median board age is 57 years for the manufacturing companies and 57.5 years for nonmanufacturing companies.

Meeting Frequency

The annual frequency of regular board meetings in these firms is:

Industry	Number of Regular Board Meetings Per Year		
	Range	Median	Most Often Reported
Manufacturing	2-13	5	4
Nonmanufacturing	1-53	6	4

Committees

Board committees are ubiquitous in the Canadian corporations participating in the survey. Ninety-eight percent of the manufacturing companies and 89 percent of the nonmanufacturing companies have at least one such committee apiece. Other key statistics about these committees:

Industry	Number of Board Committees		
	Range	Median	Most Often Reported
Manufacturing	1-5	2	2
Nonmanufacturing	1-7	2	2

Industry	Number of Directors on Committee		
	Range	Median	Most Often Reported
Manufacturing	1-13	4	3
Nonmanufacturing	2-23	4	4

Industry	Number of Committee Meetings per Year		
	Range	Median	Most Often Reported
Manufacturing	1-12	2	1
Nonmanufacturing	1-70	4	2 and 4

Other statistics about Canadian boards appear in the two separate tables.

The most common committees are:

Name of Committee	Number of Companies Reporting	
	Manufacturing (42)	Nonmanufacturing (74)
Audit	35	59
Compensation	28	28
Executive	27	48

The Board Today and Tomorrow: Perspectives from Canada

Twenty-one Canadians have contributed their insights on boards of directors to this study in lengthy personal interviews. Eighteen are chairmen or presidents of their own firms and outside directors of one or more other companies; most of these hold the title of chief executive officer. One is the retired chairman of a bank; one, executive vice president of a conglomerate that owns or controls a number of subsidiaries on whose boards he sits; and one is an attorney who serves as outside director of a number of firms.

The overpowering impression gleaned from their comments is that, as in several other countries, the board is undergoing marked change: It is playing a more substantive role than it used to; it is, properly, more independent of management than it used to be; and board service is more taxing than it was only a few years ago.

Table 9-2: Principal Occupations of Outside Directors

Occupation	Percent of Companies Mentioning	
	Manufacturing	Nonmanufacturing
1. Practicing lawyers	71.4%	83.8%
2. Owners or executives of merchandising or trading companies	61.9	72.9
3. Owners or executives of financial institutions	54.7	72.9
4. Independent businessmen, financiers, consultants	52.8	59.5

What follows is an encapsulation of the views of these Canadian executives and directors on specific issues affecting the board. Perhaps not surprisingly, many of these views correspond closely to those articulated by United States directors participating in this study and in the earlier *Role, Selection and Legal Status of the Board.*

Board Functions

Although there is virtually universal support for the precept that the board must see to it that the company is run in the interest of the shareholders, the role the board plays varies by type of company. What is true of the boards of large publicly held companies is not true of boards of large privately held companies; and what is true of small-company boards is not true of large-company boards. Furthermore, there are notable differences among the boards of most large, publicly held, Canadian-controlled companies (the focus of the interviews), of banks, of crown corporations, and of the Canadian subsidiaries of foreign parent companies. Most important, what a board does, or does not do, apart from fulfilling the responsibilities laid down by corporate bylaws, is in considerable measure determined by the company's chief executive.

This much said, do boards have a significant function beyond the routine activities formerly assigned them by law and company bylaws? It is clear that boards do not and cannot, as some statutes command, "manage the affairs of the corporation." Although a few Canadian directors allude to experience on boards that have served simply as rubber stamps for domineering chief executives, it also seems clear that the majority of the boards with which these executives and directors are associated have come to play, at least in recent years, a substantive role — a role that apparently includes, in Professor Mace's famous formulation, both what boards are supposed to do and what they actually do.[4]

By far the most commonly mentioned function of the board, and the one that seems most important to many directors, pertains to the selection, monitoring and appraisal, succession and, as necessary, replacement of senior management. Of these interrelated jobs, it is monitoring that seems to be preeminent — in part because selection, succession and replacement are but occasional happenings; in part because, as one director puts it: "If management does a good job, the director shouldn't have a hell of a lot to do."

[4]Myles L. Mace, *Directors: Myth and Reality,* Boston: Graduate School of Business Administration, Harvard University, 1971.

The function next in frequency of mention — and, to some, second in importance — is deliberation and decision about policies and planning. Here, it is widely maintained, the board's role should be to review and approve, but not initiate, which is the job of management.

The board should enforce discipline on management. This function is accomplished by asking tough questions, or being ready to, and thereby keeping management on its toes; by forcing management to make thorough and adequate preparations for board meetings; by preventing sloppy practices from taking hold.

Offering advice and counsel is yet another vital function of the board. Because the chief executive is in a lonely spot within his organization — he has no peers with whom to share his deepest concerns — outside directors serve as confidants or sounding boards. Furthermore, the varied background of knowledge and experience of outside directors can raise the sights or broaden the perspectives of the chief executive and his colleagues in top management.

Other specific board functions cited by Canadian directors are: seeing that the broad social responsibilities of the company are met; that management decisions are not in conflict with public policy; and preventing conflicts of interest.

Independence vs. Harmony

An effective board, one that creditably performs the functions just described, must perforce maintain a stance of independence from management. Indeed, management should be beholden to the board, rather than the other way around. At the same time, though, the board must be a harmonious body; its individual members have to be united by a devotion to the survival and success of the firm, and have to be compatible (if not congenial) with one another; and neither the board nor an individual director can act as an adversary to management. The tension between independence and harmony — a creative tension, some call it — is manifest in the observation made by a number of Canadian directors (and U.S. directors as well) that it is rare for a board to turn down a major recommendation of management, although such recommendations are sometimes modified or deferred. For issues that are controversial, or gray rather than black or white, the chief executive typically sounds out individual directors before the board as a whole must take action and seeks to convince them of the merits of his recommendations. If he fails to convince several, he will more likely than not withdraw or postpone the matter. This is not to say, though, that there are not occasions when one or more directors will refuse to accept management's formal recommendations at board meetings and will record their dissents.

Boards of Banks, Canadian Subsidiaries of Foreign Parents, Crown Corporations

The Canadian directors interviewed perceive unique characteristics in the boards of these three types of institutions.

Banks: As compared with other major publicly held corporations, bank boards seem to have a limited function. For although the independence of bank boards is apparently guaranteed by the Bank Act, this statute imposes so many formal, routine requirements on these boards that they cannot do much in the way of playing a substantive role. The situation is exacerbated by the large size of so many bank boards, making them unwieldy and foreclosing productive discussions in meetings. Moreover, many banks have appointed outside directors with the primary objective of attracting or keeping their business.

Canadian Subsidiaries. Most Canadian respondents believe that the boards of Canadian subsidiaries of foreign parents ought to function with the same degree of independence and in the same relationship to management as the boards of Canadian-owned companies. The independence of the subsidiary board is essential, one director notes, because its members are far more familiar with Canadian problems and issues and specific investment opportunities than are members of parent-company management in the United States or other foreign countries. Another maintains that a parent company should limit its control over a Canadian subsidiary's board to firing a chief executive.

In practice there appears to be great variation in the independence of Canadian subsidiary boards, ranging from situations in which neither the directors nor the management of a parent company have more than nodding familiarity with the plans of the Canadian subsidiary to those in which very extensive Canadian businesses are simply maintained as branch plants and the Canadian subsidiary board is truly ineffective.

Although there is general approval of the requirements recently introduced in some jurisdictions that a majority of the directors of companies offering securities to the public be resident Canadians, a number of Canadian directors are skeptical that the requirement will lead to greater independence for the boards of Canadian subsidiaries. They believe that a foreign parent so disposed can find resident Canadian "yes men" to serve as directors.

Crown Corporations. Based on their current or past service as directors of crown corporations — those business firms in which the federal or a provincial government is the sole shareholder — several Canadian directors offer observations about these institutions.

While the board is supposed to monitor management and approve capital expenditures, it is the government that sets the policies for these corporations. Indeed, with respect to policy setting, one study participant maintains that the government wants the crown corporation to be an instrument of government policies. To this end, some ministers are unhappy about any manifestation of independence by boards and are moving to have more and more senior civil servants, as opposed to businessmen, appointed to the boards of these corporations.

There is sometimes a problem of accountability for the board of a crown corporation. For instance, a change of government policy can have significant consequences for a particular crown corporation, while its own laid-down policies remain unchanged. Directors may then be criticized either for being uncooperative with the changes or for not following original policy, even though they are not legally liable for consequences. One director maintains that this problem of accountability is not well understood either by parliamentary committees that review crown corporations or by the general public.

As compared with private-enterprise boards, the boards of crown corporations have the following characteristics, according to another director:

(1) Meetings are much tougher.

(2) Decisions have to anticipate government reaction, which sometimes can frustrate, even enrage, the director.

(3) It is sometimes hard to find out what the government really wants to do.

(4) Directors have to be much more careful and demand more detailed information.

(5) Directors can be criticized more openly.

Yet another respondent is disturbed that chief executives of crown corporations are not permitted to sit on the boards of private companies. This forecloses them from some very useful exposure and limits their knowledge about the management of business enterprises.

Accountability

The consensus of Canadian participants is that directors are, of course, accountable to shareholders, but

Cumulative Voting

Under cumulative voting, a stockholder has the privilege of flexibility in casting his or her votes, which are determined under such a system by multiplying the number of voting shares held by the number of directors to be elected. Thus, an owner of 1,000 shares in an election of 12 directors would have 12,000 votes, and could distribute these votes in any manner among any two or more directors or could concentrate them all on one director. This procedure, similar to that of proportional representation in political elections, contrasts with the more usual voting procedure in which the stockholder votes his shares individually for each director to be elected.

The significance of cumulative voting is that it may enable a concentrated minority of stockholders to concentrate their voting power and thereby elect one or more directors of their choice. Under straight voting, on the other hand, holders of a majority of the outstanding shares of stock can always prevent the election of a director not of their choice.

Source: *Corporate Directorship Practices: Membership and Committees of the Board,* Conference Board Report 588, 1973, p. 7.

this accountability is not truly enforced — nor, in the opinion of some, can it be.

Several Canadian directors, however, note that the board is not accountable to shareholders alone. Other groups with claims on the board include employees, customers, suppliers and the community. Indeed, one Canadian director asserts that shareholders "are now fifth or sixth on the list." Above them he places the Department of National Revenue and other government agencies; employees; customers; the general public (in one sense all Canadians, in another, the residents of towns or provinces in which the company conducts its business). At board meetings, he continues, one rarely hears comments about shareholders, most likely because most major shareholders of companies today are institutions rather than individuals.

The lack of enforcement of accountability, or perhaps its unenforceability, troubles a number of Canadian directors. They note that with management essentially in control of the proxy machinery, mounting a proxy fight is not a realistic means to this end, except in unusual

circumstances. Nor is the opportunity to speak up at annual meetings. The right to elect directors, to be sure, can be seen as a vehicle for enforcing accountability, but again the odds favor the slate of directors put forward by existing directors and management. The only realistic remedy for a disgruntled shareholder (excepting of course one with a significant holding) is to sell out. Indeed, a few study participants make the point that the great majority of shareholders are not interested in holding directors accountable, but only in the value of their shares. "Getting shareholders to ask questions at an annual meeting is like pulling teeth," one asserts.

One director insists that "there has got to be more accountability or else shareholders and society alike will wonder why a private group is entrusted with the running of a large company." Like other study contributors, he maintains that institutional shareholders could — and perhaps should — be more active in enforcing directorial accountability; for instance, they could successfully seek seats on boards of firms in which they have substantial holdings. (Most institutional investors in Canada, as in the United States, evidently prefer to maintain an "arms-length" relationship with such firms which, among other things, enables them to dispose of their holdings rapidly.)

Another director believes that the new Canada Business Corporations Act has given shareholders new opportunities to enforce directorial accountability. Under this Act, shareholders can get lists of other shareholders, examine corporate records, propose alterations in the bylaws, and five percent of them can call a special meeting. Furthermore, shareholder approval now has to be gained for the sale or lease of property and cumulative voting is provided for (see box), although not required. But, he adds, though this legislation clearly advances the interest of shareholders in terms of holding the board properly accountable, company business would be bogged down if shareholders should take full advantage of these powers.

The possibility, very new in Canada, for shareholders to institute derivative suits or representative actions against directors for neglect of their duty of due care might seem to provide an effective means of enforcing directorial accountability. But, as "The Canadian Context" notes, it is too early to tell what the consequences of this change will be.

Appraisal. If shareholders will not or cannot enforce the accountability of directors, that implies that they do precious little appraising of directors. Who, then, appraises them?

For the board as a whole, really no one, according to the Canadian study participants. A few suggest that "the marketplace," "the company's creditors," or "the investment community" judge the board, but they do not indicate how such judgment is manifested or rendered, other than by the firm's credit worthiness or the price of its securities. But individual directors evidently are subject to more focused and personal appraisal — by management and by their peers. Here are some representative comments.

- "I [a board chairman and president] quietly assess the ability of directors and note such things as health problems."
- "Board members appraise each other. Those who are a nuisance or are lazy are known to everyone. It is a chairman's responsibility to recommend, after consulting with other directors, that a bad director not stand for reelection."
- "It doesn't take long for a board to suggest that a particular director is ineffective and should be replaced."

One participant reports that a firm he serves as an outside director has established a board committee whose responsibility it is to select candidates for directorship and, more importantly in his view, to monitor absenteeism, assess performance, and review retirement policies. This firm, then, has attempted to institutionalize the appraisal of directors.

Appraising an individual director can be difficult. Take a board that has several committees. A director can contribute very well to one committee, but not so well to another, or to the board as a whole. Similarly, a major shareholder could very well insist on the election of one director whose role is to concentrate on two or three issues. That shareholder may not be concerned if the director in question does not play an active role in other board activities.

According to one director, not only is it hard to judge the effectiveness of an individual board member, but this is done only rarely. When it is, no action is taken as a rule if the appraisal is negative. Furthermore, he believes it would be dangerous to institutionalize any means of getting rid of ineffective directors.

Other participants remark on the difficulty of taking action following an adverse appraisal of an individual director; usually, the matter is allowed to slide, especially if the deficient director is close to retirement, unless the problem cannot be ignored. "It is a hell of a hard job to fire a director, believe you me!", according to one of this number. But on occasion he has asked an ineffective board member to resign early to make way for someone else, and this request has customarily been agreed to.

Fixing a retirement age seems to be a means of getting rid of some sub-par directors. And if a particular director has performed well, the company always has the option of retaining him as a consultant when he reaches that age.

Effectiveness

The key ingredient in the effectiveness of a board is the chief executive officer. Everything depends upon whether he regards the board as a nuisance or as a body to which he is accountable for his stewardship of company affairs. The other ingredient in board effectiveness is the ability and dedication of outside directors. The crucial question is: Do they have the independence of mind, sophistication and willingness to do the necessary work and ask the tough questions that will enable the board in fact to supervise the management of the affairs and business of the corporation? The required independence of mind implies the disposition to employ the director's "ultimate weapon" if necessary — resignation in the event of an unresolved disagreement with management.

Most Canadian directors surveyed believe that the boards with which they are associated are by-and-large effective — more effective than the public generally believes and more effective than they were some years ago. Two reasons for improved board effectiveness: legal developments that suggest that higher standards may be used to judge directors' performance and make it easier for shareholders and others to bring suits against directors; and a general evolution in management style toward less autocratic and more participative forms.

An exception to this general rule is found in the boards of banks. Their chief defects: They are too large (some have 50 or more directors); they are enjoined by law to deal with a great many routine, even trivial, matters; and, as noted earlier, some outside directors are appointed to such boards in the expectation they can get more business for these banks. One result of these drawbacks is that much of the substantive work of a bank board is really done by its executive committee. Some bank directors note, however, that they have a valuable role in advising bank managers in their region.

Beyond the attitudes of the chief executive officer and outside directors, there are some organizational imperatives for board effectiveness:

— A board of proper size and adequate number of meetings. One Canadian director offers these guidelines:

Board Committees

Canadian study participants offer a number of insights into board committees.

Executive committees. Opinions are divided about this committee. Some directors believe it is indispensable, especially for boards that meet infrequently or that are large in size, notably bank boards. The powers of executive committees appear to vary among the companies represented in this study. Some of these committees make decisions between board meetings. Others, however, are confined to exploring issues confronting the company in greater depth than the full board can, and making recommendations to the full board. A couple of Canadian directors are adamantly opposed to executive committees, believing that they create two classes of directors — those who are members of the executive committee and those who are not.

Audit committees. Canadians universally endorse audit committees, and practically all of them express pleasure as to the functioning of the audit committees of which they are members. Most believe that the audit committee should be composed entirely of outside directors, but a minority feel that outsiders only need to form a majority, arguing that both external and internal auditors are not at all reluctant to speak their minds to audit committees on which inside directors sit.

Compensation committees. One study participant believes that while the compensation committee should, of course, assure itself that salary levels are high enough for the firm to keep good people, the committee ought to ask more questions than it does about why increases are or are not being recommended.

Management resources committee. The same executive would like to have a management resources committee of the board created. The function of this committee would be to study the technical competence of senior management.

The board should have no more than 15 members; there should be at least 10 meetings a year, with a minimum of three hours for each meeting.

— Outside directors should form a majority (but there should be insiders other than the two top officers of the company).

— An adequate body of committees. This is essential, given the complexity and pressures of running a major business today (see box).

— Provision of adequate information by management to the board.

Information. While some Canadian directors indicate that the information they receive from management in their role as outside directors — oral presentations at meetings, written material distributed between meetings, responsive answers to the questions they ask — was in the past sketchy or inadequate, almost all of the study participants declare themselves well-satisfied with the information they receive today. A few go on to observe that a seasoned director can fill in any gaps in the information provided by management simply by making inquiries, or by initiating conversations with company executives. Putting on their chief executive hats, several Canadian directors speak of the efforts they have made to give timely and complete information to their outside directors. At least one routinely asks his outside directors if they are getting enough information.

Indeed, a number of Canadian directors speak of the dangers of being inundated with information, and some refer to efforts they have made to simplify and make more digestible the written material sent to directors. The problem is that an abundance of detail about inventories, production and sales tends to overwhelm outsider directors and discourages them from grasping the significance of the figures.

All Canadian participants commenting on the point express strong disagreement with the proposal to create an independent staff for outside directors to obtain for them information they would not otherwise get. Such an organism is not needed, because directors can get all the information they want; it would add needlessly to company expense; and it would undercut management, suggesting a loss of confidence in it by the board.

There are, of course, informal sources of information on which outside directors can and do capitalize. For example, one firm regularly schedules a dinner for directors and senior executives before each board meeting. This occasion permits not only a relaxed and open exchange of views, but also encourages outside directors to approach company executives for additional facts and figures they may want.

Most of the companies which the interviewed Canadian directors serve provide written information to directors before board meetings — e.g., the agenda, reports on operations and emerging issues and problems, background memoranda on matters on which the board will vote. The chief executive of one of the few firms that does not follow this practice says that it is unnecessary because the board meets so frequently.

One director attacks the notion that no, or very limited, written information should be distributed to directors because of the risk that confidential matters would become known outside the organization. His point: If you can't trust a person to keep a confidence, then he shouldn't be on your board.

Composition of the Board

As in the United States, most publicly held Canadian-controlled corporations have a majority of outside (nonmanagement) directors on their boards. (For statistics on this point, see *Composition and Organization of the Board,* page 113.) How are these directors selected? What criteria are used? Who should serve as inside (management) directors and why? This inquiry now turns to these and related questions.

Selection of Outside Directors

As for selection criteria, of course care is taken that a prospective director would have no conflict of interest in joining the board. Then the following factors come into play.

— Diversity. Some Canadian executives place great importance on continuing, or achieving, a pattern of diversity on the board: in occupations, in places of residence, in experience and background, in ages. Yet diversity must not be gained at the cost of harmony among board members and between the board and management.

— Personal qualities. Integrity, intelligence, diligence, good reputation — *"Ça va sans dire."*

— Ability and the willingness to make a useful contribution. This includes adequate time and freedom from commitments which would interfere with service on the board for which the individual is under consideration.

— Background and experience. These terms refer severally to the individual's occupation — when some board seats become vacant an effort is made to fill them with persons of specific expertise — past achievements, breadth of experience, familiarity with the business of the company.

— Prestige is still a factor in directorial selection, in some companies and industries, notably banking. This is often defined as preeminence in one's occupation.

There is a diversity of views about three types of directors or directorial candidates: major shareholders, business executives beneath the top rank, and certain suppliers of services to the company — bankers, accountants, consultants and outside legal counsel to the board.

— The chief arguments for having major ownership interests represented on the board is that these directors manifest a keen interest in the affairs of the company. "They will always be attentive, concerned and active about the state of the business," one respondent notes. Another asserts that directors who represent major ownership interests "are not found reading their reports on the way to the meeting." The argument against electing major shareholders to the board is that they may not be objective. For example, they may urge a larger dividend than it would be prudent for the company to pay.[5]

— Should only the top one or two executives in a firm be considered as outside directors of another firm? The arguments for confining the choice to the chief executive or chief operating officer is that, as outside directors, junior executives would not speak up to senior management. It is important to have a board composed of persons who are peers, and it would be awkward to ask the third or fourth ranking officer of a company to serve on the board without also asking the first two. On the other hand, some respondents believe that board independence is enhanced if members do not all belong in the same peer or age group.

— Most Canadian respondents (like a good many of their United States counterparts) express themselves against having the company's banker, legal counsel, or other persons supplying services to the corporation on

---

[5] "Major shareholder" in this context does not mean institutional investors. As a rule, these do not wish to be represented on boards of companies in which they have holdings.

the board. The problems with such representation are that a supplier of any one of these services cannot be sufficiently independent of senior officers because his livelihood depends on them or, particularly in the case of a banker, he will probably have an inside track on business with a company.

One Canadian director makes the point that having officers of large financial institutions serving on the boards of many companies unduly concentrates economic power in their hands. (Of course if a financial institution insists as a condition of lending money to a company that it be represented on the board, the company may not be able to protest.)

In smaller companies, it is fairly widely acknowledged, there is a benefit to having the firm's legal counsel and investment banker on the board for informed advice which may not be otherwise available.

Professional Directors. The class of professional or extra-time directors — persons whose principal occupation is to serve as outside directors of several corporations but who have no management responsibility in these corporations — is not so clearly recognized or developed in Canada as in the United States. Evidently those who most nearly correspond to professional directors are venerable corporate executives who have retired from management but still belong to a number of boards.

Most Canadian study participants venturing an opinion are not in favor of transplanting the professional director in the U.S. sense across the border for these reasons:

— The high fees paid a professional director because of the extra time spent on the business will make him a "bought man," resulting in a loss of independence.

— The appointment of professional directors might well create two classes of outside directors: higher status professionals and lower status others.

— The professional director would tend to get involved in the day-to-day operations of the business.

— Lacking a management affiliation, he or she could not provide so informed guidance in matters of corporate strategy and tactics as could outside directors who are senior executives in their own companies.

The arguments *for* professional directors adduced by Canadian respondents are:

— The exposure of such individuals to various viewpoints, businesses and boards would make them very valuable to each board on which they serve.

— They could retain objectivity and independence since they do not have a management responsibility in any organization.

— They would avoid the inevitable conflicts of interest that beset inside directors.

— A professional director could do more work than an ordinary director — make more plant visits, attend more meetings, participate in more special projects, counsel with management more frequently.

Two *caveats* about professional directors voiced by Canadian study participants: "No board should have more than two, or possibly three, professional directors; the bulk of outside directors should be executives with current management responsibilities, the traditional practice." And: "The professional director can be useful only if it is clear what his role is, what he should or should not do."

One Canadian director expresses the belief that professional directors were introduced in the United States because board members in that country were nervous about lawsuits and wanted some colleagues to spend more time on directors' business for the benefit of every other board member's security. But, in his view, professional directors have sometimes interfered with management.

"New" Faces. As in the United States, new faces have been appearing in Canadian corporate boardrooms in recent years. A number of firms that traditionally have drawn from the English-speaking business, financial and legal establishment have added Francophones — French-speaking Canadians. Women and educators and — one study participant remarks — "even a few non-Christians" have been elected to the boards of some large companies.

How do Canadian directors surveyed look at these new faces and proposals for adding still newer ones — notably, drawing from the ranks of nonmanagement employees and/or union officials? A consensus view would be that it is appropriate to draw from new sources in filling outside directorships, but not at the cost of appointing to the board spokesmen for particular groups or viewpoints.

In other words, a woman, educator, consumerist, and the like can be a good director if he or she is fully qualified for the demands that the job entails and, as the law mandates, represents the interest of *all* shareholders. But such a person ought not to be on a board if he or she is there only to represent a special interest. For there must be overriding loyalty to the company and its shareholders among its officers and directors, and this would be jeopardized if a board member served a particular interest, particularly if he or she reported to those sharing that interest on board matters. In sum: "new" faces, yes; constituency representation, no. Moreover, even if a case could be made for constituency representation, a practical problem would arise for many companies: Several groups would have to be represented on these boards, which would become inordinately large.

Nonmanagement Employees: One class of "new director" not yet found on Canadian boards — the blue-collar employee or his union representative — draws considerable comment from Canadian study participants, partly because several Canadian directors have been exposed to such employees on the boards of European corporations (see box).

This interest is manifest although Canadian unions have shown little interest in pressing for employee representation on corporate boards, preferring to confine themselves to their traditional goals of bettering wages, fringe benefits, hours of work, and working conditions.

Most Canadian directors are opposed to the election of nonmanagement employees to the board, offering arguments similar to those voiced by U.S. executives. Thus:

• Board membership would pose a conflict of interest for the employee. He would be torn between his commitment to the well-being of the enterprise and his commitment to the interests of his fellow workers or his union. At the very least he would be hard put to keep privileged information obtained in the boardroom confidential.

• Disharmony would result in the boardroom, which would be deleterious to the conduct of board business and, one director maintains, "would take the heart out of management."

• The necessary profit motive might well be diluted or compromised; if it were, this would hurt the Canadian economy which functions best when, Adam Smith-like, each enterprise strives to maximize its profits.

• Neither employees nor their union representatives are qualified by experience or training to make helpful contributions to boards of directors.

• Employee or union directors have not been effective in Europe. And with their presence, management avoids bringing to the board matters that it properly should.

One Canadian director suggests that it would be appropriate to have on his board a nonmanagement employee from *another and noncompetitive* company.

Other "New" Faces: Two other groups were singled out by the Canadian participants in discussions of "new" faces in the boardroom: women and consumers.

Consumers. A pair of contradictory comments: "They need not be on the board because their interests are met through legislation"; and "Consumers ought to be represented on boards of companies in certain industries."

Women. A typical opinion: "When their knowledge, experience or other qualifications are appropriate, there should be no question about their eligibility." A few directors, who are sympathetic to the idea of women serving as directors, say that if a board should have women among its members, there ought to be at least two. This would tend, in their opinion, to reduce (if not remove) any preoccupation of a sole woman director with the problems and interests of the members of her sex and would overcome the loneliness or "unease" she might feel in an otherwise all-male group. (Unfortunately, none of the Canadians interviewed were women, so this proposition could not be suitably tested.)

But if women seem to be acceptable as directorial material to most of those interviewed, this does not mean that they will soon proliferate in Canadian boardrooms. One director notes that at least one board with which he is associated has "blinkers on about women." Another has found it hard to get his boards interested in appointing women directors. "The process takes time. When the issue is first raised, the usual reaction is, 'interesting but not now.' Later the matter is discussed and then the usual reaction is that the person should be qualified, not a token appointee, which results in further delay. Next the reaction is that a woman would be lonely and perhaps the outside world would look at her as a token appointment. Still later their reaction is that it is tough to find a qualified woman director and very tough to find two."

Consequences – and a Difficulty: Accepting the likelihood and desirability of more "new" faces in Canadian boardrooms, one director foresees certain consequences – and a difficulty:

"Opening up boards to new groups is probably going to happen and will probably be worthwhile. Consumers, union officials, and persons with non-business or nonbusiness-related backgrounds can provide an input that would be useful. Had there been more on the board at General Motors, perhaps Nader-type questions might have been asked earlier. But with new faces on the board (1) there will be longer and more frequent meetings, and (2) therefore, directors will have to be persons who can afford to spend much time, and (3) probably will have to be paid better. And who is to select the representatives of these groups justly?"

Inside Directors

Most of the Canadian respondents commenting on the point believe that it is appropriate and desirable for companies to have inside directors, in addition to the top two officers of the firm, but that insiders should constitute a small minority of the total board.

Why, in view of the widely acknowledged ambiguous, not to say contradictory, position of the inside director – as director he is passing judgment on the person who is his boss outside the boardroom – do Canadian participants find value in inside directors?

— It is beneficial to outside directors. By observing the insiders in action, so to speak, they can evaluate these individuals in line with their responsibility for senior management selection and appraisal. Moreover, outsiders gain a broader, more diverse view of the company and its affairs by having several insiders rather than just the chief executive and chief operating officer report and comment at board meetings. In this connection, it is maintained that this purpose would not be so well served if insiders reported merely in their capacities as senior officers, since their words would not carry so much weight.

— It helps the chief executive who feels he cannot present all issues accurately to the outside directors or answer their questions fully.

— From the insiders' point of view, there are several benefits from board service: education gained through being exposed to the experiences and views of outside directors and the give-and-take of board meetings, and development as they have to put forward and defend their positions. A third benefit, in which the organization does not share of course, is the prestige attendant upon board service.

As some respondents point out, insiders never vote against the chief executive at a board meeting.[6] But they can, and do, debate with him beforehand.

[6]It is well to recall that some chief executives will not call for a vote of the board until they are certain that everyone on the board, outsiders and insiders, will endorse their recommendations.

Retirement and Resignation

According to a recent study made by The Conference Board in Canada, *Canadian Directorship Practices: A Profile,* most major Canadian corporations have a compulsory retirement age for both outside and inside directors. Insiders generally retire at the normal age for employees — most commonly 65 in manufacturing companies, 70 in nonmanufacturing — with, often, an exception made for the chief executive. As for outside directors, the most common retirement age is 70 in manufacturing companies and 71 in nonmanufacturing companies.

Most Canadian contributors to the present study believe that a compulsory retirement age is desirable, although some would like to see a younger age — others an older age — than is now specified by their respective companies. One director makes the point that while a compulsory retirement age can eliminate the problem of no-longer-effective directors, it can also deprive the board of some "very expert advice." An alternative, of course, is to appoint a superior director a consultant to the company when he reaches retirement age.

What about the situation in which an outside director retires from his principal occupation? Should the retirement policy stipulate that he must automatically leave the board? No, because the circumstances should govern; that would be a consensus view. Such a person can appropriately continue on a board if he is still in touch with the business environment, but, in the words of one director: "If one just retires and goes to Florida and comes back for board meetings, this is not to the benefit of the company."

Two directors look askance at permitting a retired chief executive to stay on his company's board, because he may well exert undue influence upon, or cause unwarranted trouble for, his successor. As one of them puts it, the retired chief executive "is neither fish nor fowl. He still has a relationship with management but is not part of it, and often gets into the new management's hair."

Suppose an outside director is well below retirement age for that board but *changes* his principal occupation. Should there be an understanding that he should resign as a matter of course? Perhaps he should offer his resignation, but again the circumstances should be the predominant factor in determining whether to accept the resignation. If, in his new occupation, it seems likely he can continue to contribute as a director, he should be kept on. But if he has been fired from his previous post, the shareholders of the firm he serves as an outside director might well lose confidence in him.

As for honorary directors — directors who have given up their active role on the board because of reaching retirement age but whom a company wishes to recognize for past services — one Canadian chief executive says that their election represents "a silly and archaic practice." Although his company has some, they are not paid and do not attend meetings, and if he has his way no more will ever be appointed.

Why Serve as an Outside Director?

The surveyed Canadian directors give virtually the same reasons for accepting outside directorships as their U.S. counterparts. Most frequently mentioned is the educational and informational benefits gained from such service: It is interesting and useful to learn about the issues and problems confronting other industries and how the meetings of other boards are conducted; and because the CEO is isolated in his own corporation — he can't get cozy with his own employees and still do his job well — outside board service is essential to enlarge one's perspective about business and the society in which it functions (this broadening benefit, one director avers, is especially manifest on boards of Canadian subsidiaries of foreign parent corporations); and outside board service helps to keep managerial skills honed, improving the CEO's ability to do his own job.

Other motives given by Canadian directors for accepting outside directorships are:

Noblesse oblige — It is, quite properly, expected of leaders in industry, finance and the professions to serve on boards of large corporations.

Quid pro quo — Chief executives who want to have competent, dedicated individuals as outside directors on their boards recognize the concomitant obligation to accept invitations for membership on boards of other concerns.

Satisfaction — One can gain considerable psychic income from contributions made as an outside director.

Prestige — Membership on the board of a prominent corporation inevitably confers a measure of prestige. Other manifestations of prestige include the power the office has and the opportunity to come to know influential fellow directors intimately.

Compensation draws mixed notices as a motive for service as an outside director. Some directors believe that, as one of them puts it: "The pay is good." But others think that the pay is not sufficient to compensate for the amount of responsibility and time involved. (One director, a chief executive, wonders whether, since his times getting adequate information; inadequate meeting preparation by, and the stubbornness of, certain follow directors.

Criteria for Accepting Outside Directorships. The principal criteria Canadian directors have worked out for responding to invitations to serve as outside directors are similar to those of U.S. executives:

— Enough time to do a thorough job on the new board. Among the factors to be considered are the frequency and length of meetings and where they are held.

— The reputation of the company and its management. Beyond meeting the obvious test of integrity and ability, management must give evidence that it wants and expects a truly independent board.

— The relevance of the board to one's own company.

— The relevance of the other company to one's interest and talents. The cognate question is: Can I make a contribution?

— The adequacy of compensation and benefits extended to outside directors.

There are some negative tests as well. The director must be assured that:

— There is no conflict of interest.

— There are not two "classes" of directors — "super directors and ordinary ones," as one Canadian phrases it.

— There are no problems with sensitive payments, either domestically or abroad.

— One is not being asked because of his name.

Only one Canadian study contributor explicitly mentions that outside directors be a majority, and none mention the existence of an audit committee, as tests for serving on outside boards. Each is a sine qua non for many U.S. directors in agreeing to such service.

Restrictions on Board Service

In Canada, as in the United States, there is no legal restriction on the number of outside directorships an individual can hold. But what is a reasonable limit for someone other than a retired person or professional director? Canadian study participants offer a broad range: two to twelve.

Whatever a chief executive's preference within this range, how does he regard service on outside boards by his subordinates? Most Canadian executives impose restrictions. For instance:

service as an outside director is on his own company's time, he should turn over his outside director's fees to that company. This, however, is an unusual, not to say an heretical, opinion.)

The Canadian directors surveyed are virtually unanimous in reporting that their outside directorships have met their expectations, although a few note that more work has been involved than anticipated and some boards are engaged in more trivia than they had foreseen. But directorial service is not without its frustrations. Some examples: It takes more time to bring about change than is desirable; the difficulty of some-

— One tends to be "very restrictive" but is more lenient as a colleague nears retirement.

— A second insists that he give prior approval (and he himself gets approval of his own board before accepting a new directorship).

— A third will permit his subordinates to serve on other boards only if it will enhance his company's image.

— Several want to be assured that such service will not be excessively time-consuming.

An exception to this general posture is sometimes made for bank boards. Here some chief executives say they are more lenient because such service is "such a good window," as one of them phrases it.

Legislation Affecting the Board

Of the various government laws and regulations affecting the board of directors, the federal and several provincial requirements that resident Canadians be a majority of corporate boards of companies whose securities are publicly traded draw the most comment from Canadian contributors to this study. Opinions about this legislation are quite diverse, although a majority seem to favor it — at least in principle.

According to one director, the requirements can lead to problems for large Canada-based MNC's that like to elect to their boards persons from the countries in which they operate. To achieve the Canadian representation called for might make such boards too large, and thus unwieldy. Furthermore, it is distasteful to imply, as the requirements do, that non-Canadians will not take Canadian interests to heart.

Canadian directors, a second director insists, do represent the Canadian point of view and it is a good idea to require them on boards of Canadian subsidiaries of foreign parents. A third adduces a specific benefit of the requirements. An insurance company which he serves as director is owned by a European concern. When that concern bought the company the European owners wanted to introduce management concepts indigenous to their own country. The Canadian directors recommended against it, saying these concepts could not be applied in Canada, and the parent company did not press the point. More generally, he maintains that it is in a foreign parent company's own interest to allow independence to a subsidiary in Canada, which the Canadian-board-majority rule fosters. "How can a decision be made in London about what to do in Calgary?"

Several directors think that the requirements will have no real effect because it will always be possible for a foreign parent determined to exercise close control over its Canadian subsidiary to find "cooperative" Canadians to put on the board of the subsidiary. On the other hand, if a foreign parent wants effective independent directors for its Canadian subsidiary, their nationality is irrelevant.

If there is support by most Canadian directors for legislation calling for a Canadian majority on the boards of publicly held companies, that does not mean that they are sanguine about leglislation that would specify other appointments to the board. Specifically, several would vehemently object to a law requiring a non-management employee or representatives of other special interest groups to serve on corporate boards.

Audit committees have recently been made mandatory in certain jurisdictions for Canadian companies whose securities are publicly traded. The Canadian directors who volunteer opinions endorse this requirement, although one points out that a great many companies had audit committees before their existence was legally required.

Securities laws evoke divided opinions. One director, for instance, says: "It would be useful to require higher levels of professionalism in this country — for example, rules could be tougher and more open regarding the reporting of salaries of senior executives." By contrast another director, while conceding that there is room for improvement in the Ontario Securities Commission and that a federal securities regulatory body might be desirable, believes that the Securities and Exchange Commission of the United States is "the originator of a great many things Canadians should not copy."

Two Canadians make more general observations about legislation affecting boards of directors. One finds it ironic that the federal government has pressed for new laws when, in his opinion, both government agencies and crown corporations are pronounced laggards — their boards "historically have been dummies," simply rubber stamping government policies, reporting precious little, and making no attempt to keep the public well-informed about their agencies' or corporations' activities. "Government should clean up its own boards first and set the pace for the rest of the community instead of lagging behind," he urges. The second director adverts to perhaps the most basic legal issue affecting the board of directors: He can't envision "any board of directors managing a company," and believes that the de facto situation should be recognized by a change in the law.

Liability

Recent legislation in a number of jurisdictions permitting derivative suits or class actions against directors for neglect of their duty of care, plus awareness of such suits or actions mounted in the United States, have raised the question of the director's liability to a new level of interest and concern in Canada. Here are the principal reactions of Canadian study participants to this legislation and to their liability as directors:

Distaste for class-action suits is expressed by several, on a variety of grounds. Such suits are basically unfair, encouraging "morning after" quarterbacking, that is, "looking back at decisions in the light of the passage of time," in the words of one director. And another complains: "The colossal expense and time that would be taken for a few aggrieved shareholders would be unfair to other shareholders and employees." Class actions, moreover, would vitiate the effectiveness of the board because to avoid them directors may well fail to sanction normal business risk taking. Still another director thinks that while it may be proper for a stockholder convinced of management or directorial neglect to sue the parties he deems responsible, it is deplorable to permit an individual to bring an action "on behalf of a class of persons. The class itself should have to be involved." A fourth dismisses class actions as "mainly a way for lawyers to make money."

Unlike the situation in the United States, lawyers in Canada cannot take contingency fees — that is, bill a client for a percentage of the sum awarded in a successful suit, while receiving no payment if the suit is unsuccessful. For class actions, this is as it should be, in the view of several Canadian directors. With contingency fees, not only would class actions be encouraged by unscrupulous lawyers, but also shareholders would encounter no financial risk in suing directors. On the other hand, at least one director believes that shareholders ought, as a matter of protection, to have the right to bring suit against directors; but in the absence of contingency fees for lawyers, this right would be academic because of the impossibility for most shareholders of paying the inevitably large fees based on a lawyer's time.

Two benefits are perceived in the otherwise gloomy specter of class actions: If U.S. experience is a reliable guide, directors will do their homework more completely, and do a better job of monitoring how management is running the company.

Risk. With varying degrees of certitude, six directors think that there is now a greater risk in serving as a director than there used to be. One of these, however, sees a silver lining in this greater risk: What a director's liability entails has been clarified by the new statutes.

Two respondents believe that, as always, there is little or no risk in serving on the boards of well-managed companies. One, though, says that it is because he is "an activist and not negligent" that he feels risk free.

Three believe that there has been no change in the degree of risk a director faces; and two have no feeling for whether or not risk has increased, one pointing out that no cases have occurred yet in Canada.

Greater difficulty in recruiting directors? There is almost an even division of opinion as to whether it is harder to recruit directors as a result of possibly greater liability than there used to be. According to one director, though the possibility of class actions "hasn't had an impact on the recruitment of directors yet, many persons are increasingly uneasy and are thinking twice before accepting invitations to join boards." He adds: "The more there are of such risks, the more the compensation for directors should be."

D and O Insurance. Unlike the situation in the United States, where most publicly held corporations provide not only indemnification but directors' and officers' insurance against lawsuits brought against management and directors, a good many Canadian companies have not done this. In one director's view, liability insurance will become more necessary because, whereas the standard for judgment for directors is still that of prudent men, more people will be "muddling in the affairs of the company and this will perhaps expose errors of judgment and lead to derivative suits. The expense of defending oneself is beyond the individual's capability and therefore insurance will be essential," he asserts.

A second director is dubious about the real protection afforded by D and O insurance, given "the increased willingness to sue"; in fact, he says, in many cases such insurance "is an open temptation to sue." Similarly a third director maintains that most liability insurance does not cover what one would want it to cover, and asserts that it is very hard to get anyway.

Changes, Both Recent and Anticipated

At the outset of this discussion it was noted that Canadian participants in this study have perceived three principal changes in directorship practices in their country: The board is playing a more substantative role than it used to; it is, properly, more independent of management than it used to be; and board service is more demanding than formerly.

What other changes have flowed from these three? What changes are likely to take place as a consequence in the future? Here is what the Canadian participants see and foresee:

— There is a new climate in the boardroom. Boards are more open than they used to be. Negative votes have been recorded, which, incidentally, has been a traumatic experience for many older board members. Nowadays it is acceptable to criticize management at a board or committee meeting, whereas formerly hard questions were put to management only in private. The result is that management can less easily hoodwink the board.

— The greater work load for directors — "the burden on boards of directors has increased two- or threefold since the war," one study contributor maintains — has had a number of consequences. The depth and scope of director's activities have been enlarged. Directors are drawn more deeply into planning; they have to confront and react to more government regulations; and they must take into account — indeed meet with — more groups on whom the corporation impinges. In terms of work routine, there are more meetings and each meeting calls for greater preparation.

— Concern about liability is much more widespread, in part because of the recently enacted legislation permitting shareholder class action suits.

— Because of the heavier burden on directors and because of greater concern about liability, it is becoming more difficult to recruit able directors — at least from the traditional sources of business, finance and the law. One result may be greater reliance on professional or extra-time directors.

— The performance of directors has improved. They are more conscientious; they do their homework more thoroughly; they challenge management more frequently. This is not to say, however, that excellence is a universal or even dominant hallmark of directors. The comment of a Canadian bank director is illustrative. "Eight years ago about five members out of 45 on this board could contribute; now about 15 out of 50 can." But, he continues, this trend should continue.

— A few respondents expect that there will be found more and more nonmanagement board chairmen who will play dominant roles in establishing guidelines for the functioning of the board as well as conducting its affairs. This should enhance not only the independence of the board, but also its efficiency, because adroit management of the board and its work requires a not inconsiderable investment of time and talent and, as one director puts it, "Organizing and chairing meetings is a very much neglected art."

— Companies in general and, some Canadian participants assert, banks in particular will get new types of directors: younger persons, women, representatives of occupations or interests (e.g., consumers) not commonly seen in boardrooms up to now. This will transpire in part because of the growing reluctance, stemming from the heavier workload and concern over liability, of business executives, financiers and attorneys who already serve as directors. It will transpire in part because of pressures exerted by society upon business. But the opening up of the boardroom to new faces will be done primarily for selfish reasons: because in the end it will be beneficial to corporations. The image that the board presents to the public is important, and enlarging the sources of directors will improve that image (this is why new faces have appeared in the boardrooms of the United States, one Canadian director observes). Also, the narrow occupational pool from which directors have traditionally been drawn means that management is too self-assured and the board is not so independent and effective as it should be.

— Finally, boards ought to become even more independent of management. This means, among other things, that there should be far less reciprocity in the selection of directors. In the striking phrase of one participant: "If I sit on your board you *can't* sit on mine" should be the rule.

Chapter 10
Venezuela

The Venezuelan Context

Government Control of and Involvement in Business

Venezuela is constitutionally a federal republic but in practice the states, while having extensive executive powers, have no power to legislate in regard to business other than by levying local taxes. All general laws applying to business are enacted by the federal legislature.

On the other hand, individual states provide financial inducement to suitable businesses to locate within a particular state in addition to the inducements provided by the central government. They also frequently engage in partnership with private investors to encourage industrial development, particularly where there is the prospect of considerable employment.

The federal government is not only a major investor (accounting in 1975 for slightly more than a third of gross fixed investment) but also plays a predominant role in industry. In the first place, there is a government planning agency, Cordiplan, which has recently become a direct arm of the Presidency, where formerly it had considerably more autonomy. The form of planning is basically indicative; that is to say, the broad lines and general targets for the development of the country are laid down for a five-year period. In the case of major projects, these are made much more specific by detailed regulations. The country is now in

The preparation of the context material and the gathering of the information on which the remainder of the chapter is based were done by Mr. Avison Wormald of the consulting firm of Lansberg, Wormald y Asociados in Caracas.

its fifth five-year planning period. The extent to which any particular government intervenes in industrial matters depends much more on its political color than in the United States. However, there seems to be some degree of consensus between the two main political parties, and Cordiplan has functioned satisfactorily with both.

The federal government has recently nationalized the oil and iron mining industries, formerly controlled by foreign companies, but it has a much longer tradition of direct investment in key sectors such as electric power, iron and steel, aluminum and communications. Involvement of government in business stems from several different causes, the most important being that, since the revenue of the country depends so largely on the oil industry, the government has the major part of investment funds at its disposal. While part of these are returned to private investments in the form of capital grants and incentives of various kinds and taxation in practice tends to be very low, nevertheless at the present time the government is the only source of capital for very large projects, particularly in the absence (until very recently) of an effective stock market. A number of the projects in which the government engages are in any case of such magnitude and long-term nature that it would probably be difficult for them to be financed, in the initial stages at least, through private financial channels. There is no fixed line between the private sector and the public sector, and mixed companies — either between the government and foreign interests or the government and private Venezuelan interests — are fairly numerous.

Apart from its role as the largest industrial investor, the federal government regulates a number of sectors of the economy fairly closely. The most important of these are banking and insurance, which have specific laws applying to them and are generally considered to be rather strictly controlled through the respective Superintendencias. There has recently also been established a Superintendencia of Foreign Investment in accordance with Decision 24 of the Pacto Andino, and this has a complex set of rules applying to all foreign investments in Venezuela, whether already sustained or proposed. Private business is also regulated through various forms of price controls and levies for such purposes as the encouragement of training of workers and research and development.

While the stock market has not been an important source of capital in the past, it is the government's intention to increase its role in the financing of business. Its activities are controlled by the Investment Law and by the Comision de Valores which regulates the stock market on a day-to-day basis. Since it has recently become evident that the oil and mineral revenues are not going to be sufficient to finance the many major industrial projects approved, it is likely that the role of private investment in industry may increase considerably, and there is an evident desire on the part of the authorities to increase savings and investment. One form which this encouragement has taken recently is the activation of SAICA, a form of company which has no nominal capital and in which at least 50 percent of the capital must be in the hands of a substantial number of shareholders. This form of company, which has recently obtained exceptionally favorable tax status, represents an attempt to persuade large private companies to encourage investments by more people, instead of having their shares held by a relatively few large investors. It should be noted that, on the whole, the Venezuelan investor tends to be very conservative, and shows a strong preference for highly liquid investment or for property.

The Position of Boards of Directors and Individual Directors

The state corporations have boards of directors and many distinguished business figures serve on them. In this respect, however, they are considered to be public servants and are consequently not affected by the general laws regarding the position of director. Private business activities are conducted mainly through corporations probably for two main reasons: (1) to obtain the benefits of limited liability, and (2) to provide a vehicle for the association of different groups of shareholders. In the most important industrial group of

the country, the majority of the companies have either foreign shareholders or outside shareholders, that is to say shareholdings not controlled by the major partner.

There are a number of different forms of corporation. In practice, for any substantial operations, there are only two: The SAICA, already mentioned, and the more prevalent Sociedad Anonima, or limited company.

With the exception of particular sectors, chiefly banking and insurance, the requirements of the law in regard to limited companies are surprisingly few. They have to be inscribed in the *Registro Mercantil* and *should* have a board of directors and *should* submit balance sheets and accounts annually — but in practice there seem to be no stringent requirements in this respect. The requirements become more stringent if a company wishes to raise money on the stock market, when it then becomes subject to the Ley de Mercade de Capitales and the executive regulation of the Comision de Valores (already mentioned).

The duties of directors of limited companies are laid down in very general terms in the Codigo de Comercio, and, in theory, directors could be prosecuted under the provisions of the Codigo. They are, of course, also subject to the ordinary penal laws of the country, particularly with respect to theft or malversation. In practice, these regulations are ineffective except in the case of extremely serious matters which might become public knowledge.

The pattern of wide shareholding ownership is not common in Venezuela. There are only a few private corporations which have a large number of shareholders, particularly the Electricidad de Caracas and its associated holding company, Tacoa. In general, corporations are owned by individuals, groups of individuals, or a number of associated financial groups, possibly with participation from investment companies which are themselves owned by the banks. The question of absentee shareholders, therefore, does not really exist, although undoubtedly it will as more companies sell shares on the stock market. The position of public corporations is, of course, quite different and the tendency has been for these to have a strong representation of whatever political party is in power, but there has also been an increasing trend toward the more or less permanent appointment of managing directors. There are a certain number of highly competent, nonpolitical figures who are much in demand on both public and private boards.

The growing importance of institutional investment should be noted. Since all public and private bodies have to have pension funds and there are also requirements in regard to termination payments, the amount of institutional funds of this kind outside the insurance companies and banks is becoming very large. This source of funds is regulated by a special law, the Ley Nacional de Cooperativas, which lays down in detail the requirements for the administration of these pension funds, the duties of directors, and the composition of the board.

Again, in theory, the nomination of directors of limited companies is subject to general meetings of shareholders, but as in other countries these exist only in theory as regulatory forces; in practice, the great majority of corporations are dominated by single owners or by groups of owners who also dominate the boards of the companies. In practice, therefore, the dismissal of directors is relatively easy unless they happen to be substantial shareholders. Then, obviously, there can be power struggles between different financial groups. Also in practice, there are some executive directors (managers) on boards who are not substantial shareholders, and their removal is also relatively easy if the board is dominated by one financial group. The fact that high-grade executives are extremely rare, however, gives some of them considerable effective power, even though they may not have a substantial shareholding.

As is well known, the checks on directors in more advanced countries, which stem from legal requirements as to auditing, are not entirely effective in the event of major inefficiency or fraud, and they are still less so in Venezuela. It is generally considered also that the rights of minority shareholders are not adequately protected either as regards the information which they receive or the power to influence the conduct of the company.

It may be asked to what extent, therefore, the boards of directors are effective — or even important — organs in the structure of corporate administration. Obviously, the answer varies from case to case, the dominant factor being the ownership representation on the board. If the board primarily represents capital, that is to say without experience of the particular industry involved, the general view is that the board is ineffective as a method of influencing the policy or administration of the company. Where the board represents capital allied to the knowledge of the business — a rare case in Venezuela — then the board may be effective. The general view is that the control of the company is effectively located with the executive management as its members are the only ones who have sufficient information about the business, or, indeed, who are competent to determine its efficiency.

The effects of this situation can be very serious. Ownership control of the board without sufficient knowledge of the business is mitigated in Venezuela by the lack of competition in many industries and the oligopolistic structure of industry. In other words, the shortcomings of boards of directors do not lead to the number of business failures which would be almost inevitable in more competitive economies. All this, however, is undoubtedly changing and there is a perceptible move toward bringing about a more effective management of businesses. The stimulation of competition by the government through a wide variety of assistance to prospective entrepreneurs is likely to make it rapidly more necessary for boards to become more effective policymaking and control instruments.

The Capital Market Law

The National Securities Commission set up under this law has broad powers regarding the offering of securities and attendant publicity issued by their sellers. Also it governs the form and content of financial statements and other measures necessary to protect the interest of investors. Audited financial statements for at least five years are required as a condition for permission to issue stock to the public, together with information regarding the directors, objectives and statutes of the company. Some protection is accorded to minority stockholders and organizations of bondholders are specifically mentioned.

The Securities Commission is still regarded as experimental, and modifications are being introduced as and when required. The general effect has not been dramatic in the increase of public issues until very recently when several important corporations have converted their companies into SAICA's, presumably in order to obtain the advantages of tax remissions. It may be expected that the specific obligations laid on directors will be tightened up with the development of the stock market.

Management-Labor Relations and Unionization

The trade union movement is fairly strong in Venezuela, and there is an overall organization called the Confederation of Venezuelan Workers (CTV) which embraces the majority of the trade unions of the country. (By one estimate, about a third of Venezuela's workers are unionized.) There are also very strong professional associations of journalists, economists, engineers, and so on, that act as pressure groups in order to secure advantages for their organizations (such as making it difficult for nonmembers to practice in their fields). Employers are grouped into an organization called FEDECAMARAS, which holds a large annual convention at which matters of public interest are discussed. The organization makes representations, publicly or directly to the President, at frequent intervals. FEDECAMARAS is officially recognized as the mouthpiece of private industry but there is also an important pressure group called PRO-Venezuela, which is listened to with some attention. These bodies, of course, by no means comprise all the industrialists of the country.

Unions are represented by law on the boards of all public corporations. In some cases, such as the national airline, the contribution of the union representative is said to have been very positive. There is no requirement as regards union representation on the boards of private corporations, and no great pressure for this at the present time. The question of two-tier boards has not been an issue of concern up to the present.

Labor legislation, however, is complex and demanding and employees are protected by requirements on such matters as the termination of service, participation in profits, and other measures. There are fairly frequent strikes, but it is quite common for the government to intervene in these and to call both sides together and negotiate or impose a settlement. It is not infrequent for the President himself to exert his authority in matters of wide public concern. Collective contracts between unions and management are quite common although there are no legal requirements in this respect. It is rather likely that this practice may be generalized in the fairly near future.

As might be expected in a country with a shortage of skills of every kind, it has been thought necessary to enact legislation reserving 75 percent of all jobs for Venezuelans, and it is very common to see the stipulation that an employee must be Venezuelan, as many firms have exceeded their quota of non-Venezuelans. These may be Colombians — who constitute an important percentage of the population — or other South American nationalities, particularly Chileans and Argentinians — and Southern Europeans. Certain disabilities are laid on foreigners employed by Venezuelan business; one is that they cannot be members of boards of directors.

Some private enterprises have shown an excellent example in social aspects of their operations by providing housing, health benefits, and so on; and in many respects the best private companies show greater concern for the worker than many of the state organizations. Mention may also be made of the movement called "Dividendo Voluntario para la Comunidad," which groups together employers who undertake to devote a percentage of their profits to social work for the community.

Current Concerns

Today in Venezuela the problems of boards of directors and individual directors are very different from those of the more industrialized countries. Because of the enormous oil income on the one hand and the strength of the government on the other, the general direction of the economy is not a subject of great concern to the average director. He sees the encroachment of the state in many directions on business and industry, but he knows he is virtually powerless to influence this and that it is only likely to be influenced either by a reduction in the financial strength of the government relative to its planned projects, or, alternatively, a change of government to one more inclined to leave matters to private business.

The major concerns of Venezuelan directors are:

(1) The knowledge of, and if necessary, the compliance with the enormous volume of legislation pouring from Congress which at least concerns directors, even if it does not directly affect them. Such legislation is in the fields of taxation, regulation of industry in matters such as the numbers of staff to be trained, amounts to be spent on technical research, and so on.

(2) The difficulty in obtaining and retaining qualified staff, which is also related to the soaring costs of executive personnel and better qualified labor.

(3) The widespread incidence of dishonesty amongst employees.

(4) Detailed government regulations in the areas of banking and insurance and of foreign investment.

(5) The increasing complexity of business and the necessity to give more authority and power to professional managers, which is a source of potential conflict with the hitherto dominant owner-management. The reorganization of business to take account of its increasing size and complexity, in particular the problems of transition from owner domination to professional independent management, has not been satisfactorily solved in many cases. Techniques such as budgeting and planning, which have become virtually universal in advanced countries, are still almost nonexistent so that many businesses, in fact, are virtually out of the control of the owners and continue to function only because of the lack of effective competition. Many boards are very conscious of this and are dealing with the matter with a sense of urgency.

Composition and Organization of the Board

Seventeen Venezuelan companies have contributed information about the composition and organization of their boards. Two of these firms are manufacturers; the other fifteen are engaged in banking and finance, insurance, communication, distribution, computer software, and technological advising. All seventeen are owned, either entirely or for the most part, by private investors or other private companies.

The number of shareholders of these firms ranges from 1 to 700, with the average 79 and the median only 6. The corresponding figures for number of employees are: range, 5-1900; average, 272; median, 80.

Table 10-1 presents basic quantitative data about these boards. Other salient characteristics with respect to their composition and organization are:

— On each of two boards the inside directors include one nonmanagement employee (but not a union representative), and on each of two other boards the employee directors include retired executives. Women are represented on four boards; they hold two seats on each of two boards and one seat on each of two others.

— By far the most popular business and professional category from which the ranks of nonmanagement directors are filled is principal owner or shareholder of the company, or agents of same. Other occupational categories from which directors are commonly drawn are, in order of incidence: banking and finance; independent businessmen and consultants; manufacturing company executives; merchandising and trading company executives; and attorneys.

— Virtually all the directors are chosen by shareholders. The only exception is a financial institution in which the government has chosen one of the six directors.

— Only five companies report that outside directors are required to own stock in the companies they serve in this capacity. The number of shares required is minimal in each case.

— The average age of board members, company by company, ranges from 30 to 60. The median figure in the range is 48 years.

— Compulsory retirement ages for outside directors are exceptional. Only two companies have fixed them, at ages 65 and 60, respectively. This is a practice which some Venezuelans would like to see become more common. On the other hand, just two companies permit employee directors to retain their board seats after they have retired from their management posts.

Table 10-1: Key Statistics of Venezuelan Boards

	Range	Average	Median
Number of board members	3—18	7	7
Number of outside directors	0—16	5	4
Number of employee directors	1— 5	2	2
Number of regular meetings per year	3—52	14	12
Term of office (years)	1— 5	2	2

Board committees evidently are very rare in Venezuela. Only five of the participating firms have them: One board has created four committees; a second, two committees; and three others each have a single committee. (See next major section for views of some Venezuelan directors who would like to see more widespread use of board committees.)

The Board Today and Tomorrow: Perspectives from Venezuela

Eighteen Venezuelan executives and directors — all but one of these speaking for the companies whose practices are described in "Composition and Organization of the Board" — contributed to this study by completing a lengthy questionnaire. Of these individuals, 16 serve as outside directors — that is, directors of firms other than those that they own outright or that employ them, or subsidiaries of those firms. The number of outside directorships these 16 individuals hold ranges from 2 to 11, with 6 the median.

Seven of these study participants are each board chairmen of at least one company they serve as outside director. Finally, five are outside directors of corporations under substantial or complete government ownership or control: one corporation apiece for four of these and two for a fifth.

Role of the Board

It is the interest of shareholders that the outside director must represent, according to an overwhelming majority of the Venezuelan study contributors. But there are other groups whose interests must be kept in mind: the company's, in terms of perpetuation; the community and the country's; the employees'; consumers' — and even the interest of the board itself.

In meeting their obligations to shareholders and other groups, the Venezuelan directors participating in this study define the primary functions of the board of directors in very much the same way as do directors of other countries surveyed. Thus there are frequent mentions of policy determination and planning; oversight – of the interests of the shareholders, of management performance, of major decisions such as mergers and acquisitions, important borrowing, and sale of assets, of the execution of policy and plans; and the election, appraisal and, as needed, dismissal of senior management, particularly the chief executive officer. There are also some references to helping the company through one's personal or business influence.

A few Venezuelan directors see the board as having a role to play in assisting management in understanding and coping with social and political factors that affect the company. One of these executives says the board should be "a place where the situation can be discussed as regards the environment in which the business is located, where the external impact of the business can be evaluated, where the political and economic pulse of the business can be taken." Another thinks the board must "establish the policy that deals with the institutional relations of the company: government, political parties, public opinion organs, and so on." To a third this responsibility has an internal as well as an external facet. In his opinion, the board has a mission "to investigate or have investigated ways in which the company can set up participative policy that would improve human relations within the company and at the same time promote its development by the improvement of productivity and consolidation of its position in a country where there is an economic and participative democracy."

Several respondents emphasize a harmonizing role for the board. It should reconcile the interests of the several groups that are affected by the activities of the company – shareholders, workers, the community, financiers – and it should "coordinate the company's operations in a way compatible with its objectives and plans, as well as with the legal structure."

Decisions Boards Should Make or Approve

The most common type of decision Venezuelan respondents insist boards ought to make or approve is in the realm of finance: major loans and credits, investments, budgets and dividends. Eleven out of eighteen respondents mention this kind of decision.

Next in frequency of mention are: the appointment of senior executives (eight mentions); policy formation or approval (seven mentions); monitoring of management performance, of possible conflicts of interest, of company programs, of the achievement of objectives and strategies, of the budget (six mentions each); the

definition of objectives and strategies (five mentions).

Less frequently cited decisions the board must make or approve are:

- Decisions affecting profitability or ensuring adequate returns to shareholders;
- Decisions affecting company image;
- Decisions "authorizing expansion or contraction";
- Labor questions;
- Selection of outside auditors;
- Sales policies, including pricing;
- Selection of major suppliers;
- Senior management salaries;
- Decisions about what powers ought to be delegated to management;
- Reconciliation of interests of those affected by the company.

Decisions about labor relations, sales matters, and selection of suppliers would in most other countries participating in this survey fall clearly within the domain of management responsibility. That boards in Venezuela – and Turkey, to give another example – become involved in managerial decisions may stem from the common presence of major shareholders on boards in those countries, some of them senior company managers as well.

Effectiveness of the Board

Only four Venezuelans surveyed believe that the effectiveness of boards in carrying out their functions is satisfactory, or better. Three other respondents believe that boards are satisfactorily effective under certain conditions; for example: "with a homogeneous team, with unity of command, discipline and unity of doctrine"; "if individual members are competent and dedicate the necessary time to do their homework." For one executive, board effectiveness also depends heavily on individual participation, including "continuity of meetings, relationships with management, and knowledge of the business."

Another Venezuelan thinks that board effectiveness covers the full spectrum, varying "from virtually nil to highly effective." Still another grades the board according to its various functions: "... 35 percent effective for establishing policies and approval of major matters such as sales of assets, major credits, and mergers and acquisitions; 60 percent effective for electing and dismissing the chief executive; and 80 percent effective for providing environmental information to the executives and representing the company."

Appraising the Board As a Whole...

A majority of the Venezuelan contributors to the study believe that in one way or another it is the shareholders, or major shareholders or, in one case, the chairman who is *the* major shareholder, who appraise the performance of the board. But in the opinion of some, the board is appraised partly or entirely by management.

What standards are used for appraisal? Profit, variously described, is the strong favorite. Several respondents also refer to the correctness or coherence of decisions.

Other standards of performance cited are more subjective: for example, confidence, character, politeness; accord with bylaws and real practical interests; effectiveness, vision, suitability of measures taken.

Two respondents are very skeptical about whether the board as a whole is, in fact, appraised. According to one of them: "It is not easy to establish a routine and systematic procedure for evaluation."

... And the Individual Director

How is the individual director's performance appraised, as distinguished from that of the full board? In terms of who does the appraising, most Venezuelans indicate that this is the function of one or more other directors; for example, the chairman, two or three influential directors, the executive committee, and all other directors. Sometimes this appraisal by one's peers is contributed to by shareholders or senior management personnel. Just five respondents indicate that it is the shareholders who are primarily responsible for appraising the performance of the individual director, and one of these indicates that appraisal by shareholders is actually carried out through a key director.

As for performance appraisal standards, the one most commonly mentioned by Venezuelan study participants relates to the thoroughness and quality of the director's participation in the work of the board. This is described by such phrases as "initiating actions subsequently supported by other directors"; "my influence with other members and sometimes with management to approve certain practices"; "contributions of opinions at meetings to decision making"; "ideas brought to discussions and recommendations made." One problem is that appraisals of this kind may not be clearly articulated by the director's peers, which forces at least one director to rely on self-appraisal, "using my own standard."

A few directors believe that more objective performance standards can and do apply. One, of course, is the progress and profitability of the concern. Another is fulfillment of specific responsibilities assigned by the chairman to the individual director. Two directors think that they are judged by the business they bring to companies on whose boards they sit.

Enforcing Accountability

Do shareholders have effective means of holding a director to account should his acts, or failure to act, dissatisfy them? Yes, say a great majority of the Venezuelan study contributors, and by far the most frequently cited means is removal from the board, or, more gently, failure to reelect. But a few participants believe this recourse is rarely effective in practice — "only in extreme cases." And, of course, only a majority of shareholders can effect removal. A discontented minority is powerless.

Several respondents speak of remedies other than removal for a director who fails adequately to represent the shareholder groups to which he is accountable. Disaffected stockholders can express their unhappiness, "spread rumors and criticisms," institute legal proceedings. Several respondents who feel accountable in part to other directors note that the threat of ostracism by their peers in the event of unsatisfactory performance is a means of enforcing accountability.

The Board or Corporate Management: Which Is More Significant?

In terms of impact on company behavior and performance, most Venezuelan respondents believe that corporate management has more significant long-term influence than the board. Practically all who hold this view believe that management's primacy stems from its deeper involvement in the business and its greater access to information. "Except for financial statements," one of this number observes, "the board knows only what it is told by management." Two respondents, however, note that there are instances in which the board can be more dominant. "If the board is well organized, it can help the company more than management," one maintains. And the other, while agreeing that corporate management usually predominates, says that the question "depends on the nature of the business, the degree of administrative difficulty, and how responsibilities are shared between directors and management." He adds that properly qualified management is absolutely indispensible for a company to be successful, but since the selection of management is the primary function of the board, it is this function that really determines the final success of the company.

The minority of Venezuelans who believe that the board has the primary long-term influence on company behavior and performance do so for several reasons:

- " . . . because it decides the general policy."
- "Because of written operating rules that the board requires almost unanimous consent on all important decisions."
- "Because the framework of objectives and strategy to achieve them is of key importance."
- "Because growth decisions, securing bank loans, and senior appointments are all vital."
- "Because in a good organization management is only the executive arm of the board and subject to its decisions."

In this camp there is one Venezuelan of an "it depends" persuasion. Though in general he finds the board is in the superior position, he asserts that "with strong, dynamic management the board is very much influenced, and in this situation corporate management has the dominant influence on the activity and productivity of the company."

Personal Reactions to Directorships

By far the most common satisfaction Venezuelan directors report from their board service is seeing firms prosper and grow. Also, several feel that such service has made a contribution to the development of their country, and one speaks of his pleasure at helping the private enterprise system become stronger.

There are also more focused rewards in directorships, according to several participants: working together with talented fellow board members; partaking of the intellectual stimulus of board service; harmonizing the interests of the various stakeholder groups; enjoying the power that a board seat confers; and, finally, persuading others of one's viewpoint. Two respondents state frankly that board service is financially rewarding.

Chief Frustrations and Difficulties

The frustrations or difficulties the surveyed Venezuelan directors have encountered have to do, for the most part, with company executives and staffs and their fellow directors. Among the reported irritating characteristics of executives: failure to supply adequate information about the company; concealment of some

of their activities from the board; the "low level" of their competence; irresponsibility; and lack of honesty. As for the shortcomings of fellow directors, these charges are leveled: unwillingness to participate in the solution of certain problems pertaining to the political and socio-economic development of the country; failure to do their homework; cliques on certain boards; the manifest conflicts of interests of some fellow directors; and a chairman with "the mentality of a bookkeeper."

Another set of frustrations has to do with the director's job, or specific aspects of it:

- Reconciling differences among shareholders of different nationalities;
- Negotiating with unions and other labor matters;
- Unjustified interference by the government;
- Being criticized when things turn out badly but not getting credit when they turn out well;
- The inevitable loneliness and toughness of the director's position.

Legal Risk of Board Service

About half of the Venezuelan directors express concern about the legal risk of serving as directors. One is especially worried about the risk entailed in serving on boards of banks and insurance companies.

Other perspectives on risk offered by this group of study contributors:

- One should take one's board activities seriously in order to avoid risk.
- Legal risk is small if the board has confidence in management and insists on a high level of managerial ethics.
- Legal risk is much less than the severe risk of damaging the esteem in which one is held, particularly in difficult moments.

Workers on the Board?

As noted in "The Venezuelan Context," non-management workers do not, as a rule, serve on the boards of private Venezuelan companies. But the respondents in that country were asked to express their opinion of this European practice. Most are opposed; a few see some merit in the idea, either now or some years hence when they believe conditions will be more propitious for this innovation.

The basic argument voiced by Venezuelan directors against electing workers to corporate boards is substantially the same as that raised by directors in other countries: The stature of the board would be diminished; its functions would not be fully or efficiently performed. This would happen in part because workers are not prepared by training or background to assume the responsibilities of directors. As one Venezuelan puts it, the innovation would be "a fraud because it would make persons responsible for decisions who have neither preparation nor ability to administer, who lack education and experience." Also, a worker director might place the interest of himself and his colleagues ahead of the interest of the corporation, which would make a political forum of the board. Indeed, another respondent, fearful of this eventuality, thinks that a "parallel organism" might have to be created to fulfill the functions of the board.

The points in favor of worker representation adduced by Venezuelan directors are: It would round out the influences to which a board should be subject and, if well implemented, it could be a power for improving productivity. Two of these respondents offer qualified views. One believes that the arrangement would have merit if the worker representatives would "look to the sake of the company" — but he is doubtful that they would. And in the judgment of the other, the outcome would depend upon how worker representatives were selected: whether by popular election, by seniority, or on the basis of merit.

Comparing worker representation on the board with worker participation in management decision making, another Venezuelan director believes that the latter would be "a more difficult step" than the former, that worker representation on the board of directors should precede worker participation in management decision making. This recommendation is in contrast to the views of several European commentators who believe that worker participation in corporate affairs must start at the bottom and percolate upwards — for example, from planning work on the factory floor to participation in more substantive decisions and, eventually, to representation on the board of directors.

As also pointed out in "The Venezuelan Context," unions are represented by law on the boards of all public corporations. A respondent who has served on the board of one such corporation has this to say about that board's worker director:

"I consider that the company was lucky to have a person of extraordinary personal qualities designated to fill the nonmanagement employee seat, since he has always maintained a balance in his position which has

---

Responsibilities of Directors in Government Corporations

Of the Venezuelans commenting on the question of whether the responsibilities of a director of a government-owned or -controlled corporation differ from those of a director of a privately held company, a majority sees no essential difference. Here is a summary of the comments of those who discern a difference (one of whom maintains, however, that the responsibilities of a director *should be* the same "independent of the source of capital"):

— A director on a government board is more advisor than a decision maker.
— State corporations have less freedom of action, especially in budget matters and in personnel policies.
— State companies give social and political considerations precedence over profits.
— Because the chairman of the board of government enterprise is elected by official shareholders and private shareholders, his function is to balance interests of both groups.

---

enabled problems of a most delicate labor-relations nature to be treated with all frankness in his presence. His advice even on this subject has always been valuable and timely. He has had the discretion not to interfere in matters beyond his capacity. This experience, I am afraid, cannot be generalized, and probably frequent conflicts could appear in cases where the labor representatives on a board of directors do not have suitable qualities. In this event it would be inevitable that partial meetings of the board of directors would take place in order to reach decisions without the participation of an unsuitable labor representative."

Desirable Changes in the Board

Venezuelan directors participating in this study suggest a number of changes — in composition, in organization, and in functions — they would like to see implemented in corporate boards in their country.

Composition, Size, Tenure:

— Reduce average age of board members.

— Appoint more women directors.

— Limit size of board to seven members to improve board effectiveness.

— Represent management, not just capital, on the board.

— Establish mandatory retirement: set a flexible retirement age, have directors retire "at the proper time."

Organization and Work Routine:

— Make it mandatory for board members to attend meetings and participate.

— Send out agenda, supporting materials, and documents on material to be discussed well before meetings.

— Give more relevant information to the directors for the decisions they must make.

— Schedule more frequent meetings of some boards.

— Appoint working committees.

— Conduct secret evaluations of each board member by his fellows.

Functions:

— Free the board from administrative work, confining it to approving policy and management and to serving as a sounding board as to what is going on in the business and outside it.

— Assert more effectively the interests of the shareholders as against those of the board.

— Manifest more social responsibility — for example, promote consumer cooperatives, nursery service for workers' children, bonuses and stock ownership plans for workers.

— Communicate more fully with shareholders and workers on nonconfidential subjects.

— Make surprise checks "on the conduct of the company."

— Originate policies to enforce a strict managerial ethic — which means that each director must set a personal example of vigorous compliance with these rules.

Two other changes advocated do not fall into any of the three categories just listed. Directors should be charged with greater legal responsibility, one respondent urges. And a second expresses a wistful wish, in the dynamics of the board-management relationships, for "less dominant presidents."

Two Final Perspectives

Asked for a final comment on corporate boards in their country, the Venezuelan study participants addressed themselves to two subjects — the inadequacy of some boards, and the apparently inevitable variability in the functions of the board. Here are some typical statements:

— "Some directors representing ownership of the company are not suitable for their responsibilities as directors. This often occurs when unqualified sons of owners or retired directors are appointed."

— "Many boards in Venezuela are not professional and resemble social clubs."

— "There are many companies with boards of directors on paper."

— "Boards normally function to establish limits of actions more than to make decisions, and are more vital in difficult situations."

— "The function of a board depends on the external opportunities the company is allowed to realize and the internal teamwork of the board and management."

Chapter 11
Japan

Composition and Organization of the Board

The 134 Japanese corporations that have contributed information about their boards of directors represent organizations with a wide range of characteristics. Of the several industrial categories in the group, the largest single one is machinery manufacture, with 30 companies. Twenty companies are in finance and insurance; the mining and metal products categories are represented by eleven companies each; and chemicals and commerce by ten companies each. There are eight textile companies, and five companies apiece in the construction and foods categories. The remaining 24 companies are made up of firms in such industries as fisheries, agriculture and forestry; pulp and paper products; real estate; transportation; utilities; and others. More than half have at least 5,000 employees.

All of these companies are owned by shareholders that range in numbers from fewer than 1,000 (16 companies) to more than 50,000 (33 companies). Forty companies have from 10,000 to 30,000 shareholders; 22 have from 30,000 to 50,000; and 23 have from 1,000 to 10,000 shareholders.

The sizes of the companies, based on their capital and annual sales, are shown in Table 11-1.

In Japan, research for this report was limited to a survey of the composition and organization of boards of directors. The survey was conducted for The Conference Board by Keizai Doyukai (Japan Committee for Economic Development) in Tokyo. The manuscript, based on the results of this survey, was prepared by Rochelle O'Connor of The Conference Board staff.

Information on the Japanese context and the perspectives of Japanese directors could not be gathered in time for inclusion in this report, but will soon be released in a supplement.

Board Size

The boards of these Japanese companies are substantially larger, on the average, than boards in most countries surveyed. The average (mean) board size is 21.6. As Table 11-2 shows, better than 50 percent of the companies have boards with over 20 members, and four boards have more than 40 directors. On the other hand, a dozen companies have boards composed of fewer than ten.

Board Composition

Japanese boards are primarily internal organs, consisting almost entirely of company executives. Well

Table 11-1: Size of Respondent Companies, by Category

Category	Number of Companies
Capital (billions of yen):	
Less than 5	32
5-10	21
10-50	57
More than 50	24
Total	134
Annual Sales (billions of yen):	
Less than 10	6
10-100	36
100-500	46
500-1,000	9
More than 1,000	17
Total	114*

*Excludes 20 financial institutions.

under 10 percent of the total directors on the boards of the surveyed companies are not full-time employees of the company or of its subsidiaries. None of the inside directors is a worker or union representative.

Table 11-3, showing the business or professional background of the outside directors of these firms, indicates that a majority of them are major shareholders or their agents. Three companies have government representatives on their boards.

Eighteen boards have directors who are former employees of their respective organizations. One company has nine such former employees, but nine companies have only one each. The remaining eight companies have from two to eight such directors.

Members of Japanese boards of directors are almost invariably selected by the corporate shareholders or by management. Of the 124 companies that replied to this question, 117 choose their 2,563 directors in this fashion. One firm reported that the government picked two of its directors; six companies said that other groups or organizations selected sixteen of their directors.

Only six companies report that they require their nonemployee directors to own stock; none says it is required by law. Of the six companies, two specify the number of shares required: 10,000 in one company and 100,000 in the other.

Two years is the predominant term of office for directors in these Japanese companies. This is reported by 125 of the companies cooperating in the study. Only one company cites a one-year term for its directors, while the remaining eight firms do not specify a term.

Retirement from the company terminates eligibility for board duty in almost four-fifths of the companies. One hundred and six companies say that these directors may not serve on the board after retiring. In six companies, they may continue as directors; twenty-two companies did not answer this question.

Table 11-2: Number of Directors per Board

Number of Board Members	Companies	
	Number	Percent
Less than 10	12	9.0
11-15	15	11.2
16-20	38	28.4
21-25	34	25.4
26-30	18	13.4
31-35	5	3.7
36-40	8	6.0
41-45	1	0.7
More than 46	3	2.2
Total	134	100.0

Table 11-3: Backgrounds of Outside Directors

Business or Profession	Number of Directors
Principal company owner or agent	128
Manufacturing executive	17
Banking executive	14
Merchandising or trading company executive	7
Other financial executive	6
Public utility or transportation executive	3
Government representative	3
Other	5
Total	183

Outside directors, on the other hand, apparently need not retire from the board at a specific age in the majority of the participating companies that have outside directors. Seven companies do have such a stipulation, however. Fifty-four companies did not answer this question, possibly because they do not have nonemployee directors.

The following tabulation shows average ages of boards in reporting companies:

Average Age	Companies	
	Number	Percent
Less than 45	1	0.7
46-50	6	4.5
51-55	28	21.1
56-60	79	59.4
61-65	19	14.3
Total	133	100.0

Meeting Frequency

A majority of the Japanese boards (57.6 percent) meet monthly — a high average compared with most other countries surveyed. The following figures show the number of board meetings in the 134 companies:

Number of Board Meetings	Companies	
	Number	Percent
Less than 5	8	5.8
6-11	18	13.5
12	77	57.6
13-19	20	14.9
More than 20	11	8.2
Total	134	100.0

Committees

Only three of the 134 companies have any board committees. One of these has a single committee with seven members that meets twelve times a year. (This committee includes two members who are not company employees.)